THE BOOK
of
OUR HERITAGE

First Volume

TISHREY — SHEVAT

ELIYAHU KITOV

The Book of our Heritage

The Jewish year

and its days of significance

Translated from the Hebrew

SÉFER HA-TODA'AH

by NATHAN BULMAN

REVISED EDITION *

FELDHEIM PUBLISHERS

Jerusalem • New York

1978 / 5738

Revised Edition

ISBN 0 87306 158 6
(3-volume set: 0 87306 157 8)

Reprinted 1988

PHILIPP FELDHEIM, Inc.
200 Airport Executive Park
Spring Valley, NY 10977

FELDHEIM PUBLISHERS, Ltd.
POB 6525, Jerusalem, Israel

Printed in Israel

10 9 8 7 6

CONTENTS

A GUIDE TO OBSERVANCE

INSIGHTS, REASONS, MEANINGS AND ALLUSIONS

מַה אָהַבְתִּי תוֹרָתֶךָ כָּל הַיּוֹם הִיא שִׂיחָתִי (תהלים קיט צז)

FOREWORD

My original intention in writing the Hebrew edition of 'Sefer HaToda'ah' was to aid the teacher of Jewish studies in Israeli schools. I tried to impart general conceptions of the vast spiritual treasures inherent in the Jewish festivals and days of significance, as well as to convey details of law and lore, background and insights — based upon authentic sources and presented in a modern and easy style. I tried thereby to lighten the teacher's burden in collecting material and to facilitate the student's comprehension.

When the book was completed, some eight years ago, I could not foresee the great interest it would arouse in the diverse Jewish public. Yet, I soon realized, to my surprise, there were many groups and individuals in Israel and in most countries of the Diaspora who found the book enlightening and beneficial. 'Sefer HaToda'ah' which appeared quietly and without the benefit of publicity, soon found its way into many thousands of homes and became a guide and handbook for fathers and sons, teachers and students, rabbis and congregants.

In recent times, I have been repeatedly requested by many in countries outside Israel, especially in the U. S. and other English speaking lands, that the book be offered in an English translation. This demand has brought about the present English edition which 'A' Publishers now presents to the Jewish public the world over.

Translating 'Sefer HaTodoa'ah' was a very difficult undertaking because of the book's special character and unique style. 'The Book of our Heritage' was meant to be a typically

Jewish traditional tract and at the same time a popular readable publication. This was difficult enough to achieve even in the Hebrew which is nourished by the very roots of the Jewish way of life with all its phases, laws and customs; the more so when we endeavored to transplant all this specific Jewish material in a language quite new and foreign to its culture, psychology and values.

American and English literature on subjects of Judaism have produced much in the field of translation from classic Hebrew scripts as well as in original writing. Still, to date no suitable modern English style has been crystalized to combine the new taste with the old flavor.

Rabbi Nachman Bulman, who undertook this almost impossible task, has shown a great deal of resourcefulness and sagacity in paving the way to a synthesis of the old with the new by developing original means of expression and syntax. His main purpose was to retain, on one hand, the traditional character of the book, while on the other hand making it an enjoyable and readable text whose every 'abstract' or 'technical' point could be easily understood by all. I hereby express my compliments and deep gratitude.

Rabbi Bulman has already won acclaim for his work in translating my previous book, 'The Jew and His Home'. In this present work he has surely surpassed himself. I am certain the reader will share my sense of indebtedness to him for his efforts.

I should also mention my thanks to Mr. Zvi Kitov and Miss Esther Karno for their help in editing ond preparing the text for print.

I should like to stress that despite all the efforts our work has not reached perfection. A reader not acquainted with the Jewish Classics will find some difficulty in understanding the Hebrew concepts abundantly referred to here. We have therefore added an alphabetical Glossary and Index to the English edition providing explanations and references for such points.

I am also obliged to ask my readers not to regard this book as an authority on religious law. The book was only meant to give general ideas of law so that cognizance of the different problems may be taken. Specific questions of practice should be referred to an authorized rabbi.

Since my main purpose in writing 'Sefer Hatoda'ah' has been to 'cause public merit', I see it as a pleasant obligation to share merit with Mr. Abraham Parshan of Toronto, Canada, who granted me invaluable and vital assistance for the materialization of this idea. 'Bless, Lord his substance, and accept the work of his hands' (Deuteronomy 33: 11).

Many thanks and deep gratitude are also due Mr. Charles Batt, of Hartford, Connecticut, whose guidance and advice were of great encouragement and benefit.

Jerusalem, Sivan 5728 (June 1968).

ELIYAHU KITOV

NOTES:

1. When Hebrew terms are first introduced in this book, they are italicized and usually followed by glossary in brackets. Later in the book, as these terms are repeated, they acquire the status of regular English words with no special distinction. If the reader comes across a 'strange' word, he should refer to the 'Glossary and Index' in the end of each volume.

2. The spelling of the Hebrew terms is in accordance with the Sephardi pronounciation prevalent in Israel and, of late, in most Hebrew schools in the U. S. Each vowel-letter always represents the same phonetic value and consonants are therefore not doubled.

These phonetic-values are as follows:

- a — [a], pronounced as u in *u*p or o in l*o*ve;
- e — [e], pronounced as e in p*e*n;
- i — [i], pronounced as *i* in s*i*t;
- o — [o], pronounced as o in b*o*y;
- u — [u], pronounced as u in p*u*t or oo in b*oo*k.

The combination ch is pronounced as ch in the Scottish lo*ch*.

3. Passages specifying details of law are usually italicized. New Hebrew terms introduced in these passages are placed between quotation marks.

TO

ABRAHAM PARSHAN

WITH GRATITUDE

Tishrey ROSH HASHANAH

THE MONTH OF TISHREY ❖ THE FIRST OF TISHREY ❖ DAY OF CONCEALMENT ❖ DAY OF BEGINNINGS ❖ DAYS ON WHICH ROSH HASHANAH SHALL NOT FALL ❖ ROSH HASHANAH — TWO DAYS ❖ THE DAY OF JUDGMENT ❖ TRANSGRESSIONS AND MERITS ARE WEIGHED IN THE BALANCE ❖ WHAT IS THE DAY OF JUDGMENT ? ❖ A YOM TOV ON WHICH HALEL IS NOT SAID ❖ THE FIRST NIGHT OF ROSH HASHANAH ❖ THE TORAH READING OF ROSH HASHANAH ❖ THE SOUNDING OF THE SHOFAR ❖ THE REQUIRED ORDER OF SHOFAR SOUNDS ❖ ONE HUNDRED SHOFAR-SOUNDS ❖ HOW SATAN WAS ONCE CONFOUNDED ❖ THE SHOFAR — A FINAL DEFENCE ❖ THE SOUNDING OF SHOFAR AND ITS BRACHOT ❖ VERSES WHICH INVOKE COMPASSION ❖ THE EFFECT OF THE SHOFAR ❖ SHOFAR IS NOT SOUNDED ON SHABAT ❖ THE TIME FOR TEKIAT SHOFAR ❖ INSCRIBE US FOR LIFE ❖ PRAYERS OF THE DAYS OF REPENTANCE ❖ MALCHUYOT, ZICHRONOT, SHOFROT ❖ TEN UTTERANCES, TEN COMMANDMENTS AND TEN PRAISES ❖ HE REMEMBERS ALL THAT IS FORGOTTEN ❖ MUSAF DURING HOURS OF COMPASSION ❖ THE PIYUT 'UNTANE TOKEF' ❖ SLEEP ON ROSH HASHANAH ❖ TASHLICH ❖ THE SECOND DAY OF ROSH HASHANAH ❖ ERUV TAVSHILIN

CHAPTER ONE

THE MONTH OF TISHREY

The Hebrew months are known by the names acquired during the Babylonian Exile (Tishrey, Cheshvan, Kislev etc.). Still, other meaningful names and identifications are found in the earlier Scriptures.

The Torah calls the month of Tishrey *hachodesh hashvi'i* (the seventh month), in accordance with the numerical order of the months beginning with Nisan.

In the Jewish Tradition, being seventh has special significance and symbolism.

'All sevenths are beloved above...' said our Sages. Chanoch, the seventh generation after Adam, was uniquely significant; of him it is said 'And Chanoch walked with God...' (Bereishit 5). Of Moshe, the seventh among the Fathers of Israel it is said 'And Moshe ascended to God...' (Shmot 19). Likewise do we find: 'And God blessed the seventh day' (Bereishit 2), 'Six years you shall sow your land and gather in the increase thereof, but the seventh year you shall let it rest and lie fallow' (Shmot 23). Seven cycles of seven years are crowned by a *yovel year* — 'And you shall sanctify the fiftieth year...' (Vayikra 25). Tishrey, the seventh of months, is also unique with its many significant phases.

No other month is endowed with so many *mitzvot* (Torah commandments) as Tishrey. No other month has as many festival days and rites. In the land of Israel, Tishrey is also the ingathering season when people witness the material plenitude God has blessed them with. These qualities are alluded, according to our Sages, by the similarity in sound between *sheva* (seven) and *sova* (satiety).

In the Prophetic-Writings, the month is also called *yerach ha'etanim* (the month of the Mighty) — 'And all the men of Israel assembled themselves unto King Shlomo at the feast, in the month of Etanim, which is the seventh month' (First Melachim 8). Our Sages commented it was thus named because the Patriarchs (Avraham, Itzchak, Ya'akov), who were the Mighty-Ones of the world, were born in Tishrey.

THE FIRST OF TISHREY

Although Tishrey is the seventh month, it is nowadays numbered the first month with reference to the calendar years. Its first day is also the beginning of a new year, 'Rosh Hashanah,' for applying the laws of sabbatical and Jubilee years, young fruit trees and harvest of grain and vegetables.

For sabbatical and Jubilee years: upon the advent of Tishrey in a sabbatical year (a year of 'shmitah,' ending a seven-year cycle) or in a Jubilee (a yovel year which comes after seven shmitah-cycles), plowing or seeding is prohibited by the Torah in the land of Israel.

For young fruit trees: all fruits which are picked during the first three years after planting are called 'orlah' and are prohibited as food or for any other use. The fruits of the fourth year are called 'neta revai' (literally: the plant of the fourth) and are to be eaten in the city of Yerushalayim (Jerusalem). If a tree is planted forty five days before the first of Tishrey, its second 'orlah' year begins on the first of Tishrey.

For the harvest of grain and vegetables: The first of Tishrey is considered as 'Rosh Hashanah' with reference to the 'trumot' and 'ma'asrot' (heave offerings and tithes). The Torah requires that the harvest of each year be tithed separately and one should not allocate 'trumot' and 'ma'asrot' from grain and vegetables harvested before the first of Tishrey upon those harvested afterwards.

DAY OF CONCEALMENT

Rosh Hashanah — the first of Tishrey, is also called *yom hakeseh* (day of concealment). 'Sound the *shofar* (ram's horn) at the new moon, at the concealed time for our festival day' (Tehilim 81).

All that transpires on this day is characterized by concealment. All other festival days fall either when the moon is full or near full, i.e. approximately at mid-month. Rosh Hashanah however, falls on the first day of the month, when the new moon may not yet have appeared. The People of Israel is symbolically compared to the moon and is radiant on its Sabbaths and Festivals. On Rosh Hashanah, however, Israel diminishes itself and conceals its greatness in awe of the Day of Judgment. The Almighty, too, places a cover of concealment over His People's sins and accords them forgiveness.

The very character of the first of Tishrey as the Day of Judgment, is similarly concealed and is not mentioned explicitly in the Torah, so that a person might be apprehensive over his wrong-doings all year and not delay his *teshuvah* (repentance) till Rosh Hashanah.

DAY OF BEGINNINGS

The first of Tishrey was, according to Rabi Eliezer, the day on which God created Adam, thereby completing the Creation of the world.

According to Rabi Eliezer, the Patriarchs — who have started a new world after sinful earlier generations — were also born in Tishrey.

On Rosh Hashanah, Sarah, Rachel and Hannah were granted Divine-Remembrance. They have been childless, and God remembered them that day with the gift of children.

On Rosh Hashanah Yosef was freed from the prison in

which he had been kept for twelve years, and thereafter his light began to shine.

On Rosh Hashanah the bondage of our fathers in Egypt ceased, and their redemption began.

The very first Rosh Hashanah of the world — on which Adam was created — was already marked with the values of Judgment and Forgiveness. On that very day, said our Sages — Adam violated the commandment God had given him (concerning the Tree of Knowledge), was judged and then forgiven by God. Whereupon God said to him: You are a sign unto your children; as you were judged before me this day and emerged forgiven, so will your children be judged before me this day and emerge forgiven.

DAYS ON WHICH ROSH HASHANAH SHALL NOT FALL

The first day of Rosh Hashanah can fall only on the second, third or fifth day of the week, or on 'Shabat', but never on the first, fourth or sixth day of the week. This regulation is a 'takanat chachamim' (an ordinance of the Sages) and will be explained in the discussion on the Jewish Calendar.

(In Hebrew, this characteristic of the first of Tishrey is marked by the expression 'Lo A'D'U' Rosh.')

ROSH HASHANAH — TWO DAYS

Rosh Hashanah is observed as a two-day-holiday, on the first and second day of Tishrey, though the Torah prescribes its observance for only one day: 'And in the seventh month, on the first day of the month, you shall have a holy convocation: you shall do no work; it is a day of blowing the 'Shofar' unto you' (Bamidbar 29).

The two-day observance is an enactment of the First Prophets, 'Nevi'im Rishonim' — who were motivated by the following reason:

The High Court in Jerusalem, 'Beit Din,' sanctified the new month upon the testimony of witnesses who saw the appearance of the new moon 'molad halvanah.' In the case of Rosh Hashanah which falls on the very first day of the month, the observance of holiday-laws necessarily began the evening immediately following the 29th of Elul (the preceding month) since the possible arrival of witnesses for the new month on the morrow, might cause the day to be sanctified retroactively as holiday. If such witnesses did come, the same day was sacred 'kodesh', and the following day was non-sacred 'chol'; if witnesses failed to appear that day, the following day was sanctified automatically, and it was then known that the previous day was non-sacred. Therefore, in order that people might not regard the first day's sanctity lightly, because of its doubtful character, the Prophets prescribed that Rosh Hashanah should always be observed for two days; that prohibition of labor, the sounding of the shofar, the order of prayer, as well as the other details of holiday observance, be mandatory equally for both days.

These days of Rosh Hashanah are called 'yoma arichta' (one long day) to indicate that the sanctity of both is not a doubtful sanctity but a definite one. However, with reference to the preparation of food, they are considered as two individual days, and it is forbidden to prepare and cook food on the first day for the second.

The 'Rambam' (Maimonides) writes:

'The Majority of the residents of the Land of Israel used to observe the 'Yom Tov' (holiday) of Rosh Hashanah for two days because of doubt (when 'Rosh Chodesh' — first day of the new month — was fixed through visual observation) for they did not know

which day the 'Beit Din' had fixed as 'Rosh Chodesh' since messengers did not go out on 'Yom Tov'.

'Further, even in Jerusalem itself, the seat of the 'Beit Din', Rosh Hashanah was often observed as a two-day Yom Tov. If witnesses failed to come forth the entire thirtieth day, the day was observed as sacred — in expectation of witnesses — as was also the following day. And since they used to observe Rosh Hashanah for two days when the new month was fixed through visual observation, they prescribed that even the residents of the Land of Israel should always observe Rosh Hashanah for two days, even today when the new month is determined by calculation. You learn hence, that the second Yom Tov of Rosh Hashanah is 'midivrey sofrim' (a Sages regulation) nowadays.' (Hilchot Kidush Hachodesh Chap. 5).

Consequently, there is a difference between the times when the month was fixed through visual testimony and the present time. When the month was sanctified through observation, if witnesses who had seen the 'molad' (the new moon) did not come, the first day of Rosh Hashanah proved to be 'miderabanan' (observed as a Sages regulation), and the second became the first of Tishrey and was observed 'min ha'Torah' (as a Torah commandment). At present, however, when the months and the festivals are fixed solely by calculation, and the first day of Rosh Hashanah falls always on the first of Tishrey, the first day is 'min ha'Torah,' while the second is 'miderabanan.'

THE DAY OF JUDGMENT

Rosh Hashanah is the day of judgment for all the world's mortals. On this day Man is judged as to the events of his life during the forthcoming year. 'The eyes of the Lord your

God are upon it (the Land) from the beginning of the year till its end' (Dvarim 11) — 'From Rosh Hashanah (the beginning of the year) judgment is rendered as to the events occurring till its end' (Tractate Rosh Hashanah 8).

Our Sages have also spoken about the manner in which God scrutinizes His people: At one and the same time He sees them all together and considers the actions of each one separately. 'All the world's inhabitants pass before Him like sheep, *benei maron* (Tr. Rosh Hashanah 16). They pass one by one like sheep coming into their shed, being scrutinized by their shepherd — and yet, this is all done in one single survey.'

'Rabi Cruspedai said in the name of Rabi Yochanan: Three books are opened on Rosh Hashanah; one of the iniquitous *(resha'im gemurim)*, one of the just (*tzadikim gemurim*) and one of these who are in the middle' *(beinonim)*. The *tzadikim gemurim* are immediately inscribed and sealed for life: the *resha'im gemurim* are immdiately inscribed and sealed for death. The *beinonim* are held over from Rosh Hashanah till *Yom Kipur* (the tenth of Tishrey). If they merit it — (and repent) — they are inscribed for life. If not — they are inscribed for death' (Tr. Rosh Hashanah 17).

For two basic reasons Rosh Hashanah was ordained to be the Day of Judgment. Firstly, on this day the world's creation was completed, and it was the original Divine intention to govern the world with the attribute of Justice (*midat hadin*). Secondly, as stated above, it was on this day that Adam was judged, that he repented and was forgiven.

These two reasons are alluded to in the *musaf* service of Rosh Hashanah: 'For You will bring a statute of Providence that every spirit and soul be visited; that a multitude of deeds be remembered and a throng of creatures without end. From the beginning You did make this known and from aforetime You revealed it. This day is the beginning of Your works; it is a memorial for the first of days.' — A memorial for the first day of Creation's completion, and a memorial for the first Day of Judgment.

Our Sages have noted: 'God's way differs from the way of a man of flesh and blood. The way of a man of flesh and blood is to judge a loving friend in an hour of good will, in order to treat him mercifully; and to judge an enemy in an hour of anger, in order to exact strict justice from him. God does otherwise: He judges the entire world — including those who violate His will — only in an hour of good will — in the month of Tishrey. This month contains numerous festivals and *mitzvot* bringing anew the affinity between Him and His creatures. During this month of reconciliation, God welcomes Man's prayer and repentance and judges him with compassion.

TRANSGRESSION AND MERITS ARE WEIGHED IN THE BALANCE

'Each person has merits and transgressions. If one's merits exceed his transgressions — he is a *tzadik;* if one's transgressions exceed his merits — he is *rasha;* if both are equal — he is a *beinoni.*

'The same applies to each country. If the collective merits of its inhabitants exceed their transgressions, it is deemed a just country. If their transgressions exceed their merits, it is deemed iniquitous. And the same applies to the entire world.

'If a person's transgressions exceed his merits, he dies immediately because of his iniquity ... If a country's transgressions exceed its merits, it perishes immediately ... The same applies to the entire world — if its transgressions exceed its merits, it is subject to immediate destruction ... This judgment is not a quantitative one however, but a qualitative one. There are individual acts of merit which weigh in the balance against numerous transgressions ... And there are individual transgressions which outweigh many meritorious acts. A judgment is made in this matter only through the discernment of God, whose knowledge is all encompassing, for He alone knows how to evaluate merit as against transgression.

'Each person should therefore see himself — during the entire year — as if he were half meritorious and half guilty. Likewise (should he see) the entire world as half meritorious and half guilty. If he commits one sin — he tips the scale of guilt for himself and the entire world and causes its destruction, as well as his own. If he commits one *mitzvah,* he tips the scale of merit for himself and for the entire world and causes its salvation and deliverance, as well as his own' (Rambam, Hilchot Teshuvah, Chapter 3).

WHAT IS THE DAY OF JUDGMENT ?

'This teaching of the Sages — that each person is judged on Rosh Hashanah — does not refer to one's meriting *Gan Eden* and life in the World-to-Come, or his being condemned to *Gehinom* and to perish. For man is judged on Rosh Hashanah only concerning matters of this world — whether he is worthy of life and well being or of anguish and death. Thus did our Sages of blessed memory say in Tractate Rosh Hashanah: 'This is the day on which Your works began; it is a remembrance of the first day; it is a statute unto Israel, a judgment unto the God of Ya'akov. And concerning countries it is stated thereon — which is for the sword and which for peace, which for famine and which is to be sated — and creatures will be visited thereon for remembrance unto life or death.' Such then is the measure of the matter: On Rosh Hashanah a person's actions are weighed, and he is inscribed and sealed for merit or guilt in this world. And when a person departs to his final abode, they (his actions) are weighed and his portion in the world of souls is prescribed, in accord with what he deserves' (Ramban, quoted by Abudraham).

Even if a person has sinned all year he ought not lose hope in his capacity for repentance; let him rather return to the way of righteousness before he comes to judgment.

Let him believe at heart that he is always capable of tipping the scale of merit for himself and the entire world. For this reason, the whole house of Israel practices charity, good deeds, and the pursuit of *mitzvot* in greater degree from Rosh Hashanah till after Yom Kipur than during the remainder of the year.

'A person is judged only in accord with his present actions' (Tr. Rosh Hashanah 16). Though they may be immersed in sin all year, God testifies that the People of Israel desire to do His will; when they repent on the Day of Judgment and they do God's will, they are judged as they are, (not as they were).

A YOM TOV ON WHICH HALEL IS NOT SAID

Since Rosh Hashanah is the Day of Judgment, each person should feel anxiety and awe; he should guard against levity, and against anything which distracts him from the awe of judgment.

So great is the fear of judgment among Israel on Rosh Hashanah, that they do not recite the 'Halel' (Psalm 113—118, *recited on New Moon and festivals as a Song of Praise) although 'Rosh Hashanah' is a 'Yom Tov' (a festival). For the People of Israel utter the Halel before God only when their hearts are filled with joy, whereas during the days of judgment there is more fear and trembling in Jewish hearts, than rejoicing.*

'Said the ministering angels before God: Lord of the Universe, Why does Israel fail to utter song before you during Rosh Hashanah and Yom Kipur? Said He to them: When the King sits on the chair of judgment and the books of life and death are before him — can Israel utter song? (Tr. Rosh Hashanah 32).

Nevertheless, a person ought not be saddened by fear of judgment; one should cut his hair and wash in honor of the festival, and dress in his Yom Tov clothing, thereby showing trust that God would vindicate us in judgment. For the same reason, we do not weep on Rosh Hashanah. (During prayer, however, some authorities permit shedding of tears. We therefore find persons of piety who shed tears like infants during the prayers of the 'Yamim Noraim' (the Days-of-Awe, Rosh Hashanah and Yom Kipur), to awaken the mercy of our Heavenly Father upon His children. For though we all be wise and understanding, we are each before God like a child who unashamedly weeps before his father over the desires of his heart.)

We find that when Ezra the Scribe read the Torah before the assembly which gathered on the first day of the seventh month, and all the people wept on hearing the words of the Torah — Ezra and Nehemiah said to them: 'Do not mourn and do not weep, go eat delicacies and drink sweet drinks and send gifts to whomever has no food prepared, for the day is sacred to our Lord; and do not grieve, for the joy of the Lord is your strength' (Nehemiah 6 10).

'For what great nation is there which has statutes and judgments so righteous as all this Torah...' (Dvarim 4) — Which people is like this people? It is the way of the world that if a person has a judgment pending against him, he dresses in black, wraps himself in black, lets his beard grow for the uncertainty of the outcome. Israel however, is different. They dress in white; they eat, drink and rejoice, in the knowledge that God will perform miracles in their behalf (Jerusalem Talmud, Tr. Rosh Hashanah, Chapter 1).

THE FIRST NIGHT OF ROSH HASHANAH

The first night of Rosh Hashanah after prayer, greetings are exchanged. One says to each other:

'Leshanah tovah tikatev vetechatem l'alter lechayim tovim' (may you be inscribed and sealed immediately for a good life).

After the first night, it is considered improper to continue extending this greeting. One avoids wishing his friends Good Inscription at a time when all 'tzadikim gemurim' (the righteous) have already been inscribed for good life. Rather, each person should consider his fellow as completely righteous, though it may seem otherwise. For Man judges by appearances, while God sees the heart. Perhaps this or that person has repented in thought, and is hence a 'tzadik gamur'. In the communities of the Sepharadic Jews however, it is customary to extend this greeting after the Rosh Hashanah morning service as well.

Our Sages of blessed memory, have said: 'A sign has reality'. We therefore perform symbolic acts as a sign for good — an expression of prayer that we emerge meritorious in judgment and that the new year may be a good one for us. These symbolic acts are performed during the first evening meal of Rosh Hashanah, and in the Sepharadic custom, the second night as well. A morsel of the 'chalah' (festival bread) is dipped into honey, and when there is no honey, in sugar, Some follow the custom of dipping the morsel both in salt and honey. After a 'kazayit' (the equivalent of an olive in size) of the morsel has been eaten, a sweet apple is dipped in honey, the 'brachah' (benediction) for fruit-of-the-tree is uttered over it, and the following prayer is said: 'May it be Your will to renew in our behalf a good and sweet year'. (This last prayer however, is not to be said between the 'brachah' and the eating of the fruit.)

Various vegetables are eaten whose names contain (through alliteration) a symbolic allusion for the good, such as 'silki', 'karti', 'ruviyah', 'kara', and 'tamri' (Aramean names). After each of these the appropriate prayer is recited:

'silki' — to remove. Hence, 'may our enemies be removed.'

'karti' — to cut down. Hence, 'may our enemies be cut down.' (The reference is also to the evil brought about by one's own wrongdoing).

'ruviyah' — to increase. Hence, 'may our merit increase.'

'kara' — to read. Hence, 'may our merit be read before you.'

'tamri' — to consume. Hence, 'may our foes be consumed.'

Obviously these foods should themselves be good for eating, and not bitter or sour.

It is likewise the custom to partake the head of a sheep or a fish, and to say: 'May it be Your wish that we be as a head and not as a tail.' Hence also, some particularly eat fish as a mark of hoped-for blessing.

All this serves to remind man that he stands in judgment and needs self-awakening towards penitence. On this day one should especially guard against anger — which is always considered by our Sages among the severest of transgressions — but which is to be avoided all the more on 'Rosh Hashanah'. Rather, should one clothe himself in the joy of God, and fill his heart with good will and love, so that it be a sign for good to him.

On Rosh Hashanah nuts are not eaten, since they increase phlegm and saliva, and distract one during prayer. Another reason: The numerical value of the Hebrew term for nut, 'egoz', is the same as that of 'chet' (Hebrew for sin) and we refrain from alluding to sin on Rosh Hashanah.

The later Sages add another explanation for the use of these signs on Rosh Hashanah evening: On the Day of Judgment we pray, not for matters of this world but only for the Kingdom of Heaven. However, all the matters of this world are also allusions to the Kingdom of Heaven and our quest for these matters are expressed only in symbolic terms through roundabout signs.

THE TORAH READING OF ROSH HASHANAH

On Rosh Hashanah two Torah scrolls are withdrawn from the Ark. Five men are called up for the reading in the first scroll (five 'aliyot'); one is called up for the reading in the second as a 'maftir' (one who concludes the reading of the Torah and later recites a portion of the Prophetic-Writing called 'haftarah'). On the first day of Rosh Hashanah, the Torah reading in the first scroll deals with the birth of Itzchak (Bereishit 21) since it was on Rosh Hashanah that Sarah, his mother, was remembered by God with the promise of his birth. The reading of the 'maftir', in the second scroll, recounts the prescribed sacrificial offering for Rosh Hashanah (Bamidbar 29). The maftir then reads the 'haftarah' which consists of Hanna's prayer in the Book of Shmuel. Hanna, too, was granted Divine remembrance on this day and her prayer is the basis on which the nine 'brachot' of the day's 'musaf' service are founded.

The second day, the Torah-reading consists of the 'Akedah' (the testing of Avraham with the commandment to sacrifice his son — Bereishit 22), and again there are five 'aliyot'. The maftir, in the second scroll, is the same as that of the previous day. The haftarah in the Book of Irmeyahu contains an account of Israel's future redemption; the hope that future merit may also enable the People of Israel to endure their immediate Day of Judgment, and to emerge the recipients of Divine Mercy. In addition to this, the haftarah also contains an account of our mother Rachel's refusal to be consoled for the exile of her children, and of God's assurance that her hope for their redemption would be vindicated. The fact that Rachel too was granted God's remembrance on Rosh Hashanah, is another reason for selecting this passage as a haftarah for this day.

THE SOUNDING OF THE SHOFAR

We are bidden by the Torah to sound a 'shofar' (a ram's horn) on Rosh Hashanah: 'And in the seventh month, on the first of the month, you shall have a holy convocation; it shall be a day of 'tru'ah' unto you' (Bamidbar 29).

'Although the sounding of the shofar on Rosh Hashanah is a decree of the Torah (which is observed without reasoning), it contains an allusion: Awake you sleepers from your sleep, and you slumberers, arise from your slumber — examine your deeds, repent and remember your Creator. Those of you who forget the truth in the vanities of the times and dwell all year in vanity and emptiness, look into your souls, improve your ways and actions, let each of you forsake his evil path and his thoughts which are not good' (Rambam, Hilchot Teshuvah, Chapter 3).

Rav Se'adiah Gaon recounts ten symbolic meanings in the sounding of the shofar on Rosh Hashanah:

1. The day marks Creation's beginning; thereon God created the world and became its Sovereign. And at the beginning of a reign, it is customary to sound trumpets before the newly crowned king, and to proclaim his ascent to sovereignty throughout the realm. Similarly do we accept the Creator's sovereignty upon ourselves.

2. Rosh Hashanah is the first of the Ten Days of Repentance, 'asseret yemei teshuvah', and shofar is sounded thereon to proclaim and to warn: Whoever wishes to repent — let him repent; if not, let him have remorse later. And this is the way of kings; first they forewarn the people through decrees, and whoever transgresses has no complaint.

3. To remind us of the stand at Mt. Sinai, of which it was said, 'And the sound of the shofar was exceedingly strong.' So that we might accept upon ourselves what our fathers accepted when they said, 'We will do and we will hear (understand and accept).'

4. To remind us of the words of the 'Nevi'im' (the prophets), which were compared to the sounding of a shofar: — 'And whoever hears the sound of the shofar (i. e. the call of the Prophets) and takes no warning — if the sword comes and takes him away, his blood shall be upon his own head; whereas, if he had taken warning, he would have saved his soul' (Yechezkel 33).

5. To remind us of the destruction of 'Beit Hamikdash' (the Sanctuary in Jerusalem) and the trumpet-blasting of the enemy attack. When we hear the shofar's sound, we are to pray to God for the rebuilding of the Sanctuary.

6. To remind us, through the sounding of a ram's horn, of the binding of Itzchak (the 'Akedah'), who offered his life to God, and of the ram slaughtered in his place. Likewise, are we to offer our lives for the sanctification of His Name, so that our remembrance may ascend before Him for the good.

7. When we hear the sound of the shofar, we are to feel fear and trembling, and are to humble ourselves before the Creator. For this is the effect of the shofar — that is arouses fright and trembling, as it is written: 'If a shofar is sounded in the city, shall the people not tremble?' (Amos 3).

8. To recall in fear the forthcoming great Day of Judgment, as it is said: 'Near is the great day of the Lord, near and exceedingly soon is the day of shofar and shouting' (Zephaniah 1).

9. To recall our faith in the future ingathering of Israel's dispersed, and to awaken our yearning for it. As it is said: 'And it shall be on that day — a great shofar will be sounded, and those who have perished in the land of Assyria, and those who were dispersed in the land of Egypt will come...' (Yeshayahu 72).

10. To recall our faith in the future resurrection of the dead. As it is said: 'All you inhabitants of the world, and you who dwell in the earth; when an ensign is lifted on the mountains you shall see, and when the shofar is sounded you shall hear' (Yeshayahu 18).

THE REQUIRED ORDER OF SHOFAR-SOUNDS

The Torah mentions the word 'tru'ah' (a shofar sound) three times with reference to blowing the shofar. Each tru'ah is known to be preceded and followed by a straight sound called teki'ah. Hence, a person is obligated to hear on Rosh Hashanah at least nine shofar-sounds: 'teki'ah-tru'ah-teki'ah, teki'-ah-tru'ah-teki'ah, teki'ah-tru'ah-teki'ah.

Concerning the tru'ah to which the Torah refers — doubt has arisen among us as to its manner, through length of years and the extension of exile, and we no longer know how it is sounded: whether it is a wailing tone, such as women utter among themselves when they lament; or is it a sigh, such as a person might repeatedly utter in a state of acute anxiety; or is it a combination of both sighing and wailing tones which is called tru'ah. For such is the way of one who feels anxiety — he first sighs and then laments. Therefore, we sound all of these shofar tones.

To differentiate between both possible tones, we call the wailing sound 'tru'ah' and the sighing sound we call 'shvarim.'

The order of the shofar-sounding is therefore as follows:

The man who sounds the shofar utters the brachah (benediction said over the performance of a 'mitzvah') and sounds a teki'ah, then a shvarim-tru'ah and finally a teki'ah. He repeats the same order 3 times, thereby sounding 12 sounds: 3 times shvarim-tru'ah — hence 6 sounds, 3 teki'ot preceding the shvarim-tru'ah sounds and 3 teki'ot following — a total of 12 sounds.

He then sounds teki'ah-shvarim-teki'ah 3 times — a total of 9 sounds.

He concludes with the sounding of teki'ah-tru'ah-teki'ah 3 times, also a total of 9 sounds.

The total number of shofar sounds (thus far) are 30 — with all the doubts (concerning the three possible definitions of tru'ah) resolved.

These thirty teki'ot (the term 'teki'ot' is used for both the particular 'teki'ah' sound, as well as for the sounds of the shofar in general) are first sounded after the Torah-Reading and before the 'musaf' prayer. They are called 'teki'ot-meyu'shav' — that is, the teki'ot that are sounded before the silent musaf prayer which is said while standing. It is customary, but not obligatory, for the entire congregation to stand during these first teki'ot too; the man who sounds the shofar (the 'toke'a') is required to stand.

Later, when the congregation stands during musaf, another 30 teki'ot are sounded — 10 after each of the 3 central 'brachot' of the musaf prayer: 'mal-

chu'yot,' 'zichronot' and 'shofrot.' These teki'ot are called 'teki'ot-me'umad,' since the entire congregation is then obliged to stand.

ONE HUNDRED SHOFAR-SOUNDS

The custom became widespread in time, to blow a total of one hundred shofar sounds. (The last forty are blown at the end of musaf.) This number of one hundred sounds has been related symbolically to the one hundred and one letters of the lament uttered by Sisera's mother as she anxiously awaited his return from battle with Israel (Shoftim 5).

The shofar sound is intended to awaken mercy for the offspring of Itzchak, who was bound like a ram on the altar. The sounds of lamentation however, uttered by Sisera's mother, were suffused with incomparable brutality.

When a mother laments over her son's anguish, she experiences compassion for other mothers who likewise weep over their children's death. Sisera's mother, however, is different. She seeks consolation in a strange hope: 'Are they not finding, are they not dividing the spoil ? A maiden, two maidens to each man.' Her son Sisera is presently inflicting death agonies upon Jewish captives and shattering the limbs of their infants. Such thoughts seem to assuage her grief. Can there be greater cruelty ? Let the one hundred shofar sounds of compassion, nullify every one of those other outcries of brutality, except one. For, even the most brutal of mothers, is not devoid of mother's compassion. This one lament of compassion the shofar does not seek to nullify.

The Sephardim add one additional teki'ah to the customary one hundred shofar sounds, at the end of the service, directly before *aleinu.* Their total number of one hundred one shofar sounds corresponds to the numerical value of *Michael,* the name of Israel's protecting angel on high.

It is customary to sound a *teki'ah gedo'lah* as the concluding teki'ah in order to 'confound the Accuser' (Satan), that he might not contend against the people of Israel —

who rejoice with food and drink after their prayers as if they lack fear of Divine Judgment. When Satan hears that many more shofar sounds are blown than the Torah prescribes, he is apprehensive lest he be hearing the *shofar-of-the-Messiah* — and in anticipation of Israel's redemption he ceases his accusations.

It may be asked: Is the Accuser — cunning as he is to trap all mortals — so devoid of understanding as to be frightened by the sound of a shofar, which even children know is not the *shofar-of-the-Messiah* ?

We learn from this, however, that when the people of Israel hear the shofar, they are indeed capable of bringing about the final redemption. When the people of Israel sound their *shofrot* in fulfillment of the precepts-of-the-day, their locked hearts are opened, they shudder over their sins, and in a brief moment their reflections turn to *teshu'vah.* They barely conclude their *teki'ot,* and the sound of the shofar-of-the-Messiah is already heard. The shofar sounds blend — his and theirs — and behold, redemption comes.

Certainly, the Accuser knows these matters better than we do. He knows Israel's strength and the strength of the shofar sounds. They may originate in human blowing, but may well end at the hand of the Messiah, the son of David.

HOW SATAN WAS ONCE CONFOUNDED

An awesome event occurred once in Spain after the Expulsion. Many of the Jews had accepted Christianity under duress. Having held high government offices and having attained great wealth, they found it difficult to forsake all they had toiled for, and the prospect of wandering great distances in famine and destitution struck terror into their hearts. They therefore publicly abjured their faith, but remained inwardly loyal to the God of their fathers — whose precepts they secretly strove to fulfill to their utmost capacity.

There was one among them by the name of Don Fernando Aguilar, who was conductor of the royal orchestra in

Barcelona. The days of Elul arrived; the days of judgment were approaching, and Don Fernando's soul yearned to hear the sound of shofar on Rosh Hashanah. His yearning was shared by many of his brethern.

What did he do?

He announced publicly that on such and such a day (the date of Rosh Hashanah), he would present a concert featuring instrumental music of various peoples...

Many of the *marranoes* (the forcibly converted Jews) came... to hear the sound of the shofar... and they did! Many varied compositions were played by the performers, among them also the shofar sounds: teki'ah, shvarim and trua'h, in full keeping with the prescribed order of the mitzvah of shofar, under the very direction of Don Aguilar himself without any of the clergy aware of it.

It has been said: No one ever succeeded in confounding the Accuser through Shofar-sounds, as did Don Aguilar. All the emissaries of the Accuser were present; the leading figures in the Hierarchy and the Inquisition — they all heard and saw, but knew nothing...

THE SHOFAR — A FINAL DEFENCE

The *Magid* (preacher) of Dubno tells a parable:

'A person once wandered lost in a forest inhabited by wild, predatory animals. He was in possession of a bow and arrows with which to defend himself. As he walked along in the forest he kept imagining that whatever he saw from afar, was a bear, a lion or wolf. He kept aiming arrows at the objects of his fears, but repeatedly found that he had been wasting his arrows on some mirage. Finally he was left with only one arrow. He was hence forced to refrain from shooting his one remaining arrow on a doubt, for that last arrow might later spell the difference between life and death in a moment of danger.

'The moral of the parable: ...when we were still in God's city, and had many instruments of deliverance: the Sanctuary, the altar, the offerings, *the Cohen Gadol*, we felt sufficient strength to counter any raging storm, any predatory, roaring threat. Not so now, when all that remains of those many, mighty instruments of deliverance, is the humble, lowly shofar. Open your eyes therefore, my friend, and see; prepare your hearts and do as wisdom dictates.'

THE SOUNDING OF THE SHOFAR AND ITS BRACHOT

For every 'mitzvah' between Man and God, which is either prescribed by the Torah or the Sages, we are obliged to utter a 'brachah' of thanksgiving and praise to God who sanctified us thereby, and commanded the performance of the mitzvah, Human reason also dictates the recitation of such a brachah.

If a person eats fruit, drinks water, or inhales a fragrant odor for pleasure, he utters a brachah for the pleasures of transitory existence. How much more is he obligated then, to utter a brachah over 'mitzvot' which give him life both in this world and in the World-to-Come!

The fixed phrasing of most brachot is: 'Blessed are You, Lord our God, King of the Universe, who has sanctified us with his commandments...' — The first part is phrased in the second person (Blessed are You...) while the concluding part is phrased in the third person (who has sanctified us with His commandments). For when a person begins to utter a brachah he experiences Divine benevolence directly; he feels the nearness of God and addresses praise to Him directly, as the benevolent source of all that exists. But instantly his heart is filled with fear and trembling; how dare he stand before the King of Kings, the Holy One, Blessed is He, and address Him as 'You'? He therefore concludes — as if apologetically: 'who has sanctified us with 'His' commandments, and has commanded us... How then can I refrain from uttering a brachah to Him?'

Two brachot are uttered in connection with the mitzvah of teki'at shofar: one for the mitzvah itself (birkat hamitzvah), and the other, 'shehecheyanu,' because it occurs irrergularly, and at infrequent intervals. The 'birkat hamitzvah' always precedes 'shehecheyanu,' and both precede the performance of the mitzvah.

The mitzvah of hearing the shofar sounded, falls upon each individual and does not require the presence of a congregation. Whether one is part of a congregation or is alone, he is obligated to sound the shofar (or hear it sounded), and to utter the required brachot (or to hear them). It is commendable to 'enhance' the mitzvah of shofar by hearing it sounded among a multitude, since 'shofar' proclaims our enthronement of God and our acceptance of the laws by which He governs the world, and 'A King's majesty is enhanced in a multitude of people' (Mishley 14).

For this reason all gather in the synagogue, and villagers who have no synagogue or 'minyan' (a gathering of at least ten adult Jews for congregational prayer) of their own, come to the larger towns. An individual sounds shofar for all present after reciting the required brachot, and both he and the listeners are required to have the intention of fulfilling the obligation of the mitzvah.

If both the 'tokea' and the listeners each have the appropriate intention — the 'tokea' to enable his hearers to fulfill the mitzvah, and the listeners to fulfill their obligation — then both are equal in the performance of the mitzvah.

Interruption — even with a word — is prohibited from the utterance of the brachot till the end of all the teki'ot. If one did however converse, he is not required to utter the brachot again, though he committed a transgression.

VERSES WHICH INVOKE COMPASSION

Before the teki'ot and the brachot it is customary to recite Psalm 47 in *Tehilim* (the Book of Psalms) seven times. The Divine Name *'Elokim,'* which connotes the *midat hadin* (attribute-of-justice), is contained seven times in this passage — whose content in general reflects the theme of Rosh Hashanah. Following Psalm 47, seven verses invoking compassion are recited. The first letters of the latter six of these verses form the acrostic, *kerah Satan* ('Cut off the Accuser!'). The required two brachot follow, and the shofar is sounded.

THE EFFECT OF THE SHOFAR

'One is obligated to listen intently to the sounding of shofar on Rosh Hashanah. He should know and understand it to be a Day of Judgment — a day on which God occupies the seat-of-judgment. As sheep pass before a shepherd who stands and says, 'This one for life, that one for slaughter,' so do all the world's inhabitants pass before God — with each one's deeds inscribed in the Divine record, and read before Him, as it were, and with none knowing whether the verdict had marked him for life or death. One should therefore listen intently to the shofar, for it reminds Man to repent and return to God — in order to receive Divine mercy on the Day of Judgment' (Menorat Hama'or).

'...And it is stated in Midrash Tehilim: 'Sound the shofar at the advent of the new month.' — Rabi Brachyah said in the name of Rabi Abba: Beautify (*shapru-shofar*) your deeds, sanctify your deeds! And just as the shofar is sounded on one side, with the sound emerging on the other, similarly — as all the indictments in the world come before Me — do I listen here and extricate there...' (Abudraham).

SHOFAR IS NOT SOUNDED ON SHABAT

Although shofar is a 'great mitzvah' since it heralds the coronation of the Divine King, and awakens 'compassion-in-judgment,' nevertheless the Sages prohibited the sounding of shofar when the first day of Rosh Hashanah falls on 'Shabat.' They did so because of the stringency of Shabat — out of fear lest an ignorant individual go to a scholar for instruction (in the blowing of shofar), or to request the latter to sound shofar in his behalf — in the course of which he might either carry the shofar a distance of four 'amot' (approx. seven feet) in a public domain, or transfer it from one domain to another, thus desecrating Shabat. Such is the stringency of Shabat that its possible desecration even by an individual, postpones the performance of a great mitzvah for all. And the same applies even where there is no public domain, or in a place enclosed by an 'eruv,' which renders carrying permitted even by Rabbinic law.

Nevertheless this mitzvah of shofar can never be totally nullified at any one Rosh Hashanah. As has been said, the two Rosh Hashanah days are considered as one long day. If one, therefore, sounds shofar the second day, it is as if he sounded it on the first. And since the second day cannot fall on Shabat, it could never happen that shofar would not at least be sounded on the second day of Rosh Hashanah.

When it was decreed that shofar not be sounded on Shabat, the decree applied only to places lacking a 'Beit Din' (a Rabbinical court). As long, therefore, as the Sanctuary stood in Yerushalayim, and the 'Beit Din Hagadol' functioned therein, shofar was sounded in Yerushalayim and its environs. In the remainder of Israel's cities, however, it was not sounded.

THE TIME FOR TEKI'AT SHOFAR

The time for sounding shofar is during the day only — from sunrise till sunset; but 'the diligent perform 'mitzvot' as early as possible.'

Why, then, did it become a prescribed custom to sound the 'teki'ot' publicly after the Torah-Reading, and also during 'musaf', rather than during the earlier 'shacharit' service?

Because of an occurrence which transpired:

During a time of persecution, enemies suspected the Jews of sounding the shofar in crowded synagogues as a call to war; and they wanted to slay the Jews. The practice was consequently adopted of sounding shofar later, and also during musaf. The sight of the Jews reading the 'Sh'mah,' standing in prayer, reading the Torah and then sounding the shofar, would provide convincing proof that the Jews were engaged in the performance of mitzvot and not in a call to war.

Another reason for the postponement of the teki'ot till musaf: A prohibition was once issued forbidding the sounding of shofar. The Jews were spied upon by their enemies till six hours of the day had passed. Upon seeing that the shofar was not being sounded, the latter relaxed their watch, whereupon the Jews finally did sound the shofar. Later, the decree was nullified, but the new time was not rescinded, for fear that the earlier prohibition against shofar might be revived.

INSCRIBE US FOR LIFE

One's Rosh Hashanah prayers ought to be essentially directed towards the establishment of God's Sovereignty, and the fulfillment of communal needs, rather than individual ones; their aim ought to be that Mankind might emerge meritorious-in-judgment — that peace might increase, and that God's Sovereignty might be revealed over mankind. As all Mankind passes before God, to be remembered either for life or death, their essential prayer should be: 'May every existing being know that You have made it; and may every creature understand that You have created it; and may all that breathes declare: The Lord, God of Israel is King, and His Kingdom rules over all.'

If a person knows that he faces judgment for all his actions — how can he be concerned with the fulfillment of personal needs ? Even if he knows that he will emerge meritorious-in-judgment, how could his heart enable him to seek his own good, as the entire world is weighed-in-the-balance, for penalty or acquittal? Let him rather seek compassion for himself and the entire world, that all might be inscribed for good life; and He who portions out life to every living being, will then provide all that they lack. For thus did the Sages say: 'He who gives life gives sustenance.'

PRAYERS OF THE DAYS OF AWE

The prayers uttered by Israel before God during the Days of Awe (Rosh Hashanah and Yom Kipur) are distinguished among the 'tefilot' (prayers, of the remaining festivals by their mode; by addition to those of their brachot which are standard in prayer; by their melodies and by the number of their brachot.

All year the weekday 'amidah' (prayer uttered while standing) contains eighteen brachot (excepting 'velamalshinim'). Shabat and Yom Tov, (other than Rosh Hashanah), it contains only seven brachot. Of these, the first three and last three are the same as those of the weekday 'amidah,' while the fourth, central brachah, relates to the particular sanctity-of-the-day, 'kedushat ha'yom.' On Shabat it concludes: 'Who sanctifies the Shabat,' and on Yom Tov it concludes: 'Who sanctifies Israel and the times-of-festival.'

The form of the festival 'tefilot' is the same for the various 'Yamim Tovim,' except for mention of the specific festival in the indicated places. During musaf, the fourth, central brachah, recounts the sacrificial offerings prescribed for the specific festival. Otherwise there are no differences. The Rosh Hashanah prayers however, differ in many respects.

1. In the first two and the last two brachot, four passages are respectively added:

a) 'Remember us for life...' — ('zochrenu').
b) 'Who is like you...' — ('mi kamocha').
c) 'Inscribe us for life...' — ('uchtov').
d) 'In the book of life...' — ('besefer').

These passages are said the entire ten days of penitence till the conclusion of 'ne'ilah' on Yom Kipur — with the one further change for 'ne'ilah,' of substituting 'chatimah' (sealing) for 'ketivah' (inscription), in praying for life (since the Divine decree is sealed at the close of Yom Kipur).

2. The third brachah concludes with 'the holy King,' instead of 'the holy God.' This, too, applies to the entire ten day period of penitence.

3. The third brachah ('You are holy') is lengthened, and petitions are added for the manifestation of Divine Sovereignty; Israel's honor; the honor due those who serve God; the joy of the righteous and Jerusalem; the passing of evil from the earth; and the manifestation of the light of the Messiah. These passages are added to the third brachah of the Yom Kipur 'amidah' as well, but they are not added to the 'amidah' during the remaining days between Rosh Hashanah and Yom Kipur.

4. During the other festivals the fourth brachah ('kedushat hayom' — the sanctity of the day) makes reference to the day and to Israel; on Rosh Hashanah however, it also invokes the spread of God's Sovereignty over all the Earth; over Israel; and over all the world's peoples.

5. It is the custom in most Sephardic and in many Ashkenazi communities to include various liturgical poems, 'pi'yutim,' prior to the amidah — and in the 'chazarat hashatz' (repetition by the cantor), during the amidah as well. 'Avinu Malkenu' is recited upon the conclusion of 'shacharit,' excepting the times when Rosh Hashanah falls on Shabat. In the Sepharadic communities, however, 'Avinu Malkenu' is said on Shabat also. Likewise, Psalm 130 is recited during shacharit in all communities, before the 'kadish' or 'barchu.'

6. The cantor intones the traditional Rosh Hashanah chants and melodies, and dwells on them at greater length than would be his practice any other Yom Tov. Of these various additions and changes, some were transmitted to us from the 'Anshei K'nesset Hagdolah' (Rabis of the Great Synod), who fixed the mode content of all the 'tefilot' of the year; while others are a heritage from the greatest of the Sages, who knew how to approach their Maker on the Day of Judgment, and how to awaken fear of Heaven, and trembling before God's judgment.

7. The essential difference which characterizes the Rosh Hashanah prayers is the inclusion of three lengthy brachot in the musaf service: the order of 'malchu'yot,' 'zichronot' and 'shofrot.'

MALCHUYOT, ZICHRONOT SHOFROT
(Sovereignty, Providence, Revelation)

In the year-round musaf prayers, the Rabis-of-the-Great-Synod included seven fixed brachot, but for the Rosh Hashanah musaf, they prescribed nine brachot. The first three and last three are essentially the same on Rosh Hashanah as in every other 'musaf' (with the exception of the several previously cited changes and additions). The three central brachot are called 'malchuyot,' 'zichronot' and 'shofrot.'

The 'order of malchuyot' is included in the fourth brachah ('kedushat hayom' — the sanctity of the day). No individual brachah is prescribed for 'malchuyot,' since the essential sanctity of the day consists in making God Sovereign over all His works. For the 'order of zichronot' and that of 'shofrot' however, separate brachot are prescribed. The total number of brachot in the Rosh Hashanah musaf is therefore nine.

These nine brachot correspond to the nine 'azkarot' (utterances of God's Name) uttered by Hannah in her prayer: 'My heart rejoices in the Lord...' (First Shmuel 2).

'Mar stated: On Rosh Hashanah Sarah, Rachel and Hannah were granted Divine remembrance' (Tr. Brachot 29). Corresponding to the nine utterances of God's Name in Hannah's thanksgiving for the Divine gift granted her on Rosh Hashanah, we utter nine brachot in our observance of Rosh Hashanah.

In the 'order of malchuyot' we acknowledge God's creation of all existence, His Sovereignty over the entire universe, and our acceptance of His dominion unto eternity.

In the 'order of zichronot' we proclaim our faith that the Creator's relationship to all He fashioned is a providential one; that all of Man's actions are subject to Divine remembrance; that God bestows reward and inflicts punishment in accord with Man's actions.

In the 'order of shofrot' we accept the yoke of Torah as if it were given once again with thunder and lightning, and mighty shofar blasts. We also await the final redemption which is to be heralded by the 'shofar-of-Messiah.'

The three orders of malchuyot, zichronot and shofrot are all cast in one form: each order begins with an introductory plea on its respective theme; it continues with the citation of ten scriptural verses on the same theme, and ends with a concluding paragraph, on a note of brachah.

TEN UTTERANCES, TEN COMMANDMENTS AND TEN PRAISES

With ten utterances God created His world and became its Sovereign ('and He said: Let there be...' occurs ten times in the account of Creation in the Book of Bereishit). In accepting His Sovereignty on Rosh Hashanah we too utter ten verses of malchuyot.

Through the Ten Commandments spoken at Sinai, God 'folded' His entire Torah and gave it to Israel, through whom He made it known to the world's inhabitants; He thereby became the world's lawgiver and judge. When standing before His seat of judgment on the Day of Judgment we too utter ten verses of zichronot — that we might be remembered for good and emerge meritorious.

With ten expressions of *halel* (praise), His anointed King David concludes *Tehilim* (the Book of Psalms) — which contain redemptive correction for all transgressions of all generations, till the Earth will behold God's revelation, and all that breathes will praise Him. When we hear the shofar sound, we too utter ten verses of shofrot, to know and make it known that the Torah by which we shall walk till the end of days, derives for us from Him alone; and that from Him alone deliverances and salvation will be forthcoming for all the world's peoples.

In allusion to these three themes of Sovereignty, Providence and Revelation (malchuyot, zichronot, shofrot), the prophet Yeshayahu says: 'For the Lord is our Judge, the

Lord is our Lawgiver, the Lord is our King, He will give us salvation' (Yeshayahu 33).

The prophet begins at midpoint in world history — when we became a people and God became our Judge and Lawgiver. He then returns to the beginning of days — from which time God's Sovereignty endures. He finally concludes with the end of days — when the power of God's actions and His salvation will become manifest for all. We, however, begin with Sovereignty and then continue with Providence and Revelation.

Why did the Sages choose to begin with malchuyot and then to continue with zichronot and shofrot? — First, make Him your Sovereign and then seek compassion from Him, so that you might be remembered before Him. And how? — With the shofar of liberation...' (Sifri Beha'alotecha).

HE REMEMBERS ALL THAT IS FORGOTTEN

It is quoted in the name of a particular *tzadik* (a pious man) that he explained the Divine Attribute of 'remembering what is forgotten' as follows:

It is the way of God to remember what Man forgets, but to forget what Man remembers. How?

If a man commits a transgression and forgets it without penitence, then God remembers it, and brings the offender to judgment.

If a person commits a transgression, but always remembers it, as did David who said: 'And my sin is always before me' — then God does not remember the offence.

If a person performs a mitzvah and remembers it always, in conceit, then God does not remember it, for 'the Lord hates the haughty.'

If a person performs a mitzvah and forgets it, and it is as naught in his own eyes — then God always remembers it, treasures it, and rewards its doer appropriately.

ROSH CHODESH IS NOT MENTIONED IN THE DAY'S PRAYERS

Rosh Hashanah is also a *Rosh Chodesh* (New Moon) — the first day of the month of Tishrey, and in the Sanctuary (Beit Hamikdash), the prescribed sacrificial offering for Rosh Chodesh was brought. Nevertheless, no mention is made of Rosh Chodesh in any of the prayers prescribed for the day.

The matter may be likened to a king who arrives in a city accompanied by dukes and ministers. None of the princes or ministers who come with the king are mentioned: only the king is. Likewise Rosh Hashanah: if Rosh Chodesh comes with the King (Rosh Hashanah), it remains unmentioned (Tashbetz).

MUSAF DURING HOURS OF COMPASSION

If an individual prays at home on Rosh Hashanah, he ought not pray musaf the first three hours of the day, since these hours are hours of Divine anger towards, and judgment of, idolators.

'We have learned in the name of Rabi Meir: When kings place their crowns upon their heads, and bow down to the sun (at the third hour of the day, which was the time for rising on the part of gentile kings), then God is immediately angered.

'Rabi Yosef said: Let no one pray musaf the first three hours of the day, on Rosh Hashanah if he is alone. During these hours Divine judgment is stern, and the individual might be rejected in judgment. If so — shall the congregation also not pray the first three hours? — The congregation is not rejected because its merits are many' (Tr. Avodah Zarah 4).

THE PIYUT 'UNTANE TOKEF'

'Rabi Amnon of Meintz was a *gedol hador* ('great of his generation'). He was wealthy, of aristocratic ancestry and handsome in appearance. The ministers and the ruler sought to prevail upon him to convert to their religion, but he would not hear them. Each day they spoke to him, but to no avail, and the ruler began to press him strongly. One day when they became particularly insistent, he said: 'I wish to take counsel and to deliberate on the matter for as many as three days.' He spoke thus only to put them off.

'On departing from the ruler's presence, he took it to heart that he had allowed an expression of doubt to pass his lips — as if there were a possibility that he might deny the Living God. He returned home, and would not eat or drink, till he became ill. All his near-and-dear-ones came to console him, but he refused to accept consolation, saying, 'I will go down to the grave in mourning.' He wept and grieved.

'The third day — in his state of pain and anxiety — the ruler sent for him, but he said, 'I will not go.' The tyrant thereupon sent officials of higher rank and in greater number than his first emissaries — Rabi Amnon still refused. The ruler finally ordered Rabi Amnon brought forcibly — which was promptly done.

'The ruler addressed him: 'What is this, Amnon — why didn't you appear before me after taking counsel — at the time you yourself set for a final response to my request?

'Whereupon Rabi Amnon answered: 'I will decree my own penalty. The tongue which spoke lyingly to you — shall be severed.' For Rabi Amnon wanted to sanctify God's Name after having spoken adversely.

'No,' said the ruler, 'I will not have your tongue cut out for it spoke well. Rather will I sever the legs which failed to come at the time you appointed and I will also inflict punishment on the remaining parts of your body.'

'The tyrant then had Rabi Amnon's hands and legs severed at each joint successively. As each joint was severed, he was asked: 'Do you finally want to convert to our faith?' He repeatedly answered in the negative. After the amputations were complete, the evil tyrant had Rabi Amnon sent home with his severed limbs at his side. Not for naught was his name Rabi Amnon — for he placed his faith (Amnon — *Emunah* — faithfulness) in the Living God, and endured the severest of tortures in behalf of his faith.

'Shortly afterwards, the time of Rosh Hashanah arrived, and Rabi Amnon asked to be brought to the synagogue with his severed limbs, and to be placed near the cantor. This was done, and when the cantor reached *kedushah,* Rabi Amnon said to him: 'Wait a while, and I will sanctify the great Name of God.' Rabi Amnon then began aloud: 'And thus shall holiness ascend to you...' He continued with '*untaneh tokef kedushat hayom*' ('And let us convey the mighty holiness of this day...') which proclaims God's judgment of Man's action on Rosh Hashanah and Man's acquiescence in the rendition of Divine justice. At the hymn's conclusions, Rabi Amnon expired and departed from this world — taken by God. And of him it is said: 'How great is the good which You hold in concealment for those who fear You' (Tehilim 31).

'The third day after Rabi Amnon had been called on High, in purity, he appeared in a vision of the night to Rabenu Klonimus, the son of Rabenu Meshulam; he taught Rabenu Klonimus the hymn *untaneh tokef* and bade him to send it to the entire Diaspora, so that he might be remembered thereby. The *Gaon* did accordingly' (Or Zaru'a — The Laws of Rosh Hashanah).

'HAYOM HARAT OLAM'

The reason for saying '*hayom harat olam...*' ('This is the day of the creation of the world...'), during the musaf prayer of Rosh Hashanah, is because on this day the world has first come into existence and it is being renewed again, as at first, to continue its existence until the next Rosh Hashanah.

We say '*hayom harat olam*' at the end of each of the three 'orders' of *malchuyot, zichronot* and *shofrot,* since the renewal of the world on this day of Rosh Hashanah resembles the three fresh starts that the world has experienced: On the Six Days of Creation, after the Flood and on the day of the Giving of the Torah.

In the Six Days of Creation the world was formed to be ruled by the system of *malchuyot* (Sovereignty). After the Flood the system was changed by diminishing Sovereignty and adding a new rule of *zichronot* (Providence). On the height of Mt. Sinai the system was changed anew and the world was now founded on three elements: *malchuyot, zichronot* and *shofrot* (Revelation).

For a thousand, six hundred and fifty six years, God treated Man with the attribute of Sovereignty alone. The Lord, King of the Universe on-High, has crowned Man over the lower creation. He endued him with honor, gave him power and might, made his life long and let him do in the world as he wished. He did not give him the Torah, nor the Seven Laws of the gentiles (save by allusion), He did not promise him any award nor warned him with punishment. Those of a King's household do not require any codes, they are only demanded to live up to their greatness, retain the Honor of Kingdom and be worthy of their high standing by upright deeds and thoughts as prescribed by the wisdom of their hearts.

Man however, did not stand this test of Sovereignty. Instead of bestowing the world with graciousness through the mighty powers that were given in his hand to rule the entire creation, he filled the whole world with lusts, ugliness and wickedness. Instead of being an associate of the Lord Who had created His world with grace and love, he became a partner of the Corrupting Devil and used his greatness only to corrupt.

For a long period, the descendants of Adam were treated with patience and tolerance. When 'their measure was full' and they showed no sign of repentance, the Flood came and washed them away.

It became apparent that a world based on the foundation of Sovereignty alone could no more exist. Man's earthly instincts would always overpower him. Even if he possessed tremendous abilities but lacked fear and worry, his lusts would drive him towards evil and destruction.

Thus, for the next seven hundred and ninety two years, God combined the attribute of *zichronot* with that of *malchuyot* to be jointly ruling the world. Perhaps Sovereignty together with Providence would secure the world's existence. Man was not derived of his crown and superiority, but he had to come under a yoke of explicit laws and commandments. He could no more do as he wished but had to beware of supervision, of awards and punishments. God also shortened Man's life, and diminshed his powers so that even if he wished, he would not be able to corrupt the world in a short while.

Yet, the world did not stand even this second test. Ten generations from Noah to Avraham were continuously defying God's laws although they well knew their behavior would surely cause a second collapse.

Sovereignty and greatness were not sufficient to defend Man against his evil instincts. Providence did not suffice either. The knowledge that he would be called upon to account for his deeds was not enough to prevent Man from his wrongdoings. Even if you restricted him by warnings and penalties, he would still break laws and pursue wickedness. His philosophy would be: 'Eat, drink and be merry, for tomorrow we die.'

And the world was on the brink of a second disaster, till a nation arose, of the descendants of Avraham, Itzchak and Ya'akov, and undertook the responsibility to care for the whole creation. They took upon themselves to straighten the crooked and restore Honor to those who were created in God's image. They have saved the world from regressing into void and emptiness and when they received the Torah at Mount Sinai, it was as if the world was reborn; this time, unto eternity.

In this renewal God has added a third element to form, with the other two, a basis for everlasting existence. This was the element of *shofrot*, that is, the ability of Man to perceive Revelation of God; to hear the voice of prophecy, the call of his conscience, ringing inside him and making him tremble as when a shofar blasts, always demanding and imploring, 'Where are you!'

From the moment the Israelites said, 'We shall do and we shall hear,' — 'we shall do' what none had done before, 'and we shall hear' the Voice of God coming out of our hearts and from all being — from that moment the world has become truly established.

The recognition of Man's esteem and august standing through his power of Kingdom, elevates him and makes him capable of exalted tasks; —

his knowledge that all his deeds are supervised and remembered before God's Seat of Judgment and that he is to account for all he does — deters him from abandon to sin without reckoning; —

and now comes the 'voice of a shofar' bursting forth from the depths of his heart, awakening him from sleep and forgetfulness, reminding him what he is and what role he has to play and showing him a way of repentance and rise when he has sinned and fallen.

With thunder and lightning God revealed Himself unto the entire nation and with mighty shofar blasts he appeared upon the children of Israel, till they became like prophets. Even after those sounds stopped, their echoes remained and have unceasingly done their parts in the inner conscience of every Israelite, everyone according to his conception.

The echoes of those *shofrot* are always prevalent. At times they are strong and at times they get weaker and then strong again. When the Great Day of the Lord comes, they shall burst with their full might and be heard by all mankind — 'And it shall be on that day, a great shofar shall be sounded, and they that were lost in the land of Assyria shall come, and they that were dispersed in the land of Egypt... and they shall bow to the Lord on the Mount of Holy, in Jerusalem...' (Yeshayahu 27).

On each and every Rosh Hashanah, as the year is renewed from the Source of the early Creation and its three starts, we pray to God, our Creator, that He shall strengthen within us these three elements on which the world is based — until the day comes when the world reaches its ultimate salvation, in the End of Days, through malchuyot, zichronot and shofrot:

'Let all the inhabitants of the world know and recognize..' and let them come under the yoke of Your Sovereignty...'

'Remember us with Providence of good before You.. for You remember all that is forgotten..'

'Blow the great shofar for our liberation... (greater than the first one on which it is said — Shmot 19:) It came to pass on the third day, when it was morning, that there were thunders and lightnings and a thick cloud upon the mount, and the voice of a shofar, exceedingly loud; and all the people that were in the camps trembled...'

SLEEP ON ROSH HASHANAH

It is customary to refrain from sleep during the day of Rosh Hashanah, and rather to study Torah, or to recite 'Tehilim' (Psalms) in congregation. If one is idle, it is as if he slept.

It is stated in the Jerusalem Talmud: 'If one sleeps at the year's beginning (i.e. on Rosh Hashanah), his good fortune likewise sleeps.'

And if one's head aches and he would find it difficult to utter the 'minchah' prayer with proper concentration, because of fatigue, he is permitted to nap briefly during the afternoon.

TASHLICH — (The Casting away of Sin)

'Minchah' of Rosh Hashanah begins with 'ashrey — uva letzion.' (On Shabat, a Torah reading from the weekly portion follows). The silent prayer is the same as that of shacharit, and 'Avinu Malkenu' is said after the cantor's repetition. If Rosh Hashanah falls on Shabat, Avinu Malkenu is not said, and the same applies if the second day of Rosh Hashanah falls on Friday. The Sephardim however, say Avinu Malkenu on Shabat also.

After minchah, the prayer of 'Tashlich' is said near an ocean or river. In the absence of an ocean or river, the prayer may be said near a spring or well, or even an ingathering of rain water. The following verse is recited: 'Who is a God like You, Who pardons iniquity and passes over the transgression of the remnant of His chosen people! He does not retain His anger forever, because He desires benevolence. He will again have compassion upon us; He will subdue our iniquities; And You will cast all their sins into the depths of the sea' (Michah 7). Other 'verses of compassion' follow, as well as passages from 'Tehilim'. Some add a prayer composed by Rabi Chaim David Azulai (known by the acrostic 'Chida'). One's pockets are shaken empty three times to symbolize the heart's intention to cast away sin, and to achieve total purification from its effect. This custom also finds symbolic support in a verse in Nehemiah: 'Also I shook out my lap, and said: So may God shake out every man from his house and labor, who will not perform this promise... And all the congregation said 'Amen,' and praised the Lord. And the people did according to this promise' (Nehemiah 5).

'Tashlich' also recalls 'the merit of the fathers.

When our Father Avraham went to bind Itzchak as a sacrifice over the altar (on the day of Rosh Hashanah), Satan appeared before them in the form of a large river. They entered and the water rose till their necks. Our Father Avraham then said before God: 'Lord of the Universe, The waters have reached life itself. If either I or my son Itzchak drown, through whom will the Unity of Your Name be rendered?' God thereupon 'scolded' the river and they were saved. We therefore go near seas or rivers to recall their merit in having offered their lives for the fulfillment of God's commandments.

If the first day of Rosh Hashanah falls on Shabat, Tashlich is said after minchah the second day. The Sephardim however say Tashlich the first day even when it coincides with Shabat.

THE SECOND DAY OF ROSH HASHANAH

The observance and the order of prayer for the second day of Rosh Hashanah are the same as for the first day, with the exception of the Torah-reading and the 'haftarah' (as indicated earlier).

Prior to the recitation of 'kidush' (blessings over wine made at the opening of Yom Tov dinner), it is customary to place a new fruit on the table, or to don a new garment, requiring the brachah of 'shehecheyanu.' And when one says shehecheyanu during kidush, his intention should extend simultaneously to the new fruit or garment, and the sanctity of the day, since it is doubtful whether the inclusion of shehecheyanu in kidush is obligatory the second night. Women too, follow this practice, when reciting shehecheyanu during the lighting of candles the second night. If however, neither a new fruit or a new garment had been prepared, shehecheyanu is nevertheless said, in accordance with the view of most of the authorities. The Sephardim do not say shehecheyanu during the shofar-sounding of the second day.

ERUV TAVSHILIN

When the second day of Rosh Hashanah falls on Erev Shabat (Friday), it is necessary to make an 'Eruv Tavshilin' before the advent of Yom Tov, in order to be permitted to prepare the foods needed for Shabat during Yom Tov.

What is an 'eruv'? The Sages prohibited cooking on Yom Tov for the ensuing Shabat, so that a person might not come to cook Yom Tov for an ensuing weekday. If however, one prepared a cooked food on 'Erev Yom Tov' (the day preceding the festival) for the Shabat following Yom Tov, it is permissible, (to cook Yom Tov for the Shabat following), since it is as if he had begun to cook on Erev Yom Tov the foods he would need Shabat, and now he is only completing his work. In preparing an 'eruv', he symbolically mixes ('eruv' — mixture) his cooking for Shabat with his cooking for Yom Tov, so that both are regarded as one cooking.

The eruv consists of one baked food and one cooked food. Erev Yom Tov, before dark, one takes hold of a 'chalah' or 'matzah' and a cooked food, such as meat, fish or a boiled egg, at least equal in size to a 'kazayit' (olive-size). Both foods are put aside in a reserved place and kept for Shabat. Before the eruv is 'concealed,' a 'brachah' is recited: '...who sanctified us with His commandments and commanded us concerning the mitzvah of eruv.' Now, although this mitzvah is prescribed only by the Sages and does not originate in the Torah, we nevertheless say: 'and He commanded us,' because God has commanded us in His Torah to obey the precepts of the Sages, as it is stated: 'You shall not turn away from whatever they instruct you.' And this is the general reason for referring to God as the source of the particular commandment, even in brachot recited for Rabbinic enactments.

After the 'brachah' the following is said: 'Through this eruv we shall be permitted to bake, cook, keep warm and light a fire (by contact with another fire, since new fire may not be kindled Yom Tov) and to perform whatever we are in need of on Yom Tov for the ensuing Shabat.' The eruv is kept till Shabat, when it is used for 'lechem mishneh' (the mitzvah of taking two loaves for a Shabat meal), so that another mitzvah be added to the previous mitzvah performed thereby.

A person may benefit his neighbors or anyone else through his eruv. And if he thus intends, those others are also permitted thereby to cook on Yom Tov for Shabat. This only applies however, to one who had forgotten to make an eruv. If he remembered, and failed to make an eruv because he intended to eat Shabat in a home other than his own, but subsequently changed his mind, and wishes to cook on Yom Tov for Shabat, then he cannot rely on the eruv of another.

It is proper to 'benefit' others with one's eruv. If one does so he gives the bread and cooked food to an adult member of his household — or even a minor, if the latter is not of his household — and says to him: 'Acquire these cooked foods in behalf of others.' He then recites the above mentioned, 'Through this eruv, it shall be permitted...,' but concludes: 'unto us and all who live in this city.'

Tishrey THE TEN DAYS OF PENITENCE AND YOM KIPUR

THE FAST OF GEDALIAH ❖ BETWEEN ROSH HASHANAH AND YOM KIPUR ❖ ASERET YEMEI TESHUVAH ❖ PRAYER DURING THE TEN DAYS OF PENITENCE ❖ TESHUVAH ❖ TRUTH AND PEACE ❖ THE FOUNDATIONS OF TESHUVAH ❖ THE STRENGTH OF TESHUVAH ❖ BETWEEN MAN AND HIS FELLOW ❖ TESHUVAH DURING LIFE ❖ CHILDREN ACHIEVE MERIT FOR FATHERS ❖ CHILDREN'S PRAYER ❖ SHABAT SHUVAH ❖ RETURN O ISRAEL — TO THE LORD YOUR GOD ❖ THE CUSTOM OF KAPAROT ❖ PRAYERS OF EREV YOM KIPUR ❖ CHARITY ON EREV YOM KIPUR ❖ IMMERSION IN A MIKVAH ❖ THE MEAL BEFORE THE FAST ❖ FIVE AFFLICTIONS ON YOM KIPUR ❖ PASSAGES ON TESHUVAH FROM 'HAYEY ADAM' ❖ WHITE GARMENTS ❖ TEFILAH ZAKAH ❖ KOL NIDREY ❖ ON THE RECITATION OF KOL NIDREY ❖ 'THE SONG OF THE ANGELS' — ALOUD ❖ CONFESSION OF SIN ❖ 'LIKE THE SHEETS OF SHLOMO' ❖ TORAH-READING ON YOM KIPUR ❖ YIZKOR — THE REMEMBRANCE OF SOULS ❖ PIKUACH NEFESH ON YOM KIPUR ❖ 'SEDER AVODAH' ❖ THE COHEN AT SERVICE — THE PEOPLE AT WATCH ❖ STANDING CROWDED AND BOWING SPACIOUSLY ❖ A GENTILE GUEST RELATES ❖ IN THE ABSENCE OF THE BEIT HAMIKDASH ❖ EXPRESSLY 'EMERGING' FROM THE MOUTH OF THE COHEN GODOL ❖ KNEELING DURING 'ALENU' AND KNEELING DURING 'VIDUI' ❖ THE FIVE SERVICES ON YOM KIPUR ❖ THE CLOSING OF THE GATES.

CHAPTER TWO

THE FAST OF GEDALIAH

On the day immediately following Rosh Hashanah — the third of Tishrey — the Fast of Gedaliah is observed. In the Prophetic-Writings this fast is called 'The Fast-of-the-Seventh' in allusion to Tishrey, the seventh month.

When Rosh Hashanah falls on Thursday and Friday, the fast is postponed till Sunday, since no public fast is observed on Shabat with the exception of Yom Kipur. The fast is observed from daybreak till the stars appear at night. The cantor includes the prayer *anenu* in the repetition of the *shacharit amidah.* A Torah Scroll is withdrawn (from the ark), the 'Thirteen-Divine-Attributes' are said and the Passages of *Vayechal* are read from the Torah (Shmot 32: 11—14 and 34: 1—10).

The fast was instituted by the Sages to commemorate the assassination of Gedaliah Ben Achikam, which was perpetrated by Yishmael Ben Netaniah on the instigation of the King of Ammon. As a result of Gedaliah's death the final vestiges of Judean autonomy after the Babylonian conquest were destroyed, many thousands of Jews were slain, and the remaining Jews were driven into final exile.

When Nebuchadnetzar King of Babylonia, destroyed the Sanctuary and exiled the people to Babylonia, he allowed an impoverished remnant to remain in the land, and appointed Gedaliah Ben Achikam as their Governor. Many Jews who had fled to Moab, Ammon, Edom, and other neighboring lands, returned to the land of Yehudah, tended the vineyards given to them by the king of Babylonia and enjoyed a new respite after their earlier oppression.

The King of Ammon however — hostile and envious of the Judean remnant — sent Yishmael Ben Netaniah to assassinate Gedaliah. In the seventh month (Tishrey) Yishmael came to Gedaliah in the town of Mitzpa, and was received cordially. Gedaliah had been warned of his guest's murderous intent, but refused to believe his informants, in the belief that their report was mere slander. Yishmael murdered Gedaliah, together with most of the Jews who had joined him and numbers of Babylonians whom the Babylonian King had left with Gedaliah. The remaining Jews feared the vengeance of the Babylonian King and fled to Egypt. The surviving remnant of Jews was thus dispersed and the land remained desolate. In remembrance of these tribulations, our Sages instituted the 'Fast-of-the-Seventh,' on the day of Gedaliah's assassination in the seventh month.

There is an opinion that Gedaliah was slain the first day of Tishrey, but the fast was postponed till after Rosh Hashanah, since fasting is prohibited during a festival. Concerning this fast day, the Rabis have said that its aim is to establish that the death of the righteous is likened to the burning of the house of our God. Just as they ordained a fast upon the destruction of the Sanctuary, likewise did they ordain a fast upon the death of Gedaliah.

BETWEEN ROSH HASHANAH AND YOM KIPUR

The seven days between Rosh Hashanah and Yom Kipur are called 'days-of-repentance,' or 'the ten-days-of-repentance,' since these days constitute the larger part of the total ten days period set apart for repentance: the two days of Rosh Hashanah, Yom Kipur, and the seven intervening days. And since the days of Rosh Hashanah and Yom Kipur are called by their specific names, the designation 'ten days of repentance' is applied to the intervening days. These days are also referred to by the name: *'bein kese le'asor'* (between Rosh Hashanah, which is called *kese* — as stated above — and Yom Kipur, which is called *asor*).

These names recall to Man the character of the days to which they adhere. They remind him that he is suspended between two days of judgment; between Rosh Hashanah, when his judgment is inscribed, and Yom Kipur, when it is sealed. And one who possesses this awareness will not turn his thoughts away from the fear of judgment and the obligation of repentance.

ASERET YEMEI TESHUVAH — (The Ten Days of Repentance)

'Since God loves His people and — in His benevolence — He desires not the death of the iniquitous but rather his repentance and continued life, He therefore waits for the penitence of those who transgress. In His abundant mercy He designated specific days when He draws near to us and accepts our repentance immediately — as it is said: 'See God when He is found, call unto Him when He is near.' This led our Sages of blessed memory to comment: 'We are taught therein that God at times is to be found and at times not to be found; that at times He is near and at times He is not near. When is He to be found *and* near? during the ten days between Rosh Hashanah and Yom Kipur.

'Therefore, although repentance and prayer are always appropriate, they are all the more appropriate during the ten-day Rosh Hashanah — Yom Kipur period.

'During these days additional prayers are uttered; special *selichot* (penitential prayers) are said before dawn, and greater care is exercised in the observance of *mitzvot.*

'The imposition of oaths on litigants in dispute is avoided. A *Beit Din* refrains from imposing a ban on persons otherwise subject to ban, in the hope that they might repent on Yom Kipur. It is also the custom not to hold weddings during this period.

'During this period too the wording of *kadish* is changed. The word '*l'ela*' is repeated and we say '*l'ela-l'ela.*' The year-round wording alludes to the exaltation of God beyond all earthly benediction; the usage for the ten-day penitential period bespeaks an even greater Divine exaltation, in keeping with the central motif of the Days of Awe — the acceptance of Divine Sovereignty. In addition, since the specified total number of words in the *kadish* has a particular significance, we contract two other words, so that the total number of words should remain constant: instead of *min kol birchata,* we say, *mikol birchata.*

'In the Jerusalem Talmud, it is stated: Rabi Chiya bade Rav: 'If you find it possible to eat all year in purity, do so; if not, then at least eat in purity during seven days of the year'.

'Avi Ha'ezri comments: 'I have it as a tradition that these seven days are the intervening seven days between Rosh Hashanah and Yom Kipur.'

'And the Rosh writes: 'It is therefore the custom in *Ashkenaz* (Germany and the communities deriving from the German center) that even those who do not refrain from eating non-Jewish bread all year are careful not to do so during the ten-days-of-penitence' (Abudraham).

PRAYER DURING THE TEN DAYS OF PENITENCE

The order of prayer during the 'aseret yemei teshuvah' is the same as during the entire year except that in the 'amidah' we append to the first two 'brachot': 'Remember-us-for-life...' and 'Who-is-like You...' And to the final two brachot we append: 'Inscribe-for-a-good-life...' and 'In-the-book-of-life...' If however, one forgot to say any of these four phrases till after the close of the respective brachot to which they are appended, then he is not required to repeat the brachot.

At the conclusion of the third brachah (kedushah) one says: 'Blessed are You, O Lord, the Holy King' instead of, 'the Holy God.' If he forgot — he is required to begin the amidah again. In the brachah, 'Restore our Judges,' we conclude, 'the King in

Judgment,' instead of, 'the King who loves righteousness and justice.' If one forgot, and concluded with the regular wording, he is not required to repeat the prayer, since he uttered the word 'mishpat' (judgment — justice) in any event.

Twice each day we recite Psalm 27 'The Lord is my light and my salvation' — after 'shacharit' (morning prayer) and after 'ma'ariv' (evening prayer). Some however recite it after 'minchah' (afternoon prayer) rather than 'ma'ariv'. The Psalm is said from the beginning of Elul till the festival day of 'Shmini Atzeret' — which concludes the period of Divine judgment. The Sephardim however follow the practice of saying this Psalm every day of the year, except for Shabat.

TESHUVAH (Repentance)

Repentance atones for all transgressions. Even if one sinned all his days and practiced *teshuvah* only at the end of his life, he is not to be reminded of his iniquity. For it is said: 'And as for the iniquity of the wicked, he shall not stumble on it, on the day he returns from his iniquity' (Yechezkel 33).

Just as a person needs to repent from sins of commission such as robbery, theft and similar transgressions, likewise does he need to examine his evil character traits; and to turn away from anger, hate, envy, scoffing, the pursuit of money and vainglory, excessive indulgence in eating, and the like. Of these transgressions the prophet Yeshayahu says: 'Let the wicked forsake his way, and the iniquitous person his thoughts...' (Yeshayahu 55). If a person is immersed in such transgressions, it will be extremely difficult to abstain from them; they are hence even more severe than transgressions of commission.

Each person is especially obligated to focus his mind upon repentance from habitual misdeeds or negative character traits. Let him not postpone repentance in such matters, lest he fall into the category of those who say: 'I will sin and repent, I will sin and repent.' For of such persons the Sages say: 'He is not given sufficient opportunity to repent,' since his anticipation of future repentance becomes the very cause of his present wrong doing: If not for the thought that repentance would provide an escape from punishment, he might refrain from transgressions. Therefore, since it is the very factor which causes him to commit wrong, repentance is denied him.

On the other hand, if one who has habitually committed a transgression, strives towards repentance, and 'uproots' himself from its grasp, till he forsakes it entirely — then he finds favor before God as if he had brought a rich offering upon the altar, and his reward is exceedingly great.

The same applies with reference to place, time and age:

If you see a place whose inhabitants wantonly commit a particular transgression, you may know that this particular transgression 'stands in accusation' against them beyond all other transgressions. Hence, repentance from this specific wrong also takes precedence over other meritorious acts, and is more highly regarded before God than other good deeds. Further, repentance of this one sin makes repentance easier for all others. On the other hand failure to practice repentance in such an instance may even nullify the practice of other good deeds, for it is as if one were immersing for purification while holding an object of defilement in his hand.

If a given generation wantonly commits a particular transgression, then those who are sensitive of heart in its midst are bidden to rectify that particular failing before other failings so that their contemporaries might learn from their actions and follow them in the path of repentance.

The same is true with reference to the stages of a person's life. The stage of childhood is unlike that of youth, and both are unlike that of mature adulthood. In each stage of a person's life, his evil inclination incites him towards varying transgressions against God's Will. Hence repentance attains its highest value when a person focuses his heart to know what transgression he is most prone to commit, and strives with utmost strength to attain purification from its effects — to the end that the One Who knows all that is concealed shall bear witness that he will not again revert to his folly.

TRUTH AND PEACE

Truthfulness and the keeping of peace are exalted and beloved virtues for all, but especially for youth. Youths who cultivate these traits will not come to wrongdoing. And whoever has committed wrong, will achieve repentance and rectitude if he resolves to speak truth and maintain peace. In times when lying and quarreling are rampant, truth and peace are all the more vital for the achievement of repentance.

It happened that a person became immersed in many severe transgressions. He stole, robbed, lied and committed a variety of other abhorrent deeds. Once a penitential thought rose in his heart, but he did not know what to do. He came before a *tzadik* (a righteous man) and said to him: 'I have transgressed against all that is written in the Torah — teach me a way of repentance to expiate my old sins and to guard against further transgression.' The tzadik replied: 'If I show you a way of repentance which is exceedingly difficult, will you take it upon yourself?' Said he: 'Even if you decree that I cast myself into a fiery furnace!' Said the tzadik: 'The way I will show you is even more difficult — do you take it upon yourself?' 'Yes,' he answered.

The tzadik then placed an oath upon the sinner concerning one matter alone, and said to him: 'Go home in peace, eat whatever you wish, and do whatever you desire, but if you are subsequently asked, 'what did you do?' — admit the truth. This is your total repentance.'

The man acted as he had pledged. He was about to steal

again but at the last moment he reflected: 'If I am caught, I will be asked: 'Did you steal ?' I will have to admit the truth, whereupon I will be cast into prison.' He therefore refrained from stealing. The same happened whenever his evil inclination incited him to commit wrong. Because he had sworn to confess the truth, he repeatedly refrained from misdeed. Once his inclination seized him, and he succumbed to sin. Upon being apprehended, he immediately confessed. And that confession saved him from stumbling in sin again.

Just as truthfulness is a preventive fence which restrains a person from sin and leads him to repentance, likewise is peacefulness a force which draws one towards right. Whoever loves peace, and does not quarrel with his teachers, parents and friends will learn goodness from them, and will consistently walk in their righteous ways. And they too will learn from the propriety of his ways. He thus achieves merit himself and bestows it as well upon others. Such a person is assured that sin will not come his way.

THE FOUNDATIONS OF TESHUVAH

The foundations of *teshuvah* are threefold; regret, confession and forsaking the committed sin.

'Rav Bibi the son of Abayey said: How is a person required to utter confession Erev Yom Kipur? He is required to say: I admit every evil act which I committed before you — I stood on an evil path. I will not again do likewise. May it be Your will, Lord my God, to forgive my transgressions, to pardon my iniquities, and to grant me atonement for all my sins. Thereof it is written: 'Let the iniquitous forsake his way and the man of evil intention his thoughts' (Vayikra Raba Chapter 3).

THE FORSAKING OF SIN

The Sages said: 'Teshuvah must include the forsaking of the committed sin. To what extent ? Till He Who knows what is concealed shall testify concerning him (the sinner) that he will never again revert to the same sin' (Rambam, Hilchot Teshuvah, Chapter 2). If however, one repents from his misdeed for a given time, but then reverts to his earlier delinquency, he is not considered as having committed teshuvah, despite the reward he may receive for having temporarily refrained from wrong. His previous transgressions remain unforgiven, and continue to cast their burden upon him, for they continue to be a stumbling block for him.

Since teshuvah is of such great import, one ought always to feel anxiety lest he had never properly fulfilled the *mitzvah* of teshuvah. His new misdeeds are perhaps an outcome of those earlier ones which he had not totally forsaken. He may never have achieved a state of teshuvah throughout his days. The verse states: 'Seek the Lord when he is found,' which the Sages interpret as referring to the ten days between Rosh Hashanah and Yom Kipur. And one ought to reflect: 'Rosh Hashanah has passed, the ten days of teshuvah are gone, and I have not yet achieved teshuvah.'

For this reason many pious Jews never allow the Ten Days of teshuvah to pass without having rectified at least one misdeed. Each successive year they thus rectify some additional failing, and build for themselves another fence which they never again breach.

Even if the particular incident is trivial, and even if it is easily rectified, their easily attained state of teshuvah is nevertheless of great worth. For it enables them to experience an attachment to genuine teshuvah all their days.

This practice is worthy of adoption by all — the great as well as the humble — as a means of achieving genuine teshuvah and of constantly ascending upwards on the way of the Lord.

THE STRENGTH OF TESHUVAH

'Teshuvah draws near those who were distant. Yesterday, prior to his teshuvah, the sinful person had been considered hateful before God — abhorred, banished, held in abomination. Today, having repented, he is beloved, precious, near to God, a devoted friend.

'How exalted is the virtue of teshuvah! Yesterday the sinful individual was separated from the God of Israel, as it is stated: 'Your transgressions separated between yourselves and your God.' He cried out and was not answered, as it is stated: 'Even if you abound in prayer I shall not hear.' He performed mitzvot and they were cast in his face, as it is stated: 'Who requested it from your hand to trample My courtyard?' And today — he is attached to the *Shechinah*, as it is stated: 'And you who cleave to the Lord your God...' He cries out and is answered immediately, as it is stated: 'And it shall be that before they call I shall answer.' He performs mitzvot and they are pleasurably and joyously accepted, as it is stated: 'For God has already willingly accepted your deeds.'

'All of the Prophets prescribed teshuvah, and Israel is to be redeemed only through teshuvah. The Torah has already given assurance, that Israel will in the end do teshuvah — at the end of its exile — and will be redeemed immediately, as it is stated: 'And it shall be when all these things are come upon you... and you shall return to the Lord your God... and the Lord your God shall return your captivity and shall gather you from among all the peoples whither He dispersed you' (Dvarim 30. Rambam, Hilchot Teshuvah, Chapter 7).

The Sages have said of the virtues of teshuvah: 'Where those who do teshuvah stand, perfect *tzadikim* can not stand' (Tr. Brachot 39).

'Great is teshuvah for it transforms willful transgressions into meritorious acts' (Tr. Yoma 81).

'Wisdom was asked: What is the penalty of the sinner? Its answer was: Evil pursues sins. God was asked and He said: Let him do teshuvah' (Jerusalem Talmud, Tr. Makot Chapter 2).

'Whoever does teshuvah, is regarded as if he had gone up to Jerusalem, built the Sanctuary, built the altar, and offered upon it all the offerings prescribed in the Torah' (Vayikra Raba 7).

'So Great is the strength of teshuvah that when a person reflects at heart to do teshuvah, he rises immediately to the highest Heaven, to the very presence of the Throne-of-Glory' (Pesikta Rabati 44).

'Rabi Eliezer said: The first day of the week Adam entered the waters of the upper Gichon till the waters reached his neck; he fasted seven weeks, till his body became as a sieve. Said Adam: Lord of the Universe, Remove my sin from me, accept my teshuvah and let all the generations learn that there is teshuvah' (Pirkey d'Rabi Eliezer).

'If you wish to know the strength of teshuvah, come and see: Ahab, the King of Israel, committed many transgressions — he robbed, envied, and murdered. But afterwards he did teshuvah and summoned Yehoshafat, the King of Judea, who daily administered stripes to him, he fasted and prayed morning and evening before God, engaged in the study of Torah all his days, did not revert to his evil practices and his teshuvah was willingly accepted — as it is stated: 'Have you seen how he (Ahab) humbled himself before Me — because he humbled himself, I will not bring evil in his days' (First Kings 21; Pirkey d'Rabi Eliezer).

BETWEEN MAN AND HIS FELLOW

Since teshuvah does not attain repentance for wrongs committed against another (without the latter's forgiveness), it is customary to seek mutual forgiveness, lest one had unknowingly wronged his fellow. And if one knows of a wrong he committed against another, he ought not rest till the aggrieved is reconciled to him. Nor ought a person cruelly withhold forgiveness when asked.

Our Sages, of blessed memory, relate: 'It once happened that Rabi Abba was sitting in the gateway to Lod, and saw a fatigued person approach from the road. The stranger entered a ruin, sat down beneath a tottering wall and fell into a slumber. Rabi Abba observed a serpent approach the slumbering stranger, but suddenly an animal emerged from the ruin and struck the serpent down.

'When the sleeper awoke and saw the dead serpent close by, he rose to leave. As he walked away, the wall collapsed directly upon his previous place of sleep. Whereupon Rabi Abba approached him and asked: Tell me of your behaviour. For God has wrought two miracles in your behalf. And not for naught did you merit them. Said He: Never did anyone inflict harm upon me without my effecting a reconciliation with him, and extending him my immediate forgiveness. And if it happened that I was unable to effect an immediate reconciliation, I never went to sleep till I had forgiven him, and I never paid attention to any harm he inflicted upon me. More than this — from that day I sought ways to extend him favors. Said Rabi Abba: He is worthy that God should perform miracle upon miracle in his behalf. Rabi Abba wept and said: This one's conduct is greater than that of Yosef. In Yosef's case, his own brothers were involved, and he would have been merciful towards them; while the action of this person excelled Yosef's behaviour' (Zohar Miketz).

TESHUVAH DURING LIFE

'In his youth Rabi Shimon Ben Lakish was a member of a robberband. But he returned to God wholeheartedly, in fasting and prayer. For the rest of his days he was engaged in the study of Torah and the practice of mitzvot, and his teshuvah was accepted.

'On the day of his death, two of his erstwhile friends, who had remained robbers, also died. Rabi Shimon Ben Lakish was granted entry into Gan Eden, while his two robber friends were consigned to the abyss. Said they: Lord of the Universe, Is there any arbitrary preference before You ?' Said He to them: He repented while still alive, but you did not. Said they: Leave us and we will repent. Said He: Teshuvah is only possible till the day of death.

'To what is the matter likened? to a person who departs on a sea voyage; if he fails to take along bread and water from land — he will not find them at sea. Or, to a person headed for a trip through the wilderness; should he fail to take along bread and water from civilization, he will not find food and drink in the wilderness. Likewise, if a person fails to achieve teshuvah during his lifetime, teshuvah is no longer possible for him after death' (Pirkey d'Rabi Eliezer 43).

Our Sages relate: 'Rabi Eliezer said: Repent one day before your death. Whereupon his disciples asked Rabi Eliezer: Does a person then know on what day he will die? Said he to them: All the more so — let him repent today lest he die tomorrow, so that all his days might pass in teshuvah' (Tr. Shabat 153).

CHILDREN ACHIEVE MERIT FOR FATHERS

Said the *Magid* (preacher) of Dubno in his parables:

'Holy children! Precious youths! I shall tell you a parable, so that you might understand how fervently you ought to pour forth your souls before our Holy King, Blessed be He, in the approaching Days of Awe.

'A father once walked along a road with his young son. Whenever they reached a difficult or narrow crossing, a river, a mountain or a valley, the father would lift his son upon his shoulder to enable the child to cross over. Once they came to a fortified city, at the approach of dusk. The gate was securely closed, and the only openings in the wall were small windows. Said the father to his son: Know my son that till now I behaved towards you with great compassion. I bore you upon my shoulders and carried you in my arms. But now your eyes surely see that there is no way to enter the city. We are unable to pass through the gate, unless you, my son, will exert yourself to climb through the slits and windows in the wall, and open the city gates for me from within.

'The moral: You are surely aware — holy children — that we do not burden you with our troubles and involvements. Whatever you need your fathers provide. Not so this day, when we approach God's courtyards in prayer and penitence, only to find the gates locked. As it is stated: Since the day when the Sanctuary was destroyed the gates of prayer are locked. Our prayers cannot enter other than through you, who are 'lighter than eagles.' You alone can rise like flying birds to open for us the gates of light and mercy, through prayer from the depths of the heart. For the outcry of children is formed by the breath of mouths unblemished by sin, and is therefore capable of piercing the windows of Heaven.'

CHILDREN'S PRAYER

Another parable by the Magid of Dubno:

'Holy children! Precious youths! I shall tell you a parable so that you might understand how fitting it is for you to shed tears in prayer this day. Though no worries or distress burden your hearts, since your every need is provided by your parents, nevertheless, do not remain silent, you who call upon God's Name!

'It once happened that a youth became dangerously ill. His father summoned a wise physician and spent money unsparingly in his behalf — but to no avail. He sent afar to seek out the most outstanding physicians, but they all told him that the matter was hopeless. One thing remained for him to do — to say Tehilim (Psalms) and plead for Heavenly mercy, before the most exalted of physicians — the Omnipotent God above.

'The father quickly assembled his devoted friends, so that they might invoke mercy in behalf of his son. Afterwards he reconsidered and said to his son: My precious son! though parents provide for their children's needs, and shoulder their burdens — even without the children knowing how oppressive those burdens may be — this is usually true, however, only of objects that can be purchased for money; since a child is incapable of conducting business affairs, his needs are necessarily his father's concern. And you my son — my soul's desire — you have surely seen that, as long as I thought it possible to redeem you from death's abyss through expending wealth and possessions — silver and gold were as naught to me. Now however, that the hands of the physicians are withdrawn in despair, and all the medicaments are of no avail to you — one thing alone remains: to weep and seek mercy, for the tears of one ill are surely more precious and beloved above, than tears shed for him by others. Therefore, let not your eyes be sparing, and pour forth your soul before God, that He might graciously answer your cry, and heed your supplication.

'The moral is readily understood: As long as it was possible to save you with money, we did all we were capable of. But now that nothing remains to us except to cry out and seek mercy, surely your tears are more precious than ours, for they are formed by the breath of mouths unblemished by sin.

'You are asked then to utter a general prayer:

'For Zion's sake we shall not be silent, and for Yerushalayim's sake we shall not be still. May the coming year be a year of life and peace; a year in which Yehudah may be re-established as in the days of old. And may the sons return to their boundary. Amen'

Although children are not obligated to perform mitzvot and are not subject to penalty for transgressions, they too are obligated to repent for their misdeeds, and to rectify their behavior — especially with reference to the mitzvah of honoring parents; albeit for different reasons. For them an act of teshuvah is intended to prevent improper behavior from becoming habitual transgression on their attainment of maturity and becoming subject to penalty. It also has the purpose of preventing their parents from being penalized for having failed to train them properly. With reference to the mitzvah of honoring parents, the teshuvah of children has still another motivation. Since it is a mitzvah which can only be observed while parents are still alive; and since the time of one's departure from this world is unknown, one should always be apprehensive of totally losing the opportunity to honor his parents.

SHABAT SHUVAH

The Shabat between Rosh Hashanah and Yom Kipur is called Shabat Shuvah because its 'Maftir' begins with the words 'Shuvah Israel!' (Return O Israel! — Hoshea 14).

The order of prayer is the same this Shabat as that of the remaining Sabbaths of the year, except that the customary addenda to the silent-prayer for the Ten-Days-of-Repentance, are recited Shabat Shuvah as well. 'Avinu Malkenu' is not said. In the prayer 'Magen Avot' which follows the silent prayer on Shabat eve, 'hamelech hakadosh' is said instead of the usual 'hakel hakadosh.' During 'shacharit,' 'Av Harachamim' is said as is 'tzidkatcha tzedek' during 'minchah.'

Wherever Jews live, it is customary for the rabbi to expound on teshuvah this Shabat, to make known to the people the penalty for wrong, so that they might turn their hearts towards teshuvah. And the Sages have said that, 'as the 'chacham' expounds, God forgives Israel's transgressions.'

In general the Shabat was given to Israel as a time for Torah and prayer, but one ought to be especially careful this Shabat not to pass the time idly, nor to indulge in forbidden conversation, but rather to concentrate entirely on Torah, prayer, and reflections of teshuvah; thereby attaining forgiveness for the idle conversation and idle behavior which marred his remaining Sabbaths.

RETURN O ISRAEL — TO THE LORD YOUR GOD

'Return, O Israel, to the Lord your God...' (Hoshea 14) — We are taught thereby that teshuvah is incumbent upon all without exception; for there is none so righteous that he is exempt from its obligation, nor is there anyone so depraved that teshuvah does not avail him.

Even if one be an exalted tzadik, righteous in deed and pure in thought, he is enjoined: 'Return O Israel'. For the higher one ascends (in righteousness), the more exalted his teshuvah becomes, till it reaches the Throne-of-Glory. As it is stated: 'Return... to the Lord your God.'

More than this: God sets the Divine Name upon him and says to him: 'I am your God!' For the verse does not read: 'Return... to God,' But rather, 'Return... to your God.'

Thus did the Sages expound the verse, 'Return O Israel, *till* the Lord your God': So great is the power of teshuvah, that it reaches the very Throne-of-Glory.

'Rabi Yehudah the son of Rabi Shimon, said: Return O Israel to the Lord your God — even if you denied the faith.'

'Rabi Elazar said: If a person shames his fellowman publicly, but later seeks his pardon privately, the offended is likely to say: You shame me publicly, but conciliate me privately? Go and bring the people in whose presence you embarrassed me, and I will become reconciled to you. God however is different. One may blaspheme in the market place, and God says to him: Return in teshuvah 'between you and Me,' and I will accept you!' (Yalkut Hoshea 532).

THE CUSTOM OF KAPAROT

'Erev Yom Kipur' (the day preceding Yom Kipur) it is customary to perform the rite of 'kaparot.' And if it isn't possible Erev Yom Kipur the rite may be enacted the previous day. A rooster is taken for a

male, and a hen for a female. It is proper to take a white rooster in allusion to the 'whitening' (forgiveness) of sin. As it is stated: 'If your sins should be like red thread, they will become white like snow' (Yeshayahu 18). One need not however, especially seek after a white fowl unless it be easily available.

If one failed to procure roosters, he may take a duck or even a fish, but not doves, since doves are proper for altar offering, and the error might arise that kaparot take the place of altar offerings. It is customary for an expectant mother to take two fowls, a rooster and a hen.

The fowl is taken in one's right hand, and the appropriate verses in the prayer-book are recited. The fowl is then waved about one's head three times (during the waving, the right hand is placed on the fowl's head, and the fowl is held by the left hand) as the prescribed recitation is said. This procedure is followed in remembrance of an altar-offering, for when sacrifices were offered in the Sanctuary, the owner placed his hand on the head of the offering.

A person should not think that kaparot atone for his misdeeds. Rather should one seek to awaken in himself the awareness that he may deserve death because of his transgressions, and that he ought to exert all his strength to repent and seek Divine Mercy. The kaparot are slaughtered (in accord with Halachic procedure), and their inner parts are then cast out where birds may come upon them. Since roosters obtain sustenance through robbery, this practice serves as a warning to Man against deriving benefit from robbery. Another reason for this practice is that we thereby bestow mercy upon the 'birds-of-freedom,' though their sustenance is not obligatory upon us. For just as God's 'mercy is upon all His works,' so should a person be merciful towards all living creatures —

especially during these days when we seek Divine mercy for ourselves. In the words of the Sages: 'Whoever bestows mercy — is treated mercifully.' A third reason: If a harsh decree has been promulgated that Jewish bodies be food for the fowl of the heavens or the beasts of the earth, let the decree depart through the kaparah which replaces us, whereupon we may enter upon a life of goodness, long years and peace.

It is customary to redeem the kaparot for money, which is then given to the poor. Some give the kaparot themselves to the poor. Others perform the entire rite only with money. They recite the prescribed verse and give the money to charity.

PRAYERS OF EREV YOM KIPUR

During 'shacharit' of 'Erev Yom Kipur,' the psalm 'mizmor letodah' is omitted because it is recited in the place of the 'todah-offering' which was brought while the 'Beit Hamikdash' still stood. On Erev Yom Kipur however, 'todah-offerings' were not brought, for the 'todah' was to be eaten during the day (when it was offered) and the ensuing night — till midnight.

Since however on Erev Yom Kipur the offering could only be eaten till the approach of sunset, it was more likely to reach the state of 'notar' (lit. leftover: the eating of, or derivation of benefit from, was forbidden. Allowing an altar-offering to become 'notar' was a grave transgression). 'Todah-offerings' were therefore not brought Erev Yom Kipur.

On Erev Yom Kipur only a few 'selichot' (penitential prayers) are recited, and fasting is prohibited. 'Tachanun' is omitted, as are 'Avinu Malkenu' and 'lamnatze'ah ya'ancha Hashem beyom tzarah,' since the day is of partially festive character. There is less study of Torah, and more attention to the mitzvot-of-

the-day. When Yom Kipur falls on Shabat, however, 'Avinu Malkenu' is recited on Erev Yom Kipur after shacharit.

If one has failed to perform 'hatarat nedarim' (the repeal of vows) in the presence of three on Erev Rosh Hashanah, he does so following 'shacharit' on Erev Yom Kipur.

During 'minchah' (afternoon prayer) 'vidui' (the order of confession) is added to the silent prayer, and is recited immediately preceding 'elokai netzor.' Since Yom Kipur does not atone in the absence of teshuvah, and since vidui is the essence of teshuvah, therefore one utters vidui earlier, during minchah, lest misfortune befalls him during the meal, and he be unable to utter confession later.

CHARITY ON EREV YOM KIPUR

During all the days-of-teshuvah charity is given liberally, but Erev Yom Kipur even more so, since the merit of charity is a shield against evil decrees.

'It once happened that Mar Ukva, who habitually sent a certain poor man in his vicinity 400 *zuz* every Erev Yom Kipur, once sent the 400 zuz by the hand of his son. The son returned with the money, saying: 'He needs no charity.' Whereupon the father asked: 'What did you see ?' Said he: 'Old wine is poured for him.' Said Mar Ukva: 'Is he then habituated to such delicacies ?' He doubled the amount, and sent him 800 zuz' (Tr. Ketubot 67).

'Plimo was wont to tease Satan (by never obeying him). He would say: 'An arrow in your eye, Satan!' One day, on an Erev Yom Kipur, Satan appeared to him in the guise of a poor man. He came to Plimo's door. Bread was brought out for him. Said he: 'On such a day as this, when all sit within, am I to remain outside ?' They brought him in, and served him bread. Said he : 'On such a day as this, when all are dining at the table, am I to sit alone ?' They sat him at the table. His entire body was covered with oozing wounds, and his behavior was repulsive. Said Plimo to him: 'Sit properly!' Said he: 'Pour me a cup of wine.' They poured one for him. He spat into the cup. They scolded him. He then simulated death. Plimo heard a voice: 'Plimo took a life, Plimo took a life!' He fled and hid in a place of retirement. When Satan saw how anguished Plimo was, he revealed his identify' (Tr. Kidushin 81).

EATING ON EREV YOM KIPUR

It is a *mitzvah* to eat and drink on Erev Yom Kipur. Our Sages, of blessed memory, have said: 'It is written in the Torah: 'And you shall afflict your souls on the ninth of the month, in the evening.' Do we then fast on the ninth? Is it not on the tenth alone that we fast? One is, however, taught thereby, that if one eats and drinks on the ninth and fasts on the tenth, the Torah accounts it as if he had fasted the ninth and the tenth.'

Feasting on Erev Yom Kipur is of such import because one thereby reveals joy over the arrival of his time of atonement; and, by inference, a previous anxiety over his transgressions.

Another reason: During other festivals we partake of fixed meals as an expression of joy over the practice of mitzvot and such joy merits reward. Since, however, there cannot be a fixed meal on Yom Kipur, we hold one on Erev Yom Kipur.

A third reason: So that we might be physically strengthened for prayer and supplication on Yom Kipur, and for deeper reflection on the essentials of teshuvah.

'And it is out of God's love of Israel — and His concern for their good — that he prescribed fasting for only one single day in the year — to atone for transgression; and He bade them eat and drink first, so that they might be able to fast without harm' (Tur, Hilchot Yom Kipur 604).

Many endeavor to have fish as part of their morning meal on Erev Yom Kipur.

'Rabi Tanchuma said: It once happened in Rome on Erev Yom Kipur that a certain tailor went to buy fish. Only one fish was available but there were two buyers: the tailor and the servant of the city mayor. Each bid against the other till the price offered for the fish rose to twelve dinarim, and finally the tailor bought it. During the meal the ruler said to his servant: 'Why did you not bring me fish ?' Said the servant: 'I will not conceal it from my master — I went to buy, but only one fish was available, and I and a Jew bid against each other till the price rose to twelve dinarim. Do you then want me to bring you a fish for the price of twelve dinarim ?' Said he: 'And who is this man ?' He sent for him, and the latter came. Said he : 'What caused you — a Jewish tailor — to eat a fish bought for twelve dinarim ?' Said he: 'My master ! We have one day which atones for all the transgressions we commit all year; shall we not honor that day when it comes ?' Said he: 'Since you justified your deeds, you are free.'

'How did God recompenes him ? The tailor cut the fish open and God had 'summoned' a fine gem therein for him — one from which the tailor drew sustenance all his days' (Bereishit Raba 11).

Although the mitzvah of eating Erev Yom Kipur is great, one should take care to eat only light, easily digestible foods.

IMMERSION IN A MIKVAH

Each person is obligated to purify himself in a 'mikvah' (ritual bath) on Erev Yom Kipur for the sake of the sanctity of the day, and for the sake of teshuvah. This immersion was ordained by the prophets, and the 'Ge'onim' (heads of Babylonian Torah-academies after the Talmud-era) consider it mandatory and requiring a brachah. Our custom however, is not to utter a brachah.

THE MEAL BEFORE THE FAST

After 'minchah' the 'se'udah hamafseket' (meal of-cessation) is eaten. This meal has no set time, except that it should be concluded while it is still day, i. e., before sunset, since it is obligatory to 'add from the non-sacred to the sacred.'

This addition has no measure that is prescribed by the Torah but it has become customary to cease eating not less than half-an-hour before sunset, to provide sufficient time for the recitation of 'birkat hamazon' (prayer-after-meal) with proper intention, and for arriving at the synagogue before the announcement of 'Kol Nidrey' — which is begun before sunset.

It is customary not to partake of fish at this meal. The drinking of intoxicating liquors is prohibited, lest one become drunk, and his prayers be an abomination. Garlic is avoided; the meal thus consists only of light foods.

After the meal's conclusion birkat hamazon is uttered, preceded by 'shir hama'alot' ('A song of ascents: 'When the Lord returns Zion's captivity' — Psalm 126). The psalm is said tearfully, and with fervent intention, in the recollection that though 'the reaping is past, and the summer is gone,' we have not been redeemed, and Zion's captivity has not yet ended. Likewise should all of birkat hamazon be said with fervent concentration, for it contains intense pleas in behalf of Jerusalem; the rebuilding of the Sanctuary; a good life and sustenance, and the coming of the Messiah — as well as petitions regarding various aspects of the spiritual life.

We honor the festival with festive clothing and lights. The table is set, the beds are made, the house is cleaned.

After the meal, 'Yom Tov' lights are kindled, over which two 'brachot' are uttered: 'lehadlik ner shel Yom Kipur,' and 'shehecheyanu'. 'Candles-of-the-soul' (for the departed) are brought to the synagogue. Before departing for the synagogue, the parents bless the children, and although there is no set formula, and everyone may bring forth from the heart whatever blessings he desires, the following formulas have become standard:

'May God make you like Ephraim and Menashe' (for a son): or, 'May God make you like Sarah, Rivka, Rachel and Leah' (for a daughter).

'And may it be the will of our Father in Heaven to place in your heart love and fear of Him. May the fear of God be upon your face all the days of your life, that you might not commit wrong. May your desire be directed toward Torah and mitzvot. Let the gaze of your eyes be straight forward. Let your mouth speak wisdom, and your heart feel awe. Let your hands be engaged in mitzvot, let your feet run to do the will of your Father in Heaven. And may He give you righteous sons and daughters who will be engaged in Torah and mitzvot all their days. May your life-source be blessed, and may He provide your sustenance in a permitted manner, with ease and abundance, out of His open hand, and not through gifts from men of flesh and blood; sustenance that will leave you free for the service of God. May you be inscribed and sealed for a good and long life among all the righteous of Israel, Amen!'

We then go to the synagogue with awe and reverence.

FIVE AFFLICTIONS ON YOM KIPUR

Not only eating and drinking, but all bodily pleasures are prohibited on Yom Kipur. The Sages have listed five afflictions for Yom Kipur — abstinence from eating, drinking, washing or anointing the body, the wearing of shoes containing leather (shoes made of cloth or rubber without any leather are permitted) or sexual cohabitation.

These five afflictions correspond to the five books of the Torah, which we are to accept without allowing the curtain of our physical pleasures to intervene. They also correspond to the five senses with which Man commits mitzvot and transgressions; to the five times the term 'nefesh' (soul) is mentioned in the Yom Kipur Torah-reading; to the five immersions of the 'Cohen Gadol' on Yom Kipur; and to the five services prescribed for the day: ma'ariv, shacharit, musaf, minchah and ne'ilah.

PASSAGES ON TESHUVAH FROM 'HAYEY ADAM'

'Since God loves His People — in accord with His attribute-of-benevolence — and does not desire one's death but rather one's repentance from the paths of evil so that one might live — and not because it would benefit God, for, if one is righteous what does it avail Him — but only to bestow good upon one in the end — therefore He waits, not one, or two days, for the repentance of the wicked, but rather gives us abundant time, and opens the gates of repentance and forgiveness, from the beginning of the year, till the time of the 'closing-of-the-gates' on Yom Kipur. And a proclamation goes forth from Him: 'Return you errant children, I would heal your wantonness!' And who is there who can remain unafraid upon hearing the sound of the shofar proclaiming: 'Awake you slumberers from your slumber, arise and call out to your God, for He is gracious and compassionate!'

'Great is one's transgression, if he fails to set his heart upon increased Torah study and good deeds during these days. For — would that we be regarded as among those of median piety, whose judgment is suspended till Yom Kipur. But while a man still lives, God does not practice the 'attribute-of-benevolence' towards him if he is a *beinoni* (one of median status), by adding slightly to his scale of merit, or subtracting slightly from his scale of guilt. For this attribute is practiced only after one's death, when man is incapable of achieving further merit. During one's lifetime, however, God says: 'The door is open — it is within your power to achieve the merit of any mitzvah at all; if you are indolent, you forfeit your own life.'

'Each person should therefore anxiously strive to achieve repentance for the past, and to increase mitzvot and good deeds, in order that he might be purified before the arrival of the sacred day (of Yom Kipur). As it is written: 'Before the Lord, you shall purify yourselves.'

'Nor should a man say: 'Do I not don *tefilin* and *tzitzit*, and utter brachot and prayers, so that the scales will surely be tipped on the side of merit for me?' Only one without heart would say this. For it is also necessary to consider what 'packages of transgressions' one has committed daily — idle talk, slander, all manner of forbidden conversation, and in general, sins committed with each limb of the body. In truth, this error is widespread among people, who think it necessary to repent only for severe transgressions, such as idolatry, adultery, the shedding of blood, desecration of Shabat, and the like. But such a view is totally false. For there are transgressions, which are more severe than the above three.

'Note the scriptural interpretation of the Sages of blessed memory, to the effect that slander is more severe a transgression than idolatry, adultery, and the shedding of blood. It is further, a widespread transgression among people, and the Sages testified: 'All are culpable of slander.' Note also that its effects are so powerful as to make one guilty of 'the dust of slander,' if he merely says: 'There is a fire at so-

and-so's' (that is, 'where is fire found, if not in so-and-so's house, where there is constant cooking ?').

'There are likewise 'packages of transgressions' to which men are habituated, which are beyond recounting:

False and vain oaths — it being habitual for people to swear: 'May God thus help me,' when recounting some falsehood, or selling some object... The sin of such an oath has been compared to idolatry and is even more grave than it; as it is written, 'For the Lord will not hold guiltless, one who bears His Name in vain;'

cursing oneself or another in God's Name — without distinction as to whether one does so in the Holy Tongue, or in any other language;

the utterance of brachot, or the pronouncing of God's Name for naught. (Indeed, if one were to reflect on all his prayers and brachot, he would find... that they were all devoid of proper intent, and had become mere habit);

shaming one's fellow-man;

glorying in a fellow-man's embarrassment;

inflicting anguish on any Jew, whether in word or deed (as it is stated, 'You shall not afflict each his fellow man');

causing anguish to a widow or orphan which makes one liable to 'death at the hands of Heaven;'

hatred of one man for another;

anger;

lewd gazing at women;

flattery;

scoffing;

idle talk;

discussion of business on Shabat and Yom Tov;

the lending of money for interest without a 'heter iska' — each individual deciding for himself arbitrary grounds for permission, without inquiring of qualified rabbis — all the more is this true of merchants and bankers, who almost universally do not avoid infraction of the prohibition against usury.

'All of these are exceedingly widespread, and are committed habitually. Even Torah scholars would find on reflection, that most of them generally fail in these matters, with many — beyond number — still remaining, and with neglect of Torah study outweighing them all. For one who is distant from the study of Torah is distant from the service of God. And therefore the prayer was phrased: 'Return us our Father to Your Torah, and (then) draw us near our King, to Your Service.' The more one is engaged in the study of Torah, the more is one drawn close to the service of God.

'Our Sages prescribed the sounding of shofar beginning with *Rosh Chodesh Elul,* so that a person should take it to heart that he is like one summoned to judgment; and that his heart might tremble over the arrival of days of reckoning, in which his every action and slightest movement will be reviewed by God in judgment for good or bad. Now, when one is brought for judgment before a king of flesh and blood he is surely in great fear. As Rabi Yochanan Ben Zakai expounded (concerning a mortal king) : 'Should he punish me,' through a money penalty, 'his penalty is not eternal,' for I will be able to earn other monies; 'should he imprison me,' bodily, 'his imprisonment is not eternal,' for he might die, and his successor might free me; 'if he should slay me,' my death is not eternal, for he can only impose his rule over my body, whereas my spirit returns to God who gave it. Nevertheless, one would assuredly be filled with great awe, and would strive with utmost diligence to devise ways of escape. Nor would it occur to him to turn in the slightest, towards his other concerns. He would not cultivate his soil, and in the day of travail he would assiduously shed all other thoughts or involvements, but would set his heart and thoughts only upon escape, as would a deer fleeing capture. And if it is thus in the presence of human judgment, all the more when one stands for trial together with his children, and all that is his, before the King of Kings, the Holy One, Blessed-be-He, whose penalty — whether it be poverty, or illness, a penalty affecting his children, or his very life — is eternal.

'How foolish are those who engage in their customary pursuits all day, during these penitential days of judgment, without giving thought to the verdict which faces them.

'Each person ought therefore to take the matter to heart; to diminish his usual activities, and set special hours, during the day and night, for introspection and self-examination. One should rise early to dwell on the ways of teshuvah and rectitude, to pour forth prayer before his Creator, to utter confession for his sins. He ought to practice mitzvot and good deeds the more, engage in more study of Torah than is his custom during other days, and disburse more charity, for the time is one of Divine good will, and prayer is more readily accepted then.

'It is a positive commandment in the Torah to practice teshuvah before Yom Kipur, as it is written: 'Before the Lord you shall purify yourselves.' It is therefore proper for a person to adhere — during the *aseret-yemei-teshuvah* — to *chumrot*, (restrictions beyond the requirement of the Law) by which he does not abide all year, since God also, behaves with loving-kindness towards His creatures. It is thus proper for those who eat non-Jewish bread all year, to eat only Jewish bread; and to act likewise in all matters.

'A person should rectify relations with his fellow man, for in such matters neither *Yom Kipur*, nor even death atones, till one returns the object he had acquired unjustly, and receives forgiveness from whomever he had wronged. Otherwise, even if he fasts a hundred years, brings a multitude of sacrificial offerings, and utters confessions a hundred times a day, atonement will not be granted him, as the *Mishnah* asserts: 'If one brings his guilt-offering before he returns what he had robbed, he has not discharged his obligation.' For if one wrongs another person, he sins doubly: Once, towards Man: and once, towards God, whose command he has violated. And until he has sought his friend's pardon, how can he utter confession (to God)? ...Is he not like 'one who immerses himself in a *mikvah*, with the *sheretz* (a dead insect which is a source of defilement) still in his hand?' He should therefore first attain his friend's pardon, whereupon only what is between him and God will remain, in which case teshuvah can be of avail. In King David's words (Tehilim 51 — the Psalm of teshuvah): 'To You alone have I sinned;' i.e., 'surely, this sin is not between me and another person, but only between me and You,' and therefore it is in Your hand to forgive me. After one has thus set right his misdeeds, he may utter confession for them.

'There are some people who err and give to charity what they have acquired unjustly. But this is a total error, as it is written: 'Hand to hand (the hand giving its unjust gain to the hand of the poor) will not be held guiltless of evil.' And though the Sages have stated: 'If one has robbed, but does not know from whom, let him expend those monies for public needs,' they only said so of one who does not know from whom he robbed. But if one does know, nothing will avail him till he returns (what he had robbed); or, if his victim had died, till he returns (his unjust gains) to the latter's inheritor. He is required to utter confession by mouth and at heart, — in great humility — with tears and in contrition. Then he is himself likened to a sacrificial offering, as it is said: 'A broken and humbled heart, O God, You do not despise.' He ought to resolve also not to revert again to the likes of his previous sins, for confession is like a sacrificial offering, and the Torah has said of a sacrificial offering without teshuvah: 'The sacrificial offering of the wicked is an abomination.' One is therefore required not only to repent, but to resolve not to revert to his earlier behavior.

'Let him utter confession, with weeping and bitter remorse, over having angered the Lord of Hosts, and having blemished the soul granted him by the Lord for his ultimate good, by besmirching it with iniquitous deeds. Let him grieve at heart and feel ashamed to lift up his eyes before his God, in recalling the foul deeds he committed from youth through old age — and let him say to himself: 'What have I done? Why have I despised God's words? I have not remembered that He created me from naught and bestowed all manner of good upon me. I was debased in behavior, and repaid goodness with evil. Woe to me! Woe to me! For I will go down to the abyss in mourning!' Through grief and weeping, his heart will surely become contrite, till he resolves to strive, with all his strength, not to revert to evil. And one achieves true teshuvah, only when he can call upon God Himself to testify as to the integrity of his teshuvah, on achieving the merit of such depth of remorse, he may be certain of being granted atonement...

'It is of great importance for everyone to go to the Synagogues and Houses of Study to hear the words of admonition which are expounded there, as our Sages praised 'one who cherishes admonition.' One who hates admonition, however, is very remote from teshuvah, as it is stated (Mishley 10): 'And whoever forsakes admonition, misleads.' And it is said: 'Whoever loves reproof, loves knowledge, but whoever hates admonition, is a boor... Reproof is a friend to one who forsakes the path (of right); one who hates admonition will die... An ear which hearkens to admonition for life, will dwell in the midst of the wise... A scoffer dislikes being admonished, to the wise he will not go.'

'It is proper for a person to frequently repeat King David's prayer: 'Teach me, O Lord, Your ways, guide me in Your truth, Unite my heart to fear Your Name' till the words come spontaneously to his lips at any hour. One may of course choose similar verses, bespeaking fear and reverence of God, for this purpose..., and he will assuredly be safe from sin.

'It is certainly an absolute obligation upon each person to study works inculcating piety, daily, for such study is more obligatory than all his other studies, even if he is thereby distracted from a chapter of *Mishnah*, or another study. 'For what does the Lord Your God require of you, but only to fear Him.' And as the Mishnah asserts: 'If there is no fear there is no wisdom.' For, what can Torah avail one, should he not be of a mind to fulfill its commands? Indeed, fear of God alone would not suffice him, without study of Torah — for, if one does not know how to act, of what avail is fear of God to him ? As the Mishnah states: 'If there is no wisdom, there is no fear.' That is to say, his fear of God is as naught, though it is certainly much better for a person to be God-fearing despite his ignorance, than to be learned but lacking in fear of God. As it is written: 'Better a poor man who walks in whole-heartedness, than one who distorts with his lips:' Better one who is poor in Torah but whole-hearted in piety than one who studies Torah without fear of God — for his Torah is regarded as mere 'distortion of the mouth.'

'The general principle of the matter therefore is, that a person ought to clear his thoughts for the study of Torah whenever his time is free, day and night; but on condition that his intention should be to practice what he learns; and let him not learn only to fulfill the mitzvot of studying Torah, but rather to study and to do, and then his Torah will be desirable (before God).'

WHITE GARMENTS

Many customarily wear white garments on Yom Kipur in imitation of the ministering angels. There are many also who wear an outermost garment called a *kitel* — which is the clothing of the dead — as a reminder of the day of death, and as a recall to teshuvah. The *kitel* is not decorated with gold, nor does its collar contain gold, since gold recalls the sin of the golden calf, and the 'Accuser cannot become the Defender.' It may however be beautified by a silver crown, since silver is white — the color which symbolizes loving-kindness.

It is the established practice to pray in a *talit* Yom Kipur evening. We wrap ourselves in the *talit* while it is still day, in order to be able to recite the brachah. (At night the brachah is not recited because of the fact that the mitzvah of *tzitzit* does not apply at night.)

The talit too is white, and therefore symbolizes loving-kindness, while its bars of sky-blue symbolizes Divine mercy.

It happened once that a tzadik delivered a sermon to his congregation before *Kol Nidrey*. They were all clad in white and wrapped in white. He said as follows:

'Our brothers, the children of Israel! Take to heart that in these clothes which we wear now, we will go the to world-on-high to give reckoning before the King of Kings, the Holy One, Blessed-be-He. Let us then imagine that we are now standing in these clothes before the Throne-of-Glory, to give reckoning, and let us repent, for when one stands before the Throne-of-Glory he truly repents — but repentance does not avail after death, whereas now it does avail. Let us therefore wholeheartedly regret our previous sins, let us truthfully take it upon ourselves, not to sin again and let us ask for atonement before the King who grants atonement.

TEFILAH ZAKAH

It is customary in many Jewish communities — upon arrival at the Synagogue after the *se'udah hamafseket,* and preceding *Kol Nidrey* — to fervently utter the *tefilah zakah* prayer. Tefilah zakah is a prayer worthy of its name — pure in its every word, purifying in its effect upon the hearts of its readers — as a preparation for the proper acceptance of the Day of Atonement.

The substance of tefilah zakah is the acceptance of the fast's five afflictions, and the opening of the heart to remorse and *vidui* (confession). An essential aspect of the prayer, however, is that — in addition to words of *teshuvah* — it contains words of forgiveness for sins between man and his fellow.

The heart of the Jew is open at that hour to remorse and teshuvah, but many are the obstacles which prevent him from attaining atonement for most of his transgressions. For most transgressions are between man and his fellow. How can he now find all his fellowmen — scattered as they are to the ends of the earth — to conciliate them ? And how can his fellow men find him to conciliate him over having wronged him ? Tefilah zakah, however, places in the mouths of all who practice teshuvah — wherever they be — words of wholehearted, mutual forgiveness, which remove the obstacles in the way of atonement, and open the doors of Divine Mercy.

The following is the formula of forgiveness in tefilah zakah :

'Since I know that there is hardly a pious man on Earth who does not commit misdeeds that are between man and his fellow — whether in monetary or personal matters, in deed or speech — my heart inwardly grieves, for Yom Kipur does not atone in matters between man and his fellow, till the offender conciliates the one he agrieved. And over this my heart is broken, and my bones tremble, for even the day of death does not atone for such sins. I therefore offer supplication before You that You bestow mercy upon me — and that grace and favor be granted me, before Your eyes and the eyes of all men.

'I hereby extend total forgiveness to all who have wronged me, whether personally or financially, or by slandering or defaming me; to all who have committed against me any of the wrongs that are between man and man. Let no one be penalized because of me. And just as I forgive all men, grant me favor in the eyes of all that they might also extend total forgiveness to me.'

This petition is said before Kol Nidrey, if there is still time; otherwise it is said after the Kol Nidrey service.

KOL NIDREY

Before sunset, the Ark is opened, and two of the most honored of the congregants withdraw two Torah scrolls. They leave the ark open, circle the 'Bimah' (synagogue pulpit) and say aloud the verse: 'Light is sown for the righteous, and for the upright of heart (there is) joy.' The congregation repeats after them while kissing the Torah scrolls joyously and enthusiastically — like children lovingly hovering about the mother who bore them. When the 'hakafah' (the circling about the 'Bimah') is completed, the two step near the 'shaliach tzibur' (the precentor) and remain standing by his side with the Torah scrolls in their hands, till they complete the Kol Nidrey service.

The Yom Kipur prayers begin with the chanting of Kol Nidrey before sunset, since it is a form of the repealing of vows, and vows are not repealed Shabat and Yom Tov, other than for the sake of Shabat and Yom Tov. Just as the scholar who repeals a vow says to the one who made it: 'It is repealed unto you' three times, so is Kol Nidrey repeated three times.

Before Kol Nidrey the Sephardim chant the hymn, 'To You my God, is my desire,' which opens the heart and fills it with yearning for God. The hymn also contains a formula of confession, which is required — according to many authorities after the 'se'udah hamafseket' and before the 'sanctity-of-the-day' sets in.

In the petition of Kol Nidrey there is a declaration which nullifies future vows, and according to many authorities — also a repeal of past ones. For our Sages have stated: 'Whoever wants his vows for the coming year not to be binding, let him rise on Rosh Hashanah and declare: 'Any vow which I will make in the future, shall be nullified.' Such a declaration renders invalid any vow made later, in forgetfulness of the original declaration; the reason being, that we surmise it to be the thought of one who later makes such a vow that — were he to remember his earlier stated unwillingness to accept vows — he would refrain from uttering one. His later vow is to be considered as made in error.

The order of the saying of Kol Nidrey is as follows: The shaliach tzibur takes place at his stand and two of the honored congregants — holding Torah scrolls — stand on either side of him, one to his right, and one to his left. The two lend moral support to the shaliach tzibur as he seeks mercy for the community; this procedure is similar to Moshe Rabenu's prayer in behalf of Israel, when Amalek came to wage war against them in Refidim. ('And Aharon and Hur supported his hands, on this side one and on the other side one.') Further, the cantor and both 'assistants' together form a tribunal of three, as is required for the repealing of vows. The three declare: 'With the consent of God, and with the consent of the congregation, in the court on High, and in the court below, we permit prayer with the transgressors.' They repeat these words three times.

Afterwards the shaliach tzibur says Kol Nidrey three times — the first time in subdued tones, but sufficiently loud to be heard, the second time in higher tones, and the third in full voice. The prayer is said in trembling, in awe and with intense devotion, and in many communities the congregation simultaneously says Kol Nidrey in a whisper.

The reason for the subdued tones is, that one who enters a palace to plead for his life before a king, is at first too frightened to draw near, he speaks quietly. But, as he acquires confidence, he lifts his voice and makes his petition heard.

After Kol Nidrey the shaliach tzibur — followed by the congregation — recites the verse, 'And it shall be forgiven unto the entire congregation of the children of Israel...,' three times. He follows with the verse, 'Forgive now the transgression of this people,' and both the congregation and he conclude with the verse: 'And the Lord said, I have forgiven in accord with your words.' The final verse is repeated in full voice three times.

Afterwards, 'shehecheyanu' is said; loudly by the shaliach tzibur, and softly by the congregation. The brachah is said with fervent joy, and in thanksgiving to God over His having enabled us to live and fulfill the day's precepts, and to attain atonement. The congregation concludes the brachah before the cantor, in order to respond with 'Amen' after his brachah, since one may not say 'Amen' after his own brachah.

ON THE RECITATION OF KOL NIDREY

The reason for the recitation of Kol Nidrey at the advent of Yom Kipur is that Yom Kipur does not nullify the obligations of an assumed vow. If one made a vow and forgot to abide by its terms, he has jeopardized the atonement he seeks on Yom Kipur. His only recourse is the advance repeal of future vows by which he may fail to abide; and thereby he may enter Yom Kipur without bearing the sin of violated vows.

In addition to the repeal of future vows, Kol Nidrey also retroactively repeals all the vows which one might have made during the course of the previous year, but which he had forgoten.

As for the Rabis' great apprehension over the violation of vows, they were motivated by the fact that the Torah regards the sins of speech as more grave than those of action. In the words of the Rabis: 'One who speaks (evil) is worse than one who does (evil).' Man's excellence over other living creatures lies in the power of speech. '...And Man became a living soul,' is translated by Onkelos: 'And Man became a speaking spirit.' But this excellence was given him only for proper use. One who misuses it, debases himself to a level beneath that of animals, for the animal does no harm by its power of mouth, whereas he does; he is therefore subject to harsher penalty, and the repeal of his vows is one means of rectifying the sins of speech.

The formula of permission to 'pray with the transgressors,' which is recited immediately preceding Kol Nidrey was prescribed at the time of the imposition of forced conversion upon Spanish Jewry. Cruel gentiles had subjected Spanish Jewry to harsh persecution, to force them to abjure Judaism and to accept the Christian faith. There were many Jews — unable to withstand the tortures they suffered — who publicly accepted Christianity, while secretly continuing to observe Judaism. All year these *anusim* (forced converts) refrained from gathering for religious worship, but the night of Yom Kipur they risked their lives, and assembled in multitudes in secret dungeons to accept upon themselves the sanctity of the day, and to plead for Divine Mercy over their seeming apostasy all year, For God never abhors the prayers of a multitude, even if they be transgressors.

It was with reference to those transgressors that the Rabis prescribed the declaration: 'We permit prayer with the transgressors.'

The formula was retained down to our days. Now too, many of those who come to the synagogues the night of Yom Kipur violate the precepts of the Torah all year, and if it were not for this permission to join with them in prayer, their presence would — God forbid — blemish the prayers of the pious. Once however this permission is extended — even their prayers ascend together with the prayers of all Israel. For they are all the seed of Avraham, Itzchak and Ya'akov, and they all desire to obey God's will — were it not for the effects of Exile, and the seduction of the evil inclination. Now however, that they enter the synagogues to pray, to accept upon themselves the mitzvot of the day, and to ask forgiveness for their sins of the entire year, they again become sanctified, pure and worthy of the acceptance of their prayers before Him who hears prayer.

This matter of including willfull transgressors in the prayers of all Israel, is likened to the blending of *chelbenah* with the other ingredients in the preparation of *ketoret* (incense) in the Sanctuary. The Sages have stated: 'Any fast which does not include some of those who violate the Torah, is not a fast, just as *chelbenah* is listed in the Torah among the *ketoret* ingredients, though its odor is unpleasant' (Tr. Kritot 6).

'We are taught thereby that it should not appear unworthy in our eyes to include in our midst — in the bands of our fasting and prayer — the 'transgressors-of-Israel,' so that they might be counted among us' (Rashi, Shmot 30).

THE SONG OF THE ANGELS — ALOUD

During *keriat shemah* (the recitation of the passage 'Hear O Israel') of both evening and morning prayers on Yom Kipur, we pronounce aloud the verse: *'Baruch Shem Kevod Malchuto Le'olam Va'ed'* ('Blessed Be The Name of His Glorious Majesty Forever'). All other days of the year, however, this verse is uttered in a whisper since it is a song of praise sung by the angels.

An explanation is given in Midrash Va'etchanan:

'The Rabis say: When Moshe ascended on high, he heard the ministering angels say before God, 'Blessed Be The Name of His Glorious Majesty Forever,' and he brought this verse of praise down for Israel. Why then does Israel fail to pronounce it publicly ? Rabi Ami said: To what is the matter likened, to one who had stolen an ornament from the palace. He gave it to his wife, but said to her: Do not wear it publicly, but only in your house.'

On Yom Kipur however, when Jews are pure like the ministering angels, they rightfully pronounce this song of the angels.

CONFESSION OF SIN

Oral confession of sin is one of the essentials of *teshuvah*. As it is said: 'And they shall confess their sins' and, 'One who confesses and forsakes his sin — is accorded mercy.' It is also necessary to specify the sin. As it is said in Moshe's prayer for forgiveness: 'This people has indeed committed a great sin, and they have made for themselves gods of gold.' Confession is therefore obligatory on Yom Kipur, as part of the act of teshuvah which is the central purpose of the day.

Vidui (confession) does not however avail one, unless he has resolved to forsake his sin. Otherwise he is like one who immerses himself (in a purifying *mikvah*) while holding a *sheretz* (a dead insect which defiles) in hand, in which case, immersion does not avail till the *sheretz* has been cast away. Therefore vidui is repeated a number of times on Yom Kipur, so that, if one recitation did not avail, for lack of proper intention, then another vidui recitation might avail.

We follow the custom of uttering vidui ten times on Yom Kipur: one during *minchah*, on Erev Yom Kipur; eight times during *ma'ariv*, *shacharit*, *musaf*, and *minchah* (once during the silent prayer of each service and once during the cantor's repetition — which adds up to eight); and once during *ne'ilah*. These ten confessions correspond to our violations of the Ten Commandments.

Vidui is said standing, and its order follows the order of the alphabet — as an aid to memory, and also to rectify the blemishing effect of our misdeeds on the twenty two sacred letters with which the Torah was given. The Sephardim recite vidui both after the order of the alphabet and in the reverse order.

One is required to recite the entire order of vidui without omitting even sins of which he knows himself to be innocent. All Israel is responsible for one another. On the verse: 'And they shall stumble each over his brother,' the Sages have commented: 'And they shall stumble each over his brother's sin.' Therefore vidui was prescribed in the plural. Further, no one can be absolutely certain that he has never committed this or that particular misdeed, since sin has many degrees and he may have committed it in part, even if not in whole. God alone, who probes Man's innermost parts, knows a man's inner thoughts and ways.

It happened once that a pious man told the Rambam (Maimonides) that he was unwilling to utter the prescribed order of vidui, since he knew that he had not been guilty of its specified sins, and it was wrong to speak falsehood before the King. The Rambam replied: 'If you knew the gravity of the service of God, may He be exalted; and to what extent the service of God is required, you would know with certainty that not a day passes on which you fail to do everything specified in vidui, and much else in addition; for each man is judged in accord with the extent of his wisdom. We find thus that the sin of adultery is ascribed to King David — though Batsheva was divorced from Uriah; that the slaying of Uriah is ascribed to David as a sin, though the former had himself incurred a death penalty; that the cutting off of the corner of King Saul's cloak, is ascribed as a sin to David, though Saul was pursuing him unto death. Similarly, is each person judged in accord with his own stature as a man. And even for these very words which you have spoken you will be subject to judgment.'

If one knows that he has committed one of the specified sins, he should weep over it and utter profuse confession.

And if one has committed a sin which is unspecified in the vidui he should specify it himself — in a whisper — in heartfelt contrition and weeping — but not aloud, lest his sin become widely known; it being better for him, that his sin remain unknown ('Happy is he whose willful transgressions are forlorn, whose misdeeds are covered' — Tehilim 32). If however his sins are widely known, it is permissible to utter confession over them aloud.

While saying vidui, one should beat upon his breast or heart with his fist, at mention of the sin — as if saying to it: 'Your counsel and ruminations caused me to sin.'

A man may say: How can we dare to specify all of Man's sins in a holy place, on the holiest of days, while standing before a holy and awesome King? How do our mouths dare to express every abomination with which we have become besmirched: Is not our silence better than our speech — so that it might not be as if we were casting refuse before the Majesty of God while standing in prayer before Him on the Day of Judgment? Not so! Rather it is a joy before Him when His children expel from within themselves every filth or stain — even if they be found that very hour on the threshold of His house, and before His chair of judgment. For whoever expels his uncleanness, besmirches what is external, while purifying what is within; whereas if he fails to expel it, he remains pure externally but unclean internally.

God's way is unlike Man's way. The way of one of flesh and blood, is to see what appears to the eye, and to love external gloss. God's way is to see what is within the heart, and He loves purity of the soul's inner recesses, even if His palace is besmirched, as the soul casts out its uncleanness.

Thus did the Sages say:

'Days are fashioned and one of them — is His' (Tehilim 139) — this refers to the meaning of Yom Kipur for Israel. For it (Yom Kipur) was a source of great joy before God, and He gave it to Israel with great love. To what may the matter be likened? To a king of flesh and blood whose servants and household cast out the garbage and place it at the doorway of the king's dwelling. When the King sees the expelled refuse, then he rejoices...' (Tana Devey Eliyahu Chapter 1).

Better that the refuse should be cast upon the doorway of the King's dwelling, rather than that is should remain hidden in the recesses of Jewish souls. Even more! When the King sees the refuse expelled from the heart, it may become transformed into precious gifts offered by the sons to their King and Father. For the Sages said: 'Willful transgressions become unto them like meritorious acts.'

Therefore the people of Israel are not embarrassed to utter vidui before God all day.

'LIKE THE SHEETS OF SHLOMO'

'I am black but comely — daughters of Jerusalem, like the tents of Kedar, like the sheets of Shlomo' (Shir Hashirim Chapter 1).

'Like the tents of Kedar' — Just as the tents of Kedar are filled with precious stones and gems, though they appear ugly, dark and shabby; likewise are the Torah scholars: though they appear ugly and dark in this world, yet within them there are; Torah, *Mishnah*, *Midrashot*, *Halachot*, *Talmud*, *Toseftot*, and *Agadot*.

'Can it be that just as the tents of Kedar require no washing (since they are always black) neither does Israel? We are taught: 'Like the sheets of Shlomo'. Just as this 'sheet of Shlomo' becomes repeatedly dirtied and is repeatedly washed, likewise Israel — though they become besmirched with transgressions all the days of the year — Yom Kipur comes and atones for them, as it is stated: 'For on this day He will atone for you...' And it is written: 'If your sins shall be like red thread — they shall become white like snow' (Midrash Shir Hashirim 1).

TORAH READING ON YOM KIPUR

The Torah-readings prescribed for Yom Kipur differ from those of the other festivals. During the other festivals five persons are called to the reading; on Yom Kipur, six are called. On other festivals which fall on weekdays, there is no Torah-reading during 'minchah'; on Yom Kipur, there is a minchah Torah-reading, with three persons called to the Torah — as is done during minchah on Shabat.

For the 'shacharit' Reading, two Torah scrolls are withdrawn, and the appropriate introductory passages are said, as indicated in the 'machzor' (festival prayer-book). In the first scroll, the account of the Cohen Gadol's Yom Kipur Service in the Sanctuary (Vayikra 16) is read, and six persons are called. The 'maftir' is read from the second scroll; it recalls the prescribed sacrificial offering for Yom Kipur, and is followed by the 'haftarah' (from Yeshayahu). For minchah one scroll is withdrawn, and three persons are called for a reading of the concluding passage of the portion in Vayikra read in the morning. The third also reads a 'haftarah' consisting of the entire Book of Yonah — for which reason this 'maftir' is called 'maftir d'Yonah'.

The contents of the minchah Torah-reading has no direct relation to Yom Kipur, lacking as it does any reference to the mitzvot prescribed for the day. The passage rather lists the prohibited sexual relationships and forwarns Israel against adopting the abominable practices of either Egypt or Canaan.

One Sage commented however: We are to learn from this Torah-reading that even if a person rises in holiness to the Heavens, he ought not feel secure against the coarsest temptations. For at the end of the holiest of days, when all Israel are purified as angels, the portion of forbidden sexual relations is read for them, in which they are forwarned against practicing the abominations of the most debased of nations — Egypt and Canaan. A person ought not therefore distract his attention for a moment from the enemy lurking in his heart's recesses, who seeks to trip him with all that is shameful.

As for the 'haftarah' from the Book of Yonah:

'We are taught thereby that Man is incapable of escaping God, if he has committed transgressions.' 'Where shall I go from Your Spirit, and where shall I flee from Your Presence)' said Yonah. We are also stirred towards teshuvah as were Ninveh's inhabitants, who were delivered when God observed their teshuvah' (Ma'te Moshe).

YIZKOR — THE REMEMBRANCE OF SOULS

The Sages prescribed that children recall to memory, the souls of their departed parents during prayer every Yom Tov; at which time they are also to pledge charity to 'increase the merit of the departed and to enable their souls to ascend.' 'Hazkarat neshamot' follows the Torah-reading but precedes the return of the scrolls to the ark. 'Hazkarat neshamot' is recited the last day of 'Pesach'; the second day of 'Shavu'ot', and on 'Shemini Atzeret'. Rosh Hashanah and Yom Kipur are considered as one in this matter, and hazkarat neshamot is said 'Yom Kipur' for both.

Hazkarat neshamot is of greater significance on Yom Kipur though, than it is at other times, since the very essence of the day is the quest for forgiveness and atonement; which are as necessary for the deceased as for the living. And although it is written: 'Among the dead, there is freedom' which the Rabis expounded to mean that: 'Once a person dies, he becomes free of Torah and mitzvot,' nevertheless, charity pledged by children for 'the ascent of their parents' soul,' avails their parents. For the Sages also expounded (Sifri) the verse: 'Atone for Your people Israel whom You have redeemed,' as follows: 'Atone for Your people Israel' — these are the living; 'whom you have redeemed' — these are the dead. We learn thereby that the dead are in need of atonement.' This atonement is the prayer and the charity of the living in their behalf.

Further, if the way of life of the parents was upright, and they taught their children to worship God, to perform mitzvot and to dispense charity freely, and if the children abide by their parents' teaching, then the parents' strength endures in the childrens' deeds, and it is as if they were still living and practicing mitzvot.

If one's parents are still alive, he leaves the synagogue during Yizkor, because of the possible envy of the orphaned. Another reason is that he might err and recite Yizkor with the congregation, and he would be like one 'opening his mouth for Satan.' A third reason: So that he might not stand silent while all pray. Among the Sephardim however, the entire congregation remains in the synagogue. The 'Chazan' alone recites 'Hamerachem' (Yizkor), and each individual gives him the names of his own deceased for mention in the collective prayer. The Sephardim recite hazkarat neshamot every Shabat and every Yom Tov.

PIKUACH NEFESH (the saving of life) ON YOM KIPUR

If one is afflicted by an illness which poses a possible danger to life, and if fasting might aggravate his illness, he is forbidden to fast, because it is generally stated of all the mitzvot: 'And he shall live by them, but not die by them.' It is likewise stated: 'You shall take exceeding care unto your lives.' Such a person should eat as bidden by his doctors and as instructed by a competent rabbi, and his eating is regarded not as a sin but rather as a mitzvah, since the saving of life takes precedence over all the mitzvot (excepting the three cardinal transgressions: idolatry, adultery and murder). A person is therefore forbidden to impose excessive strictness upon himself in this matter, lest he enter a state of danger, and hence — one of transgression.

Minors who are not obligated to fast, but who excessively exert themselves to fast, act improperly, since their strength is still infirm, and they might be endangered by fasting. Parents should therefore restrain them from doing so.

Minors younger than nine, should not be permitted to fast. They should eat as is their usual habit, excepting Yom Kipur night, when it is customary not to feed them. From the age of nine till that of twelve they wait one hour or two longer than usual before eating. During the year preceding 'Bar Mitzvah' they complete the fast (as a Rabbinic requirement) if they are fully healthy. Nowadays however, we do not strictly impose completion of the fast on twelve year olds, since our generations are weaker than previous ones, and wherever there is possible danger to life, the law of saving-of-life is more stringently applied. A child however, who is mature in strength and fully healthy should complete the fast.

For this same reason of 'pikuach nefesh,' the Sages did not prescribe the observance of a second day of Yom Kipur,' outside the land of Israel, because of 'sfeka deyoma,' as they did in the case of the other festivals.

Even when the new months were sanctified upon observation of the new moon, and remote communities did not know on which day Rosh Hashanah fell —

whether on the thirtieth of 'Elul' or the following day — they relied upon the fact that during most years the new moon was observed the night following the twenty-ninth of Elul, and the following day — the first of Tishrey — Rosh Hashanah; ten days later they observed Yom Kipur and the following day was 'chol' (non-sacred). Such practice was likewise based on the consideration of 'pikuach nefashot', since most people would endanger themselves were they to fast two successive days. There were however rare individuals outside the Land of Israel who observed the Yom Kipur fast for two days because of 'sfeka deyoma.'

'SEDER AVODAH'
(The Order of Service in the Sanctuary)

Our early Sages prescribed the inclusion of the *Cohen Gadol's* order-of-service on Yom Kipur, in the cantor's repetition of *musaf*. This part of the service is hence called *seder avodah* (the order of service.) The *Chazan* chants it in a special awe-inspiring mode, with the congregation responding softly and in reverence. When the *Beit Hamikdash* (the Sanctuary) stood, the 'eyes of all Israel were raised' towards the *Cohen Gadol's* order-of-service, which began before the break of dawn on Yom Kipur and lasted till the end of the day. On this *avodah*, atonement for all Israel depended ('And he shall atone in his own behalf, in behalf of his household, and in behalf of the whole congregation of Israel' (Vayikra 16).

When the Cohen Gadol's service was performed properly, Israel's total forgiveness was made manifest for all eyes to see. A cord of red painted wool had been tied by the Cohen Gadol between the horns of the scapegoat. Another such cord had been tied by him around the throat of the goat reserved for the sin-offering, so that it might not be commingled with other goats held for the remaining offering-of-the-day. The cord used for the scapegoat was later divided in two — half remaining between the scapegoat's horns, and the other half hung upon the opening of the hallway leading to the Sanctuary, so that all might see it. (In a later period, the cord was no longer hung upon the opening of the hallway, but was tied to the top of the cliff from which the scapegoat was cast.) In years when the avodah was accepted by God and atonement was granted Israel, both parts of the cord turned white like snow, in accord with the verse: 'If your sins should be like red thread — they will turn like snow.' (Yeshayahu 1). Thereupon, all eyes saw God's forgiveness and the hearts of the people rejoiced.

THE COHEN AT SERVICE — THE PEOPLE AT WATCH

Each of the 'services-of-the-day,' from the slaughter of the daily-offering-of-morning till the afternoon 'tending-of-the-lights' (some say, from the 'removal-of-the-ashes' during the night) was exclusively done by the Cohen Gadol, with his fellow cohanim assisting only in minor matters.

All night Jerusalem was filled with the echoes of Torah and prayer — emitting from all of Jerusalem's dwellings and reaching the Sanctuary. The Cohen Gadol heard those echoes — and did not succumb to sleep. If he were a scholar, he expounded Torah before the elders among the cohanim all night. If he were a disciple, Torah was expounded before him. If he fell into slumber — the young cohanim (called the 'flowers-of-the-kehunah') beat before him with a forefinger, and said to him: 'My master — the Cohen Gadol — arise, and stand on the cold floor to regain your wakefulness!' He was thus engaged till the time for the slaughter of the daily-offering-of-morning. The time had not yet come for the call of the rooster, when the 'azarah' (the temple courtyard) was already filled with people.

All that day the people stood on their feet crowded together, without moving, or emitting a sound for twelve hours consecutively, their hearts were filled with holiness and awe, and their eyes were lifted towards the place where the Cohen Gadol performed the avodah all day.

Fifteen sacrifices were offered by the Cohen Gadol this day (in addition to the scapegoat which did not require slaughtering): two oxen, two rams, three goats, nine lambs — two lambs for the respective daily offerings, morning and evening; one ox, one ram and seven yearling lambs, for the additional (musaf) festival offerings — together comprising eleven. The oxen, rams and lambs required accompanying 'menachot' (offerings made of flour and oil) and 'nesachim' (libations of wine).

In addition there were: an ox for a 'sin-offering' as an atonement for the Cohen Gadol, his family and fellow cohanim; a ram in his own behalf, a ram for the people and one goat for a 'sin-offering' — together comprising four. And finally the scapegoat on which he uttered confession in behalf of all Israel. All the sacrifices (except the scapegoat), were slaughtered by himself alone. He then received the blood in vessels, poured or sprinkled the blood, as required for each sacrifice: on the outer altar, on the golden altar within the temple (hechal), on the 'kaporet' (the ark-covering), between the two rods of the 'aron' (holy ark) in the innermost 'holy-of-holies.' He then removed the limbs to be offered on the altar, burned them on the outer altar, and also offered the 'menachot' and 'nesachim' for all the offerings requiring them. In addition to all these, there were the two 'minchot hachavitin' which the Cohen Gadol offered daily, morning and evening.

That day, the Cohen Gadol burned 'ketoret'

(incense) three times: twice — in accord with his daily practice, which was to take a hundred dinar weight of the prepared incense, divide it in two, and burn both portions on the inner golden altar — one in the morning and one in the afternoon. In addition a three hundred dinar weight of incense was prepared for him from Erev Yom Kipur, from which he took a full scoop with both his hands, and placed it on a gold spoon. He took the spoon in one hand; with the other he took a pan with burning coal from the outer altar and brought them to the holy-of-holies. He placed the pan between the rods of the 'aron'; and in the second Temple which had no 'aron,' he placed it on the 'Even Shetiyah' (the foundation-stone).

He took hold of the spoon's edge with the tips of his fingers, or with his teeth, and edged the ketoret into his palms with his thumb; and this was regarded as an extremely difficult labor in the Sanctuary. He then piled the ketoret on the coals within, in the pan, and he waited there till the chamber was filled with smoke, whereupon he emerged. So that the Cohen Gadol offered ketoret three times in the course of the day of Yom Kipur.

The Cohen Gadol changed his garment five times Yom Kipur and immersed himself in a 'mikvah' at the time of each change. He consecrated his hands and feet with water placed in a gold laver, twice; once before removing his earlier garments, and once after putting on his new ones. In the morning he removed his own (non-sacred) garments and dressed in his (sacred) gold-garments — which were eight in number. He brought the daily morning offering and morning incense; tended the 'menorah'; burned the head and limbs of the daily offering on the altar; offered its 'minchat chavitin' and 'nesachim;' offered the additional festival sacrifices (an ox and seven lambs) on the outer altar; consecrated his hands and feet, removed his gold garments, immersed himself, dressed in his white-garments (the four garments of the regular Cohen), and consecrated his hands and feet a second time; he then brought the sin-offering-ox, cast lots over the two goats — one for God, and one to serve as a scapegoat — and tied a red thread upon them; he then brought the incense and the blood of the ox and goat to the holy-of-holies for burning and sprinkling.

Why does the Cohen Gadol not enter the holy-of-holies dressed in his gold-garments? The Accuser cannot serve as a Defender. 'Yesterday,' Satan would charge, 'they made themselves a god of gold (the golden calf), and today they wish to minister before God in gold garments!' Another reason: 'so that he might be like the ministering angels, of whom it is written: 'And one among them was dressed in white linen.'

He again consecrated his hands and feet, removed the white-garments, immersed himself, dressed in the gold-garments, sanctified his hands and feet, offered the goat brought on the outer altar (this goat was one of the regular festival musaf offerings), his ram and the people's ram; afterwards he consecrated his hands and feet, removed his gold-garments, immersed himself, dressed in the white-garments, consecrated his hands and feet and entered the holy-of-holies to remove the incense-spoon and pan which he had left there in the morning.

The white-garments he was now dressed in were not the same as those he wore in the morning; both sets of white-garments were exceedingly expensive, though there was no gold in them, their value rising to three thousand gold dinar. The garments worn one year were not worn again the following year.

The Cohen Gadol then again consecrated his hands and feet, removed the white garments, immersed himself, dressed in the gold-garments, consecrated his hands and feet to bring the daily afternoon offering, with the 'minchah' and 'nesachim'; to offer the daily afternoon incense and to tend the menorah upon completion of his entire avodah, he again consecrated his hands and feet in the gold laver, removed the golden kehunah-garments, and dressed in his own clothes. All together therefore, he changed his kehunah-garments five times, immersed himself five times, and consecrated his hands and feet ten times.

On Yom Kipur the Cohen Gadol uttered confession three times: the first time, he leaned his hands on the head of the ox which was his own sin-offering, and he uttered confession for himself and his household; the second time, he leaned his hands on the same ox, and uttered confession for himself, his household and all his fellow cohanim (he first atoned for himself and his family alone, so that his own achievement of merit might avail in seeking forgiveness for his fellow cohanim); and the third time he leaned his hands on the head of the scapegoat, and uttered confession for all the people.

Ten times the 'Shem Hameforash' (the ineffable Divine Name) was uttered orally by the Cohen Gadol on Yom Kipur; three times during each 'vidui' — comprising nine times; and the tenth time, as he cast lots on the goats. Over the goat designated by lot for the Divine offering, he then spoke the words, 'Unto HaShem (the ineffable Divine Name) — a sin-offering.' When the cohanim and the people then standing in the 'azarah' (the courtyard) heard the glorious and awesome Divine Name pronounced by the Cohen Gadol, in holiness and purity, they kneeled, bowed down, and fell on their faces, saying: 'Blessed be the Name of His glorious majesty unto eternity!'

Four times the Cohen Gadol entered the holy-of-holies on Yom Kipur: the first time, he entered to offer incense and placed the incense-spoon and the coalpan between the two staves of the aron; the second time, he brought in the blood of the ox and sprinkled it between the two staves of the aron — in the air of the holy-of-holies — eight times: once upwards and seven times downwards. The upward sprinkling was to be done above a height of ten 'tefachim' (handbreadths), in view of the top of the aron, while the others were to be directed downwards, below the ark, each one successively lower. The third time, he entered to sprinkle the blood of the goat as he had done with the blood of the ox. The fourth time, he entered to remove the incense-spoon and pan which he had left in the morning.

'And there shall be no man in the Tent-of-Meeting when he enters to make atonement in the holy place.'

This verse was said of the Cohen Gadol too. For at the hour of his entry into the holy-of-holies, he was indeed not a man, but rather like an angel ministering on High. He therefore could not pray for the fulfillment of any human needs while within, but upon leaving the holy-of-holies, he did utter a brief prayer.

The Cohen Gadol sprinkled blood three times from the blood of the ox and the goat, on the 'kaporet' of the 'hechal' without, and on the gold altar within. The first time he sprinkled from the blood of the ox towards the kaporet, in the air of the hechal, once upwards and seven times downwards; the second time he did the same with the blood of the goat; the third time he mixed both and sprinkled from them upon each of the four corners of the golden altar. He sprinkled another seven times over the altar. Together with the sixteen sprinklings within the holy-of-holies the total number of sprinklings was thus forty-three.

On Yom Kipur the Cohen Gadol uttered two prayers — one brief, and the other more lengthy. After he had offered incense in the holy-of-holies and the room had become smoke-filled, he stepped backwards, still facing the holy-of-holies, till he passed through the 'parochet' (curtain) separating the 'hechal' from the holy-of-holies. In the hechal, near the parochet, he prayed briefly for rain; for Israel's material sustenance; that expectant mothers might not suffer miscarriage; for the fruit of the trees and for the eternal rule of the Kingdom of David. He was required to be brief in this first prayer lest he frighten the people, who were anxiously awaiting his emergence in peace from the holy-of-holies.

Before his final entry into the holy-of-holies he uttered a lengthier prayer in the 'azarah' (courtyard). He read in the Torah (the account of the order-of-service for Yom Kipur in Vayikra), and while the Translator followed in explanation, the Cohen rolled the scroll to another portion in Vayikra from which he read the passage relating to Yom Kipur. The Translator explained what he had read. The Cohen then rolled up the scroll, and, holding it, declared: 'More than I have read before you is written here.' He then read by heart (so as not to burden the people by further extended rolling of the scroll) the passage relating to Yom Kipur from Bamidbar. He recites eight benedictions:

1. *in thanksgiving for the Torah,*
2. *for Divine acceptance of the service in the Sanctuary.*
3. *in thanksgiving for all that God bestows on us,*
4. *for forgiveness of sin,*
5. *for the Sanctuary,*
6. *for Israel,*
7. *for the cohanim, and,*
8. *for the acceptance of Israel's prayers.*

STANDING CROWDED AND BOWING SPACIOUSLY

Happy was the eye which saw all this. Even the cohanim and the people standing in the *azarah* became like angels, no longer subject to human needs. They were not weakened by their lengthy standing, nor did they feel the crush of the enormously crowded mass. Their standing in the azarah during the Cohen Gadol's avodah, was simultaneously their own avodah and prayer, thus sustaining them in body and soul.

They saw a great miracle there. When the cohanim and the people in the azarah heard the Divine Name pronounced by the Cohen Gadol they kneeled, bowed, and fell on their faces, saying: 'Blessed be the Name of His glorious majesty unto eternity.' And despite the density of the crowd while standing, there were four ells of free space about each of them as he uttered confession while prostrate — so that none might hear the other's confession.

As the people kneeled in blessing and confession the Cohen Gadol improvised in chant while pronouncing the ineffable Divine Name, and concluded its pronouncement as they concluded their words. The Cohen Gadol then spoke the final words of the verse he was uttering: *'Titharu!'* (You shall be purified).

On emerging in peace from the Sanctuary, the Cohen Gadol celebrated, and all Israel rejoiced with him over God's acceptance of their worship, and the atonement granted them.

Even the gentiles present heard and saw that God's Name was called upon Israel, and Israel's glory was great in their eyes.

A GENTILE GUEST RELATES

Towards the end of the period of the second Temple, a Roman emissary by the name of Marcus lived in Jerusalem. Marcus related his observation of the splendor surrounding the Cohen Gadol upon his entry into the Sanctuary at the advent of Yom Kipur, and upon his departure.

'Seven days before the special day which is called 'Kipur' — the most important of their days — they prepare special seats in the Cohen Gadol's home for the *Rosh Beit Din* (Head-of-the-Court), the *Nasi*, the Cohen Gadol, his assistant and the King. In addition, seventy silver seats are set for the seventy members of the *Sanhedrin*. The eldest of the Cohanim rises to address words of admonition to the Cohen Gadol: 'See before Whom you enter, and know that if you lose the proper intention, you will instantly fall and die, and Israel's forgiveness will be lost. The eyes of all Israel are upon you. Examine your ways lest you be guilty of even the slightest transgression, there being single transgressions which outweigh many mitzvot, with judgment on the matter resting in the hand of God. Examine your brother cohanim also, and purify them. Be aware that you come before the King of Kings, who sits on the seat-of-judgment and sees all.' The Cohen Gadol responds by saying that he has already undergone self examination, and that he has repented from any sin known to him. He has also assembled his brother cohanim in the Temple courtyard, and cast an oath upon them in the name of the One Who causes His Name to dwell in the Sanctuary — to the end that each was to state any sin of which he was guilty, or that he knew concerning his companions. He would then prescribe a proper form of repentance for each instance. The king too spoke encouragingly to him and promised to honor him upon his emergence from the Sanctuary unharmed.

Afterwards they announced the departure of the Cohen Gadol to his chamber in the Sanctuary whereupon all the people came out to accompany him. And this is what I saw: The first in the line of march before the Cohen Gadol were descendants of the kings of Israel. Afterwards came descendants of the house of David. Proclamations were made before them: 'Accord honor to the House of David!' The House of Levi followed — 'Accord honor to the House of Levi!' The Levites numbered 36,000, while there were 24,000 cohanim. Then came, successively, the singers, the musicians, the trumpeteers... and those who make the incense, those who fashion the *parachot...* the seventy members of the *Sanhedrin,* a hundred cohanim with silver staffs in hand to clear a path. Finally the Cohen Gadol came, followed by the elders among the Cohanim walking in pairs of two.

'Heads of *Yeshivot* stood at street entrances and said: 'Master, Cohen Gadol! May your coming be in peace! Pray to our Maker that He may grant us life, to engage in the study of His Torah.' On reaching the entrance to the Temple-Mount they prayed for the rise of the House of David; and then, for the cohanim and the Sanctuary. The cry of the multitude who answered 'Amen' was so mighty that birds in flight fell to the ground. The Cohen Gadol then bowed to the people and turned aside weeping and in awe.

'Two cohanim-assistants led him to his office, where he took leave of his fellow cohanim. All this occurred upon his entry; when he emerged however, the honor accorded him was doubled. All who were in Jerusalem passed before him; most of them carrying lit torches of white wax, and all of them dressed in white. All the windows were decorated and filled with lights.

'The cohanim told me that many a year the Cohen Gadol was unable to reach his home before midnight because of the pressure of the milling multitude. Though they had all fasted, none would return home without having attempted to reach the Cohen Gadol in order to kiss his hands.

'The following day he held a great banquet to which he invited those near and dear to him. And he celebrated the day as a festival, over having emerged in peace from the Sanctuary.

'He then charged an artisan, to fashion a gold plate on which the following legend was to be inscribed: 'I, so-and-so the Cohen Gadol, the son of so-and-so the Cohen Gadol have ministered in the 'kehunah-gedola' in the great house which is consecrated to the service of the One Who causes His Name to dwell there; and this occurred in the year so-and-so of Creation. May He Who granted me the merit of this service, grant my sons after me the merit of standing in service before God.'

IN THE ABSENCE OF THE BEIT HAMIKDASH

The above occurred when the Sanctuary still stood, and the Cohen Gadol still ministered. The people saw and rejoiced, and happy was the eye which saw it all.

Now that the *Beit Hamikdash* is no more, and we have neither Cohen, nor altar, nor offerings for atonement, we recite the order of the avodah as prescribed by our ancient Sages instead of the practice of the avodah 'And we shall repay for the bullocks — with our lips.' By word of mouth and the intention of the heart, we discharge our obligations, while awakening anguish in ourselves over the Sanctuary's destruction and intense yearning for its speedy rebuilding.

'The order-of-avodah' which we recite Yom Kipur begins with references to the world's creation and recalls Adam's ancient sin — because of which he was expelled from the Garden of Eden. It recounts further the failure of his sons to rectify that sin and their increasing evil, till the flood swept them away and Noah and his sons alone survived for the rebuilding of the world. They too failed to rectify the sinfulness of the preceding generations, erred in their wealth and built a tower, saying: 'let us ascend and pierce the heavens to wage war against Him.' All the world was again spiritually destitute — till our father Avraham appeared and again filled the world with light. He bore Itzchak who became a perfect offering, pure of sin. After him there came Ya'akov 'the whole-hearted,' and his twelve sons, the tribes of God, all of them sacred from birth. Of them, Levi and his sons were chosen to minister in the sacred service. Of his grandsons, Aharon was chosen for the *Kehunah* — to bring sacrificial offerings, to atone for his people's transgressions, and to rectify the sinfulness of earlier generations.

The account then recalls the entire avodah practiced by Aharon and his descendants, the *Cohanim Gedolim* of all the generations, in the *Beit Hamikdash* on Yom Kipur.

When the cantor recites the passage, 'and the cohanim and the people who stood in the azarah,' the congregation and the cantor fall prostrate on their faces and say, as was said in the Beit Hamikdash: 'Blessed be the Name of His Glorious Majesty unto eternity.' And although there were ten 'kneelings' in the Sanctuary, one for each time that the ineffable Divine Name was pronounced by the Cohen Gadol, only three kneelings are prescribed in our order-of-avodah, corresponding to the Cohen Gadol's three confessionals: for himself and his household; for his fellow cohanim; and for all the people. And these three kneelings are only a memorial, since the Divine Name is not pronounced in our days.

EXPRESSLY 'EMERGING' FROM THE MOUTH OF THE COHEN GADOL

A person of flesh and blood — even the Cohen Gadol on Yom Kipur — is incapable of bringing forth the ineffable Divine Name from his mouth. Even angels cannot pronounce it; no tongue contains a word for it, because it is concealed, ethereal, and awesome beyond all else. How then did the Cohen Gadol bring it forth from his lips ?

On this Holy Day, in this sacred place, when the Cohen

Gadol — the holiest of men — purified and sanctified himself till he rose above all that was earthly, and was about to pronounce the ineffable Name — His mouth was opened, and the Holy and Glorious Name 'emerged' expressly of itself.

Because of this it is said: 'In every place where I will cause My Name to be pronounced, I will come to you and I will bless you.' The verse should have read, 'wherever you will pronounce My Name.' We learn from this that one of flesh and blood is incapable of pronouncing the ineffable Name with his lips, and that God alone pronounces it.

KNEELING DURING 'ALENU' AND KNEELING DURING 'VIDUI'

Before the order-of-avodah the cantor utters the prayer 'alenu'. This prayer too is chanted with the melody of the order-of-avodah when the cantor says: '...that He did not set our portion like theirs, and our lot like that of all their multitudes, for they bow down to vanity and emptiness and pray to a god who does not help, whereas we kneel and bow down before the King of Kings, the Holy One Blessed Be He' — the congregation and the cantor fall prostrate on their faces, and conclude the prayers. Hence, altogether, there are four 'kneelings' during the Yom Kipur 'musaf'; one in 'alenu' and three during the confessionals in the order-of-service.

'Kneeling' during alenu is also prescribed for Rosh Hashanah in the Ashkenazi custom. The Sephardi custom is not to kneel during alenu, but to kneel four times on Yom Kipur corresponding to the four times that 'vehacohanim veha'am' is said in the order-of-avodah.

The first 'kneeling' however is of different significance than the final three.

In '*Yesod Veshoresh Ha'avodah*' it is written:

'How intensely ought a person to weep as he says: 'and

when the cohanim and the people... heard the Divine Name... pronounced by the mouth of the Cohen Gadol.' How ought one to weep over the cessation of the Divine Glory which once was: when the Divine Name was heard, as it was pronounced by the Cohen Gadol in sanctity and purity, and all those standing in the courtyard... fell on their faces, saying joyously: 'Blessed be the Name of His Glorious Majesty forever...' But now, since the day of the destruction of the Sanctuary, all this has been transformed to mourning and grief... through our sins we constantly cause the desecration of his Great Name, as it were. How can we remove our shame? Woe to us for the day of judgment; woe to us for the day of admonition! And the Rabis have said: 'every generation in whose days the Sanctuary is not rebuilt, is as if it were destroyed in its day.' ...Especially when one falls upon his face saying: 'they kneeled and bowed down, and fell on their faces' — he ought to weep over the absence of God's glory.

'The intention of the three kneelings of the order-of-service is not similar to the intention of the first kneeling of *alenu.* In the case of *alenu* one should feel profound joy over his being part of God's 'portion'... whereas in the case of other kneelings every Jewish person is obligated to weep greatly over the absence of the Divine glory which once extended to him.

'At the conclusion of the avodah the *selichot* following the account of the ten martyred Sages, should likewise be said with intense devotion and weeping...'

In synagogues whose floors are of stone, it is customary to spread either straw or another covering over them, because of the prohibition of bowing down upon a smooth stone.

THE FIVE SERVICES ON YOM KIPUR

On Yom Kipur the order of prayer contains five services: 'ma'ariv,' 'shacharit' and 'minchah' (which are fixed as daily prayers as well); 'musaf', which is a fixed Service every Shabat and Yom Tov and takes the place of the 'additional-offerings' (the Hebrew term 'musaf' means 'additional') which were brought in the Sanctuary; and a fifth Service, 'nei'lah,' in honor of the specific Sanctity of the day. The name 'ne'ilah' signifies 'closing,' since its time is close to the end of Yom Kipur, when the 'gates of mercy' are about to be closed.

Since ne'ilah is said when the Divine decree is about to be finally sealed, it should be said with fervent intention in order to strengthen the attribute-of-mercy.

THE CLOSING OF THE GATES

During ne'ilah, as well as in 'Avinu Malkenu', which follows it, the term 'chotmenu' ('seal us') is used instead of 'kotvenu' ('inscribe us') — which is the usage followed during the remainder of the 'ten-days-of-penitence.'

Although 'Avinu Malkenu' is not said on Shabat, it is included in ne'ilah, when Yom Kipur falls on Shabat, even if the duration of the service extends later than the appearance of the stars. The Sephardim do not say 'Avinu Malkenu' during 'ne'ilah.'

Upon the conclusion of the Service, the cantor says 'Shemah Israel' (Hear O Israel) aloud once, and the congregation repeats the verse aloud after him. Each person should then have the intention of being ready to offer his life for the sanctification of God's Name. The cantor says: 'Baruch shem kevod malchuto le'olam va'ed,' three times, and the congregation repeats the verse aloud three times. The repetition of this verse three times corresponds to: 'The Lord reigns, the Lord has reigned, the Lord shall reign' which signifies that God was sovereign before the world's creation, that He rules this world and that He will rule the world to come.

The cantor then says: 'Hashem Hu Ha'Elokim' (The Lord, He is God) seven times. And the congregation repeats the same with all their strength seven times. These seven times correspond to the seven heavens which God opened for Israel at the time of the giving of the Torah, in order to show them that there is none beside Him. Another reason: The seven times correspond to the withdrawal of the Divine Presence, after having dwelt in our midst from evening to evening, through the seven heavens which are between the earth and the throne of Divine Glory.

The cantor says the complete 'kadish' with a joyous melody as an expression of our trust in His merciful acceptance of our prayer.

After kadish one long 'teki'ah' is sounded (the Ashkenazi custom). Or, ten 'shofar' sounds are sounded before 'titkabel', and one final 'tru'ah' follows (the Sephardi custom).

A number of reasons are given for the sounding of the shofar at the end of Yom Kipur.

1. It is a memorial to the 'yovel' (jubilee) year, which was observed when the 'Beit Hamikdash' (the Sanctuary) stood.

When the shofar was sounded on Yom Kipur of a 'yovel' year, all slaves were freed and fields which had been sold were returned to their original owners.

2. In order to confuse Satan. On Yom Kipur he has no permission to accuse. At the day's departure he wishes to stand in accusation against Israel, but the shofar confuses him.

3. It is a sign that we have vanquished Satan, just

as victorious returnees from war sound the shofar in rejoicing.

4. To recall the merit of the binding of Itzchak at the time of the final sealing of God's Decree.

5. It recalls Moshe's ascent and descent from Heaven the third time. Moshe ascended Mount Sinai the last time on Rosh Chodesh Elul, and descended on Yom Kipur, and he ordered the blowing of the shofar upon his ascent and descent.

6. It is an allusion to the withdrawal of the Divine Presence as it is said: 'God ascended with the blowing of shofar.'

7. It is an announcement that night has come and that the children who have fasted should be fed.

8. It declares that the eve following Yom Kipur is likened to Yom Tov; and that it is a mitzvah to eat a regular Yom Tov meal. As it is said in the Midrash: 'On the eve following Yom Kipur an echo-of-a-voice says: Go and eat your bread in joy.' And because the Yom Tov character of this evening is not widely known, special care is taken to publicize it.

If the 'ne'ilah' service is concluded, together with the verses which follow, and the stars have not yet appeared the congregation waits till the appearance of the stars before the 'teki'ah' is sounded.

After the shofar is sounded, 'Leshanah haba'ah biYerushalayim!' ('Next year in Jerusalem') is said.

In Jerusalem they say: 'Leshanah haba'ah bi-Yerushalayim habenuyah!' ('Next year in rebuilt Jerusalem'). 'Ma'ariv' follows (including 'Atah chonantanu'); the prescribed prayer for the sanctification of the new moon is said; mutual greetings are exchanged, and all return home, in joy and gladness of heart. 'Havdalah' is recited over wine; the brachah over light should be recited only over a light that was kindled before Yom Kipur. A Yom Tov meal then follows.

We refrain from all voluntary work this night and engage only in works involving mitzvot. It is customary to begin the building of the 'sukah' immediately following the post-Yom-Kipur meal, in fulfillment of the verse: 'They shall go from strength to strength.'

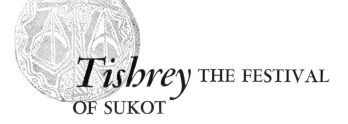

Tishrey THE FESTIVAL OF SUKOT

BETWEEN YOM KIPUR AND SUKOT ❖ THE FESTIVAL OF SUKOT ❖ THE SECOND YOM TOV DAY IN THE DIASPORA ❖ THE SEVEN MITZVOT OF THE FESTIVAL ❖ ENGAGED IN MITZVOT ❖ THE MITZVAH OF SUKAH ❖ SUKOT AND NOT HOUSES ❖ SUKOT IN TISHREY AND NOT IN NISAN ❖ AS IN THE DAY OF OUR EXODUS FROM THE LAND OF EGYPT ❖ THE BUILDING OF THE SUKAH ❖ THE MEASUREMENTS OF THE SUKAH ❖ SUKAH DECORATIONS ❖ DWELLING IN THE SUKAH ❖ THE KINDLING OF THE LIGHTS ❖ THE BRACHOT OF THE FESTIVAL ❖ IN THE SHADOW OF FAITH ❖ EXALTED GUESTS ❖ THE USHPIZIN — SHEPHERDS FOR ISRAEL ❖ THE USHPIZIN SHEPHERDS FOR THE ENTIRE WORLD ❖ USHPIZIN OF FLESH AND BLOOD ❖ GIVE THE POOR WHAT IS THEIRS ❖ TRUST IN GOD FOR THE RICH AND FOR THE POOR ❖ FOUR AND FOUR ❖ THE FOUR SPECIES ❖ THE ORDER OF NETILAT LULAV AND THE BRACHAH ❖ HIDUR AND THE FOUR SPECIES ❖ WHEN THE FOUR SPECIES ARE INVALID ❖ NA'ANUIM ❖ THE PRECIOUSNESS OF THE MITZVAH ❖ HIDUR OF THE MITZVAH — NOT OF SELF ❖ THE END DOES NOT JUSTIFY THE MEANS ❖ THE FOUR SPECIES CORRESPOND TO FOUR TYPES OF JEWS ❖ PURIFICATION FROM SIN LEADS TO UNITY ❖ ALL MY BONES SHALL SAY — NISUCH HAMAYIM ❖ WITH GREAT JOY ❖ BEIT HASHO'EVAH ❖ SIMCHAT BEIT HASHO'EVAH ❖ HAPPINESS AND GLORY ❖ THE SEVENTY FESTIVAL OXEN ❖ ISHMAEL AND ESAV ❖ 'AND YOU SHALL REJOICE ON YOUR FESTIVAL' ❖ YOM TOV OBSERVANCE ❖ THE JOY OF THE MITZVAH RATHER THAN THE JOY OF THE BODY ❖ THE DIFFERENCE BETWEEN YOM TOV AND SHABAT ❖ CHOL HAMO'ED ❖ THE SHABAT OF CHOL HAMO'ED.

CHAPTER THREE

BETWEEN YOM KIPUR AND SUKOT

The four days between *Yom Kipur* and the festival of *Sukot* are marked by a festive spirit. Fasting is prohibited, including even an individual fast on a parent's *yahrzeit. Tachanun* is not said. If they include a *Shabat* day, *av harachamim* is omitted during *shacharit,* and *tzidkatcha tzedek* is omitted during *minchah.*

The days are festive in character because they coincide with the days of the consecration of the altar in the first Temple. We too are engaged in *mitzvot* these days: in the building of a *sukah* (a booth); the purchase of an *etrog* and the other species which accompany it.

Erev Sukot one should refrain from eating during the late afternoon, so that he might eat the festival meal in his *sukah* at night, with good appetite.

THE FESTIVAL OF SUKOT

The milestones of repentance and atonement — Rosh Hashanah, Yom Kipur and the intervening days -- are followed by festival days; days of rejoicing and praise. An allusion to this sequence is found in the verse: 'And to the upright of heart, there is joy.' That is to say, after the heart is made upright through *teshuvah (repentance)* on Rosh Hashanah and Yom Kipur, it achieves joy during Sukot.

On the 15th of *Tishrey* the festivals begin, and last eight days as outlined in the Torah: 'On the 15th day of this 7th month, the festival of *Sukot,* seven days unto the Lord; on the first day a convocation of holiness, all manner of work you shall not do; seven days you shall sacrifice a burnt offering to the Lord. On the eighth day there shall be unto you a convocation of holiness and you shall sacrifice a burnt offering to the Lord, it shall be a day of assembly, all manner of work you shall not do' (Vayikra 23).

The first seven days are called the Festival of Sukot since we are bidden to observe the *mitzvah* of dwelling in a *Sukah* during this period.

The eighth day is called *Atzeret* (a solemn assembly) in the Torah. And since it is the eighth day, counting from the first day of Sukot, the day is also called *Shmini Atzeret* (the eighth day of solemn assembly).

The first and eighth days are full holidays, and work is prohibited on them, with the exception of that involved in the preparation of food. The six intervening days are called *Chol Hamo'ed* (week-day festivals). Outside the Land of Israel, *Chol Hamo'ed* consists of only five days. During these days some work is permitted, as will be clarified in the chapter on Chol Hamo'ed.

THE SECOND YOM TOV IN THE DIASPORA

With the exception of Rosh Hashanah, which is observed for two days even in the Land of Israel, all the festivals mentioned in the Torah consist of only one day. And they are thus observed in the Land of Israel. In the Diaspora however, they are observed for two days (see page 20). Yom Kipur is another exception, since it is observed for only one day even in the Diaspora.

Hence, the number of festival days in the Diaspora exceeds by five days the number of such days in the Land of Israel. These five days are: The second day of *Pesach*, the eighth day of *Pesach*, the second day of *Shavuot*, the second day of *Sukot* and *Simchat Torah*.

The first day of the festival is prescribed by the Torah, and is called simply, 'Yom Tov,' or, 'Yom Tov Rishon' (The first Yom Tov). The following day, which is observed in the Diaspora is called, 'the second Yom Tov of the Diaspora,' or, 'the second Yom Tov,' and it is of Rabbinical origin.

Why did the Sages prescribe the observance of 'the second Yom Tov of the Diaspora ?'

When the *Beit Din* (the high Court) in Jerusalem sanctified the months through the testimony of witnesses who had seen the new moon, they sent messengers to inform the outlying communities as to the day on which the new month was consecrated; so that the various communities might know the proper day for the observance of the festivals falling in the respective months. In the case of Diaspora communities too distant for the messengers to arrive on time, two festival days were observed out of doubt: Did the Beit Din sanctify the new month at the end of the 29th day of the previous month, or at the end of the 30th day ? In such instances both Yom Tov days were considered as possessing equal sanctity.

In the case of Yom Kipur however, only one day was observed, because fasting two days would endanger life. There was also reliance on the fact that during most years the Beit Din sanctified Tishrey at the end of the 29th day of Elul. In later times, the sanctification of the month through witnesses ceased, and the date of the festivals was determined in accord with a fixed system of calendar calculation. Nevertheless, the Diaspora communities did not depart from the custom of their forefathers, and they continued to observe two Yom Tov days. Likewise, do the residents of the Land of Israel, continue their earlier custom of observing all the festivals for one day, with the exception of Rosh Hashanah which they had always observed for two days (see page 21).

The laws of the first Yom Tov day apply in the Diaspora for the second Yom Tov day as well, with the exception of burial of the dead and laws involving doubts. In the case of the latter we are lenient in decision the second Yom Tov day, which is only of Rabbinic origin in contrast to the first day which is of Torah origin. Still, anyone who violates laws of

Rabbinic origin, in instances not permitted by them, is like one who violates Torah law, for the Torah has said: 'You shall not turn away from all that they shall teach you.'

THE SEVEN MITZVOT OF THE FESTIVAL

No festival is as rich in mitzvot as this one. It contains: *sukah* and the four species — *mitzvot* of Torah origin; the libation of water on the altar which is a ***halachah le'Moshe*** *misinai* (law given unto Moshe orally and not written in the Torah); the holding of an *aravah* (willow) on ***Hoshana*** *Raba* (the seventh day of Sukot) — a custom of Prophetic origin — and a specific commandment to rejoice ('And you shall rejoice in your festival' — Dvarim 16).

'...Rabi Avin said: The matter may be likened to two men who came before a judge, and we do not know who prevailed. But, whoever carries a 'sceptre' in hand (on emerging from the judge), is known to have prevailed. Likewise, Israel and the nations come and contend before God on Rosh Hasanah and we do not know who prevailed. However, when Israel emerges from God's Presence with *lulav* and *etrog* in hand, we knew that Israel has prevailed' (Vayikra Raba 30).

What constitutes Israel's victory? Their having emerged meritorious in judgment, and their attainment of forgiveness for the sins they had committed all year. Once more they become God's children. They bear the sceptre of the king; they perform His mitzvot joyously; they dwell in a sukah; they hold the four species; they pour a libation of water on the altar; they draw water joyously; they hold an aravah on Hoshana Raba. They bring offerings to achieve atonement for themselves and the whole world.

After concluding the seven festival days, they do not run home but tarry before their king, and celebrate the eighth day in rejoicing over His Torah.

ENGAGED IN MITZVOT

'And you shall take for yourselves on the first day' (Vayikra 23) — 'the first day for the calculation of sins' (Vayikra Raba 30).

A person who has won a trial, feels relieved and happy. He immediately celebrates and relaxes. Israel however, is different. After emerging meritorious in judgment on Yom Kipur, they exert themselves in the practice of God's mitzvot. They do not turn to rejoicing till *Sukot* on the fifteenth day of the month.

During the four days between Yom Kipur and Sukot they are busy building their Sukah-booths and obtaining their *lulavim,* and they do not come to sin. Neither does God engage, as it were, in recording the sins of those days. Which day is then 'the first for the calculation of Israel's sins anew? The fifteenth of Tishrey; a day which is 'replete with mitzvot like a pomegranate.'

'And you shall take for yourselves on the first day, a beautiful fruit of a tree...' (Vayikra 23) this refers to the fifteenth day. Why then is it called: 'the first day?' The matter may be compared to a province which owed payment on a penalty to a king, and which the king set out to collect. When the king came within a distance of ten *mil,* the great men of the province came out and offered him praise; the king lessened their penalty by a third. When the king came within 5 *mil,* the minor officials of the province came out and praised him, and he reduced their penalty by another third. When he entered the province itself, all the inhabitants, men, women and children, came out and praised him, and he remitted the entire penalty. The king said to them: What is past is past. From now on let us begin a new record.

Likewise, on Erev Rosh Hashanah, the greatest of the generation fast, and God reduces their sins by a third. From Rosh Hashanah till Yom Kipur, individuals fast, and God reduces their sins by another third. On Yom Kipur, all fast; men, women and children. From Yom Kipur till the festival of Sukot all Israel are engaged in mitzvot: One is engaged in his Sukah, another with his lulav, and on the first Yom Tov day of the festival all Israel stand before God with lulav and etrog in hand. God then says to them: What is past is past. From now on we shall begin a new record. Therefore, Moshe forewarns Israel: 'And you shall take for yourselves (i.e. 'for your good') on the first day.'

Happy are Israel, that they are thus immersed in mitzvot. Their hands are filled with mitzvot: the lulav and etrog. Their mouths are filled with praise to God's Name; their heart is filled with song and rejoicing before God; their entire body enters the sukah ordained by the King of Kings. In the shadow of His faithfulness, they all find protection.

The matter may be compared to a king who says to his spies: Go out and spy the house of so and so, to find out if he has not failed to pay taxes, or if he did not violate other royal decrees. They went out and found a whole house filled with gifts for the king, with a sumptuous meal being prepared in the king's honor. They returned and said to the king: So and so is your devoted friend. He does not violate your decrees but is busy all day only to enhance your glory. Happy is the one whose accuser has become his defender. On the first day that Israel's 'new sins' are recorded, Moshe Rabenu therefore forewarned Israel: 'You shall take for yourselves the four species on the first day,' and, 'In sukot you shall dwell.'

THE MITZVAH OF SUKAH

It is written in the Torah: 'In sukot you shall dwell seven days, every citizen in Israel they shall dwell in sukot, in order that your generations shall know, that in sukot did I cause the children of Israel to dwell, when I brought them forth from the land of Egypt' (ibid.). Six months before Israel came out of Egypt their bondage ceased, and they dwelt securely in their homes; homes filled with plenty. For the Egyptians sought Israel's friendship, and bestowed all manner of good upon them. Even the inquitous Pharaoh and all his servants sought to persuade Israel not to leave Egypt. They promised that all the goodness of the land of Egypt would be given to the Jews if they would stay. When the day of redemption came however it is written that: 'the children of Israel turned from Ra'amses to Sukot, some six hundred thousand on foot, the men, aside from infants. And a great mixed multitude also went up with them with sheep and oxen...' (Shmot 12). There were six hundred thousand men aged twenty to sixty. Add to these six hundred thousand children and aged, which adds up to a million and two hundred thousand males. To these add a million two hundred thousand females, besides a large mixed multitude. Hence there were three million people who left their homes and their cities, and all the goods they possessed and went after God in the wilderness, in which there were neither houses nor shade, neither food nor water, but only great and terrible desolation containing snakes and serpents. Nor did they ask their God: Where are you bringing us? And where will we find protection from heat and cold? And from whence will our sustenance come?

'From Ra'amses to Sukot.' From Ra'amses to Sukot there is a distance of 120 *mil;* a distance which it would take three days for an average person to traverse. It would certainly take twice as long or more for children and aged, with all their possessions, to cover such a distance. Nevertheless, they reached Sukot the very same day, as it is written: 'And I bore you on eagles' wings' (Shmot 19). To teach you that anyone who walks in the path of the Lord, and places his trust in God, is not forsaken by God and he experiences His miracles.

When they reached Sukot they encamped till the following day. Some of our Sages maintain that God made them actual booths. Others say that the sukot He made for them consisted of seven clouds-of-glory which enveloped them. One was placed under their feet like a carpet, one was above their heads like a shadow, four were on all their four sides; the seventh cloud went before them to show them the way, and all Israel dwelt in one sukah, in the sukah of the clouds-of-glory. And 'both views are the words of the living God' — at first he made an actual booth for them, and in reward for having forsaken their homes in Egypt, and having dwelt in temporary sukot, without complaining to God, they merited that God should surround them by the clouds-of-glory.

SUKOT AND NOT HOUSES

God was able to perform a miracle for his hosts, and to enable them to dwell in houses even in the wilderness, just as he enabled them to dwell in the miraculous *sukah* of the enveloping clouds. But He caused them to dwell in a temporary dwelling during Sukot, in order that the redeemed generation, and the following ones, might know that there is no dwelling other than one built by God. 'And if the Lord does not build a house, for naught did they strive, those who built it' (Tehilim 127). If it is His will, the houses of the wicked are overturned by Him and they become graves for their inhabitants, as when Sedom and Amorah were overturned. If it is His will He points a path through the sea, He makes habitation out of wilderness, and of the clouds in the heavens, He makes a shelter against rain.

Pharaoh and his people were mightier at that hour than any other nation. They were wealthy and strong; they felt secure in their great wealth, and they took pride in their prowess. They built Pitom and Ra'amses, saying: no one can enter our boundary and none can leave it. The river is ours and it is our god, who nourishes and sustains us.

'Now I have known' — they said: 'No slave could ever flee Egypt, since it was closed and locked. But now — He (God) has taken six hundred thousand out of Egypt.'

The Israelites of that generation were also weak in their faith. They had already been immersed in 'the forty nine gates of Egyptian defilement.' They believed that strength was the lot of the mighty; that security was the portion of the wealthy; that dominion was the province of the tyrants. The Israelites wanted only that their bondage be somewhat lightened, so that they might be likened to all other Egyptians. Then God kept His promise to Avraham, Itzchak, and Ya'akov, their fathers. He brought them forth from Egypt with great might. He cleansed them and purified them from their abominations. He showed them that God's redeeming hand was mightier than all the world's mighty ones. All this was done in order to teach Israel to forsake every vain belief, and to seek strength only in faith in God. Israel was to learn that:

The river is not God — for God smote the river and transformed its waters to blood.

A house is no security — for the frogs came up from the river and filled all the houses.

The land is not to be relied upon — for it was smitten by a lowly creature — lice.

The people are no fortress — for hordes of animals overran the cities, and cast fear and confusion among the people.

Cattle are no source of strength — for God's hand was upon all their cattle.

Pleasure is no abiding reality — dust from Moshe Rabenu's hand inflicted boils and the anguish of shame on all the Egyptians.

The laws of nature are as naught — hail fell on Egypt, such as had never been.

The trees of the field are desolate — the locust ate the trees of the field.

The sun, the moon and all heavenly hosts are Mine — for darkness covered their light.

Every first-born; every mark of preeminence and greatness

are less than naught — the Lord smote every first-born in the land of Egypt — there is none beside Him!

And now my beloved children — you are no servants of Pharaoh; you are not enslaved to their beliefs. You are My servants. I have brought you out from under the hand of Pharaoh and I shall redeem you from all his delusions. Leave every protection which is no protection. Leave their houses and their fortresses. Come and find protection in the shadow of My wings, and it shall be to you an enduring protection. Their glorious palaces will be a mark of shame to them. Whereas I will envelope you in a cloud without substance, and that cloud will bestow eternal glory upon you.

'And the children of Israel journeyed from Ra'amses to Sukot.'

They journeyed from Pharaoh's storage cities and fortresses, and they came to seek protection under the shadow of the sukah of the God of truth.

However, before they left Egypt, they had already slaughtered the Egyptian idols. They had performed the mitzvah of the Paschal lamb and had accepted God's kingdom. God had consecrated them to Himself with the blood of the Paschal offering in Egypt, and now they had entered under His *chupah* — under the shadow of His sukah — and the Lord had acquired His People as an eternal possession.

SUKOT IN TISHREY AND NOT IN NISAN

The Israelites were commanded to leave their houses for sukot on the fifteenth day of the seventh month, to recall the sukot in which God housed them when they came out of Egypt. It may be asked however: Did not the exodus from Egypt take place in Nisan? It would have been appropriate therefore, to recall the event at the time of its original occurrence — in Nisan. Why were we commanded then to observe Sukot in Tishrey? Many reasons are given; the essential one is that during Nisan, leaving one's home would not be recognized as done for the sake of God.

During Nisan or spring season as the weather becomes warmer a person usually goes away to dwell in a booth. During the days of Tishrey however, everybody returns from their booths to their houses, because of the onset of the rains, and the cold of the nights. Therefore when the Israelites take up residence in booths during the period of Tishrey, all see that they do so in fulfillment of God's decree and for the sake of His Name. As it is written: 'In order that your generations may know.' It is a mitzvah that the erection of the sukah for the sake of God should be recognizable and known as such.

The Sages have also said: 'Why do we observe Sukot after Yom Kipur ? On Rosh Hashanah God sits in judgment of all the world's inhabitants; on Yom Kipur He seals His judgment. Perhaps it was decreed for Israel to go into exile ? Therefore, they erect a sukah and go into exile from their houses into the sukah.'

Further reasons are advanced by later authorities:

We do not commemorate the first clouds-of-glory, which surrounded the Israelites during the exodus from Egypt, since those clouds withdrew from them after the making of the golden calf. We commemorate only the clouds-of-glory which returned to them later (after Yom Kipur), and did not withdraw again the entire forty years of their stay in the wilderness.

After Israel had sinned with the calf, and the clouds-of-glory withdrew, Moshe ascended on High three times. On descending the third time he brought Israel the mitzvah to erect the *mishkan* (sanctuary-tent), as a mark that God was reconciled to them and would dwell in their midst.

On Yom Kipur Moshe descended from the mountain. On the morrow after Yom Kipur it is written: 'and Moshe assembled the whole congregation of the children of Israel and Moshe said... take from among you an offering to the Lord...' And they brought their contributions the following two days — the twelfth and thirteenth of Tishrey. On the fourteenth of Tishrey the wise-of-heart (the artisans who built the mishkan) took all the contributions from Moshe. On the fifteenth they began the construction of the mishkan, and then the clouds-of-glory returned and became like a sukah (protective cover) over the camp of Israel. That day was, accordingly, fixed for them as a day when they were to dwell in sukot. Just as God left the heavens, as it were, and caused His Presence to dwell on earth in the midst of the children of Israel, so does Israel show God that they too leave their homes and dwell with Him in a sukah — in the protective shadow of His faithfulness.

Furthermore, the festival of Sukot is observed during the time of the ingathering of the harvest, when everyone stores the blessings of the soil. In order that his heart might not become arrogant, and in order that He might not set all his joy upon his worldly possessions, the master of the house rises, leaves his possessions and goes out to the sukah, to seek protection under the shadow of the wings of the Divine Presence. He declares: 'Unto the Lord is the Earth and its fullness!' And we rejoice only in You — in the shadow of Your Divine Presence.

We also read the book of Kohelet (Ecclesiastes) during the festival of Sukot (in the Ashkenazi custom), to temper our pride in our possessions, for 'all is vanity.' To what then shall we direct our minds ? To the conclusion of Kohelet: 'The end of the matter, all is heard, you shall fear God, observe His mitzvot, for this is the whole of Man.'

During the Days of Awe, Israel ask forgiveness for all the sins of the entire year. But though their repentance is accepted and their sins pardoned, they still remain agitated because of their earlier sins. For repentants usually feel as if they can find no place for themselves in the world. God therefore says: since you can find no place because of your sense of shame at your sins — I will make you a place. Come to me, and find protection in My shadow — the sukah of My Peace.

AS IN THE DAYS OF OUR EXODUS FROM THE LAND OF EGYPT

'Every citizen of Israel shall dwell in booths, in order that your generations may know, that in booths did I set the children of Israel, when I brought them forth from the land of Egypt.' When the Israelites departed from Egypt they came out with many possessions; with the spoils of Egypt, and the spoils of the sea. They came to the wilderness, in which they found neither planting nor harvest, neither water nor a dwelling place. What pleasure could they derive from all their wealth? God then said to them: Take all your silver and gold, and all your other precious objects and store them in receptacles. You shall eat bread from the heavens and drink water from the rock. Your clothes will not decay on you, your shoes will not decay from your feet. Your sustenance is upon Me. And if you will say: What will our great wealth avail us? Give it for the work of the mishkan... and I will account it unto you, as if you had sustained Me with your wealth.

Even after Israel reached their place of rest and inheritance and the land yielded its produce after they had toiled all year in field and vineyard — on gathering their blessings they immediately emerge from their houses and enter temporary dwellings: 'In order that your generations might know...' that their blessings do not come from the ground, but that 'the blessing of the Lord makes wealthy.' And just as I have blessed you, likewise shall you, My children, bless Me with what I have given you — 'and you shall celebrate it as a festival to the Lord seven days in the year.'

In the case of the festival of Pesach it was not said, 'seven days in the year,' but only 'seven days.' Whereas in the case of the festival of Sukot it was said, 'Seven days in the year.' We learn thereby: That the rejoicing of these seven days before God, through the performance of His mitzvot and through dwelling in the sukah, are regarded as if we had rejoiced all year before God: and as if all our toil during the year had been only for the sake of His glory.

THE BUILDING OF THE SUKAH

The person first erects three or four walls and then he places upon them 'sechach' (a covering) consisting of 'the grain and vine refuse.' All materials are proper for the walls of the sukah, provided that they are capable of withstanding a normal wind. Therefore one who makes the walls of canvas or sheets must make them firm enough on all sides, so that a normal wind will not displace or dislodge them. For the walls are only considered walls if they remain stationary without swaying. If one has lifted the bottom of the sukah walls to a height greater than three hand-breadths from the ground, the sukah is invalid. If one fixed poles in the ground and joins them together at the top in a wood frame, and places the sechach on top before filling in the empty places between one pole and the next, — which means that he has placed the sechach on the sukah before erecting its walls — then the sukah is invalid since a sukah is kasher (valid) only if the walls are made before the sechach is laid. If the upper frame is a 'tefach' (handbreadth) in width — even though it is not yet suitable for the insertion of boards — it is already permissible to place the sechach on top, and to fill in the boards later.

If one has first placed the sechach over the sukah, he may still make his sukah valid according to the 'Halachah' (the code of the Torah). After filling in the boards, he may lift the sechach somewhat from its place, and replace it again; which is regarded as if he had now placed the sechach on a sukah which already contains walls.

If one makes two complete walls, a third wall which

measures somewhat over a tefach, and a doorway between the walls, the sukah is kasher. Nevertheless, we seek to build a sukah with four complete walls.

Not all objects are kasher for sechach. The items used for sechach should be vegetable but detached from the soil; they must not have been used previously for any other purpose; they must never have acquired the status of a utensil and they must never have been capable of receiving defilement. Severed tree branches, strips of wood, straw and the like, are hence permitted for sechach, while planks which had been suitable for home use, may not be used for sechach. Neither are edibles usable for sechach, and if one has made his sechach of edibles, the sukah is invalid.

Boards which are broader than four tefachim, may not be used for sechach, even if they were never used for any other purpose, since they are excessively broad, and appear like a ceiling in a home.

If one builds his sukah under a tree whose branches cover the sukah, it is invalid, even if it has proper sechach of its own, since no object may be used as sechach, that is still rooted in the soil.

It is not permissible, in the first instance, to use anything malodorous, or branches whose leaves fall off easily, for sechach, since they spoil the sukah — and are likely to drive the occupant away. Further, the falling of the leaves may diminish the sechach to the extent of making the entire sukah invalid because of the 'Halachah' of, 'its sun exceeds its shadow' (which disqualifies a 'sukah').

Bundles of stalks which contain as many as 25 stalks, may not be used for sechach so long as they are bound together. If however, one placed them when they were still bound, but later unbound them, they are permissible.

A net of stalks or straw, which was originally made for the purpose of sechach, although it may also be suitable for some other uses, is not susceptible of defilement and is kasher for sechach, since it was specifically intended only for use as sechach.

There should be sufficient sechach for the shadow in sukah to exceed the light of the sun. Nor should there be so much sechach as to prevent the larger stars from being seen at night through the sechach. If there is so little sechach that the sunshine exceeds the shadow in the sukah, the sukah is invalid. If there is so much sechach that the large stars cannot be seen through it, the sukah nevertheless remains kasher.

If the sechach on a sukah is in accord with the Halachah, but the sukah was placed under a roof, a ledge, or a tree whose branches cover the sukah, the sukah is invalid. The designation 'sukah' applies only to a sukah whose shadow comes exclusively from the proper sechach, and not from anything else besides the sechach.

THE MEASUREMENTS OF THE SUKAH

The height of the sukah from its floor to the sechach should not exceed 20 'amah', and should not be lower than ten tefachim. A sukah which is higher than 20 amah or lower than 10 tefachim is invalid.

The minimal length of a sukah is 7 tefachim and its minimal width is likewise 7 tefachim. A lesser width or length renders the sukah invalid.

The maximal or minimal limitation of measurement apply only to the height of the sukah. As to the length and width of the sukah there is only a minimal limitation, namely 7 tefachim; one may however extend the width and length of the sukah as far as he desires, provided the sechach is in accord with the Halachah. Thus did the Sages say: 'All Israel are worthy of dwelling in one sukah.' And in the Time to Come God will erect a sukah from the skin of Leviathan and all the tzadikim (the righteous) who kept the mitzvah in this world will be seated in it.

The mitzvah is fulfilled in a borrowed sukah also. One who failed to build a sukah may therefore discharge his obligation in his friend's sukah. One cannot however fulfill the mitzvah in a stolen sukah. It is therefore prohibited to erect a sukah in a public domain, since, if one does so, it is as if he stole land which belongs to the public. If he did so, he nevertheless is regarded as having fulfilled the mitzvah of sukah, though he remains guilty of transgression.

It is prohibited to make the sukah walls of 'sha'atnez' (cloth combining wool and linen). No benefit or enjoyment may be derived from both the sechach and the walls the entire eight days of the festival.

SUKAH DECORATIONS

The Sages have said: 'This is my God and I shall worship Him with beauty' (Shmot 15) — beautify yourself before Him in the performance of mitzvot. Make for Him, a beautiful sukah, a beautiful 'lulav,' a beautiful 'shofar,' beautiful 'tzitzit,' a beautiful 'Sefer Torah,' and write it for the sake of His Name with beautiful ink, with a beautiful quill, with an expert scribe, and place it in a beautiful mantle.'

All the mitzvot should be performed with a regard for esthetic beauty, in accord with the insight of the Sages on the verse, 'This is my God and I shall worship Him with beauty.' This is especially true of the mitzvah of 'sukah' which is accompanied by the taking of the four-species; a mitzvah of which it is said specifically in the Torah: 'And you shall take for yourselves a fruit of a beautiful tree.'

A person is therefore obligated to show regard for his sukah, and not to bring unseemly utensils into it, not to do anything unseemly in it. One should rather decorate it as best as he can, with beautiful objects and utensils, and with beautiful fruit and flowers.

Objects set aside for either sukah decorations or the actual walls or sechach of the sukah, may be put to no other use, from the time the stars are visible the first Yom Tov night and one sat in the sukah for an hour, till after the festival of Simchat Torah. During this period they may not be removed from their place. Even if they fall down they cannot be put to any other use. If they fall down on Shabat or Yom Tov, they may not be handled. They may be put to other uses only if such a condition was specifically made at the outset.

It is customary however, even if such a condition was made not to derive benefit from the decorations which hang on the sechach.

It is proper for a person to exert himself personally in the erection of his sukah.

If one lacks knowledge of the laws of sukah, it is proper for him to show his sukah to a scholar while it is yet day, so that if he should find it necessary to rectify something, he may still do so before dark.

DWELLING IN THE SUKAH

It is written in the Torah: 'In sukot you shall sit seven days.' The tradition of our Sages is that the meaning of, 'you-shall-sit' is, 'you shall dwell.' The Torah prescribes that a person shall dwell in a sukah seven days, as he dwells in his home all year. He is to have all his meals in the sukah; he is to drink in it. and to converse there with his friends. If he happens to pray privately, rather than in the synagogue, he should pray in the sukah. Likewise, should his various other home activities, provided they are seemly, take place in the sukah, since it constitutes his home throughout the seven days of the festival. Because of the sanctity of the sukah, it is however proper to strive to be mainly engaged while in the sukah, in the study of Torah, in the pursuit of mitzvot, and in activities relating to the festival and its precepts.

It is prohibited to eat a regular meal outside the sukah. What is the definition of a regular meal? An amount of bread corresponding to slightly more than the measure of an egg; or the same measure of cakes. According to some authorities, one does not say the prescribed 'brachah' ('to dwell in the sukah') over cakes unless he intends to regard them as essential to his meal. Similarly, if a person regards a grain dish as essential to his meal, or if he sits down with friends, in a formal manner to drink wine, beer or other beverages, he would do so in the sukah. For a snack however — involving the eating of less than the measure of an egg, the eating of fruit, the drinking of water or of other beverages, a sukah is not required. Many however are stringent in the matter, and they do not eat at all outside the sukah. And one who is strict with himself and does not even drink water outside the sukah, merits blessings.

The first night of Sukot (and outside the Land of Israel, the second night also) eating in the sukah is obligatory. No one may say: I will not eat and will not sit in the sukah. One must rather enter the sukah, recite 'kidush,' and utter the brachah over the sukah and 'shehecheyanu' even if one suffers discomfort in doing so. And one may not eat in the sukah the first night before the definite onset of night; that is, after the appearance of the stars.

If it rains on the first night, and if one surmises that the rains will cease within an hour or two, he is obliged to wait. If however, he sees that the rains do not cease, or if he surmises from the beginning that they will not cease, he enters the sukah, recites 'kidush' and 'shehecheyanu' but omits the brachah over the sukah. He washes his hands, eats the equivalent of an olive and finishes his meal at home. If the rains stop before 'birkat hamazon' (benedictions said after the meal) he returns to the sukah; recites the brachah over the sukah, and eats bread of equivalent size to slightly more than an egg (and at the least, to not less than the measure of an olive), and he says 'birkat hamazon.' If the rains stop after he has already said birkat hamazon, he goes to the sukah; washes his hands a second time, says, 'hamotzi' (benediction over bread), the brachah over the sukah, eats bread in equivalent measure to an egg, and says birkat hamazon.

All other days the mitzvah of sukah is not obligatory, except for the one who wishes to eat a fixed meal but there is no obligation to eat a fixed meal in order to eat in the sukah. The Sages have however prescribed it as a mitzvah to eat a total of fourteen regular meals in the sukah during the seven days of the festival — two meals daily, once in the morning and one in the evening, with the exception of Shabat, when a third meal is also taken in the sukah. If rains fall however, and a person suffers discomfort, he is not obligated to eat in the sukah during the remaining days of the festival.

In one respect sleeping in the sukah is a more stringent obligation than eating, since the obligation extends even to irregular sleep. We are lenient with *reference to sleeping, only where the nights are excessively cold. It is most fitting though, for one to build himself a comfortable sukah, in which he can dwell and sleep together with his family, as is his custom at home throughout the year.*

A sick person is free of the obligation of sukah, even if his illness entails no danger to life. His attendants too, are free, if and when he needs them. In the case of a sick person who is in danger, his attendants are free of the mitzvah of sukah at all times; whether he needs them at the moment, or not.

Women are free of the mitzvah of sukah, but if they do eat in it they recite the brachah over the sukah. Some authorities however, prohibit women from reciting the brachah over the sukah since they are free from the obligation of the mitzvah.

Minors are free from sukah, but a father is obligated to train his son to eat in a sukah from the moment he no longer needs his mother — that is, from the age of five and above.

THE KINDLING OF THE LIGHTS

Lights are kindled the first Yom Tov night in the sukah and two brachot are said: 'to kindle the Yom Tov light,' and *shehecheyanu*. If the first day of Yom Tov falls on Shabat, the lights are lit before dark, and, in the first brachah, Shabat is mentioned first and then Yom Tov.

If the sukah is not wind proof, it is proper not to leave the candles burning there. After the woman recites the prescribed brachah over the candles in the sukah, they are removed from the sukah by another, and brought into the house. The woman may not however, do so herself, since, in having uttered the brachah over the candles, she has accepted the sanctity of Shabat, and she may no longer handle the candles, because of the prohibition of *muktzeh.*

The law which governs the kindling of lights the first day of Yom Tov applies to the second day too except that during the latter, the lights are lit at home, and not in the sukah. Outside the Land of Israel, *shehecheyanu* is recited the second night of the first Yom Tov day, as well as the night of Simchat Torah.

THE BRACHOT OF THE FESTIVAL

On entering the sukah the first night of the festival, one takes a cup of wine in hand and recites four brachot: the first over the wine; the second over the sanctity of the day; the third over the sukah; and the final one, 'shehecheyanu.' He drinks most of the wine in the cup (the proper measure of a 'kidush' cup, is a little over 3 oz.—86 gr.), washes his hands before breaking bread and takes his meal. In the case of the meals taken in the sukah which are not preceded by 'kidush,' the brachah over the sukah is said after the washing of hands and 'hamotzi,' before partaking of the meal, and not earlier, even if wine is drunk before the meal. Those however, who follow the custom of drinking wine before each meal throughout all the days of the festival, recite the brachah over the sukah, immediately after the brachah over the wine.

'Shehecheyanu' is recited over any mitzvah which comes only at periodic intervals. It is therefore recited during 'kidush' on each Yom Tov. During kidush on the first night of Sukot, shehecheyanu is required over two mitzvot: that of sanctifying the day, and the mitzvah of 'dwelling in the sukah.' Nevertheless, it is recited only once, with the intention in mind that it relates to both mitzvot.

Kidush and shehecheyanu are recited only at the advent of Yom Tov (and outside the Land of Israel the second Yom Tov night as well). The brachah over the sukah however, is recited whenever one enters the sukah for a meal through all the days of the festival.

Authorities differ on the brachah over the sukah. Some are stringent, and they require its recital whenever we enter a sukah; whether it be our own or another's, whether we enter to eat or not — even if we enter a sukah a hundred times a day. Some authorities however maintain that the brachah is required only twice daily: once over breakfast (which also suffices for any other meals for the remainder of the day, provided he has the intention that it should), and once for the evening (which suffices also for sleeping in the sukah). In this matter, a person ought to abide by the practice of his fathers and teachers.

The question may be asked: Both the mitzvah to eat 'matzah' during Pesach and the mitzvah to dwell in a sukah during Sukot, apply seven days; why is the brachah over matzah only prescribed for the first night of Pesach, while that over the sukah is required every day of the festival?

The answer is that the obligation to eat matzah applies only the first night, whereas the remaining days of Pesach, there is no obligation to eat matzah but only a prohibition against the eating of leavened bread; and if one wishes to eat only fruit, or other food which is neither leavened bread nor matzah one may do so. Therefore, since there is no obligation to eat matzah the remaining days of Pesach, no brachah is required (over the mitzvah of matzah). On the other hand, dwelling in a sukah is a mitzvah all the days of the festival. For the Sages have said: 'A person is obligated to eat fourteen meals in the sukah,' which gives it the status of a Rabbinic mitzvah. Furthermore, sleeping in the sukah is an essential part of the mitzvah since the Torah prescribes: 'In Sukot you shall dwell seven days,' and a person is unable to go without sleep for seven days. Every entry into the sukah, is therefore given the status of a Torah commandment, by implication. A brachah is therefore required over the sukah all seven days of the festival.

It is proper for anyone entering a sukah throughout the seven days of the festival, to say orally: I am ready and prepared to fulfill the mitzvah of the Almighty who commanded us to dwell in the sukah, as it is written in the Torah, 'In sukot you shall dwell seven days.'

IN IHE SHADOW OF FAITH

The way of all men is different from that of Israel. It is the way of all men to feel secure and unafraid when under the shelter of their own roofs: On emerging from their homes, their sense of security is diminished, and they begin to feel fear. Israel however, is different. While in their homes the whole year, they are apprehensive lest they become haughty at heart and forget their Maker. When Sukot comes, and they leave their homes and come under the shadow of their sukot, their hearts are filled with trust, faith and joy — for now they are shielded not by the protection of their roofs, but by the shadow of their faith and trust in God.

The matter may be compared to a person who locks himself up at home for fear of robbers. Regardless of the strength of the locks he uses, he remains afraid, lest the locks be broken. Once he hears the voice of the King and his company approaching and calling: 'Emerge from your chamber and join me,' he is no longer afraid. He immediately opens his doors, and emerges joyously to join the King. For wherever the King is found, robbers are absent. He then goes wherever the King leads him, and trust and joy never leave him.

The person (in the parable) — is Israel.

The house — his general activities throughout the year.

The robbers — the evil inclination and all who assist it.

The King — the King of Kings, the Holy-One-Blessed-be-He.

The King's company — the 'seven faithful shepherds:' Avraham, Itzchak, Ya'akov, Moshe, Aharon, Yosef, David.

The call of the King to emerge from one's house — the Festival of Sukot, as it is said; 'In sukot you shall dwell seven days.'

Those who go out to the sukah do it joyously — as it is said: 'And you shall rejoice before the Lord your God seven days.'

Come and see:

All the days that Israel is at home, it is said of them, 'Happy is the man who is constantly fearful.' Of the seven days during which they are in sukah it is however said: 'And you shall be joyous.'

Why?

When Israel leaves its home to enter its temporary dwellings — the sukot — as a memorial to the exodus from Egypt, all see that Israel finds protection — not under the shadow of its roofs, nor under the shadow of sun or earth or angels, but only under the shadow of Him who brought the world into being with His utterance.

The festival of Sukot is therefore called by our Sages: 'the shadow of faith.' The sukah is the shadow of faith and trust in God. Every Jew may merit the protection of the 'shadow of faith' by dwelling in the sukah.

EXALTED GUESTS (the 'Ushpizin')

In the Zohar it is written: 'When the people of Israel leave their homes and enter the sukah for the sake of God's Name, they achieve the merit there of welcoming the Divine

Presence and all the seven faithful shepherds descend from Gan Eden, and come to the sukah as their guests.'

The seven guests are: Avraham, Itzchak, Ya'akov, Yosef, Moshe, Aharon and David. These seven dwell with all Israel in their sukot all seven days of the festival, except that each day one of them leads the others. Others place Moshe and Aharon before Yosef and the order is as follows:

The first day, Avraham Avinu enters first, and all the others accompany him.

The second day, Itzchak Avinu enters first...

The third day, Ya'akov enters first...

The fourth day, Moshe Rabenu...

The fifth day, Aharon Hacohen...

The sixth day, Yosef Hatzadik...

The seventh day, Hoshana Raba, David Hamelech enters first and the others accompany him.

On entering the sukah, but before being seated, it is therefore customary, to invite the *Ushpizin* (guests) in, with the recitation of the formula contained in the prayer book.

Among the Sephardim it is customary to prepare an ornate chair in the sukah; to cover it with a fine cloth, to place sacred *sefarim* on it, and to say: 'This is the chair of the Ushpizin.'

THE USHPIZIN — SHEPHERDS FOR ISRAEL

Israel rejoice with their guests, the Patriarchs. And the Patriarchs rejoice with Israel, their sons. For a father has no greater joy than to see his sons going in his ways.

Of Avraham it was said: 'Go you from your land, and from your birthplace, and from the house of your father to the land which I will show you.' Israel, his sons, also leave their regular dwellings this day, for temporary ones, in accord with God's command.

Of Itzchak it was said: 'And there was a famine in the land... and Itzchak went to Avimelech, the King of Philistia, to Gerar... and Itzchak dwelt in Gerar' — in Exile. Israel his sons also wander, driven from one Exile to another and they do not doubt God; and even when they dwell at home in peace, they leave their homes in obedience to God's decrees, and they dwell in the sukah.

Of Ya'akov it was said: 'Arise, go to Padan Aram.' After the birthright had reverted to him, and he won the blessing (of his father), he enjoyed neither the birthright nor the blessing. Instead he worked for Laban with the toil of a slave for twenty years, for such was God's will; and he did not doubt God's ways. On gathering their produce, Israel his sons, also do not rejoice over their blessings, but rather go after their God, and rejoice only in Him.

Of Yosef it was said: 'Yosef was sold for a slave, they afflicted his feet in chains, his soul was imprisoned in irons.' And he remained faithful in exile as in the house of his father. Israel, his sons, also remain faithful to their Father in Heaven, and they find protection in the shadow of His faith.

Of Moshe and Aharon '...And He caused the people to journey like sheep, and He led them like a flock in the wilderness.' Israel too, have not turned away from their path; and all the wealth in the world will not make them forsake their love of God. For they have no security or strength other than in the shadow of faith in God alone.

Of David it was said: 'A song to David when he was in the wilderness of Yehudah: God, You are my God, I shall seek You; my soul thirsts for You; my flesh pines for You, in a desolate land, tired, without water.' Even in the wilderness, he had no thirst for water, and no hunger for bread: he knew thirst and hunger only for the nearness of God. Israel, His sons, also regard the nearness of God as their only good: neither a house, nor a palace; neither glory, nor pride give them joy. And there is no joy to them like the happiness they feel when they leave all the world's pleasures, to seek protection only in the shadow of faith in God.

Happy are the sons in whom their fathers rejoice! Happy are the fathers who see their sons thus!

THE USHPIZIN — SHEPHERDS FOR THE ENTIRE WORLD

The Patriarchs wandered from Exile to Exile, and they attained rest only after great toil and travail. Avraham left Ur Kasdim for Charan. He came to the land of Canaan a second time, and then he went down to Egypt... Itzchak sojourned in Philistia.

Ya'akov fled to the fields of Aram, and he and his sons went down to Egypt. Yosef was sold into slavery in a foreign land. Moshe fled to Midian. Together with his brother Aharon he led the people in the wilderness for forty years, but neither entered the beloved land. David fled to the wilderness, to Gath and Moab, and he knew no rest from war.

The King of the Universe gives life and lovingkindness to all the world's inhabitants. Is He incapable of providing those who love Him with rest and security? Why then does He make them wander from place to place without rest? So that they might shed light, goodness and blessing upon all the world.

Avraham overflows with the 'Quality of Lovingkindness;' Itzchak with 'Strength;' Ya'akov, with 'Glory;' Yosef, with 'Holiness;' Moshe and Aharon, with 'Eternity' (*Moshe* with Torah, and Aharon with *kehunah*); and David with 'Sovereignty.'

These loyal shepherds seek nothing for themselves, and whoever seeks no personal gain, is given the whole world.

Avraham was therefore made by God — 'the father of a multitude of nations.'

Itzchak — 'And all the Earth's nations will be blessed in your seed.'

Ya'akov — 'Peoples will serve you, and nations will bow down to you.'

Yosef — 'And Yosef was the ruler, he gave food to all the people of the land.'

Moshe — 'He sets boundaries of the nations according to the numbers of the children of Israel.'

Aharon — 'Like the goodly oil on the head, which runs down on the beard, the beard of Aharon..., for there God bestowed blessing, life unto eternity.'

David — 'Ask it of me, and I shall give nations for your inheritance.'

Now the children's children of these Patriarchs come; they rejoice on the Festival of Sukot before God, and say to Him: Lord of the Universe! We desire neither houses nor the field's produce; our only desire is for You. On attaining this pure joy, they become a source of blessing for themselves and all the world, and, through their merit, bounty and blessing descend upon all the world for the entire year. The very offerings they themselves bring during Sukot, are not intended in their own behalf, for they offer seventy oxen to attain atonement and blessing for all the seventy nations of the world. And only after having concluded their offerings for all the world's nations, do they bring an offering in their own behalf: 'And on the eighth day, it shall be an assembly unto you' — i. e. between Me and you alone — 'and you shall sacrifice a burnt-offering... one ox...' First make offerings in their behalf, and afterwards in your own behalf! For I had made you shepherds to sustain My entire world with love and compassion.

God said to Israel: You are shepherds, the sons of shepherds. It is fitting for the loyal shepherds of old, to dwell in 'the shadow of faith,' together with the faithful children.

USHPIZIN OF FLESH AND BLOOD

Since the festival sukah is a dwelling for the Shechinah (Divine Presence), and for such exalted guests as these, it is proper for one to also invite 'guests from below' to share his meals in the sukah; and thereby to please his 'guests from above.'

If he cannot find poor people to invite to his table, let him at least help provide the festival needs in full measure for some needy people to be able to joyously observe the festival in their own homes. And as they eat at their own tables, it will be regarded as if they were guests in his own sukah.

The master of the house sits in the middle; to his right, the 'guests from above;' to his left, the 'guests from below;' and above his head, the Divine Presence.

All year, the poor person sees others working in their fields and deriving blessing from their activities, while the poor have nothing, and are dependent completely on the gifts and leftovers of the rich. The joyous season for gathering in the harvest, has now come; all bring their blessings home, while the poor person has nothing to bring to his desolate home. With what shall he rejoice? God said therefore: In sukot you shall dwell seven days; when you gather in the produce of the earth, let all of you leave your homes, and let all of you become guests in My sukah, and the wealthy not be recognized before the poor. Three walls, and above them sechach of straw and twigs — that is the sukah of every Jew, whether poor or rich.

And every Jew speaks the same to God: Though You have given me the blessings of the field and the vineyard, my joy is not in them, but only in You, and I make my dwelling only in Your sukah. Therefore, when a Jew rejoices in his God; thanks Him for all His goodness; and acknowledges that all blessings are only from Him, it is only fittting for him to rejoice — at the time of his own joy — the hearts of those whom God loves — the poor. As it is written: 'For thus said the high and lofty One, Who inhabits eternity, and Whose Name is holy, I dwell in the high and holy place, with him also that is of a contrite and humble spirit...'

GIVE THE POOR WHAT IS THEIRS

Whoever invites the poor to his table in the sukah, does not give them what is his, but what is theirs. For, it is as if it were said to him:

You have invited the exalted Ushpizin to your sukah: the seven faithful shepherds; Avraham, Itzchak, Ya'akov, Moshe, Aharon, Yosef and David. Did you invite them only because you knew that they would diminish nothing from your table? Would you not have gone to endless trouble and expense so that those exalted guests might enjoy your food, if that were possible? But, though they themselves do not eat, they ask of you: Whatever you have prepared for us — give it to our loved ones, and it will be as if you had given it to us.

When the Sephardim provide a poor person with the needs for festival, it is their custom to say: 'This is the portion of the exalted guests.'

It is written in our sacred books: 'Whoever is God fearing should entertain a poor man at his table, and regard his guest, as if the latter were one of the Patriarchs whom he had invited for that day, and he should give his poor guest a full portion, as if one of the Patriarchs were seated with him. If it be possible for one to invite seven poor persons each day, corresponding to all seven Ushpizin, blessing will surely rest on him.

TRUST IN COD FOR THE RICH AND FOR THE POOR

We dwell in sukot seven days. For seven days we leave our permanent homes for temporary ones, in fulfillment of God's command in the Torah. In doing so we recall the sukot in which our fathers dwelt in the wilderness, and the clouds-of-glory which shielded them in the wilderness.

Reflecting on the sukah gives us an exalted insight into the meaning of trust in God, and the extent of Divine Providence.

We go out to the sukah during the 'Festival of the Ingathering,' upon having ingathered the crops of our fields. If a person has received Divine blessing; his earth has yielded its fruit bountifully; his storehouses and wine cellars are filled; happiness and trust fill his soul — then, the Torah bids him leave his home to sojourn in a frail sukah, to teach him: neither wealth, nor possessions nor land, are life's safeguards; the Almighty alone sustains even those who dwell in tents and booths. Let him reflect that all his wealth and glory are given to him only from God's hand, and that these endure for him only as long as God's will shall keep them in his possession. Let him take it to heart that wealth is no security for it often betrays its trust; that the shadow of Divine Providence alone gives reliable protection and that it does so even for one who dwells in a frail sukah, and is completely destitute of all earthly possession.

And if one is poor, and his toil has not known Divine blessing; if the earth has not given him its produce, and the fruit of the tree has not entered his cellars; if he stands forlorn and fearful as he faces the threat of hunger during the approaching winter days; then, he too will find rest for his soul in the sukah. For, he will recall how the Almighty settled our fathers in sukot, in the wilderness; how He sustained and fed them there, till they lacked nothing... The sukah will teach him that Divine Providence is better than all worldly possessions, for it will not forsake one who truthfully trusts in God. It will teach him to be strong and courageous; happy and stouthearted, even in affliction and travail...

FOUR AND FOUR

'It is written: 'And you shall rejoice in your festival, you and your son and your daughter' (Dvarim 15). God said: There are four members in your household; your son, your daughter, your manservant and your maidservant. Corresponding to them, I also have four: the Levi, the stranger, the orphan, the widow. If you will care for (those who are) mine, together with (those who are) yours, good: if not, the rejoicing will be annulled' (New Psikta).

Upon rising the first day of Yom Tov, one enters his sukah, takes hold of the four species and says two brachot over them: *'al netilat lulav,'* and *'shehecheyanu.'* If one performs the mitzvah in the synagogue, he does so before saying *Halel* with the congregation.

FOUR SPECIES

The four species are taken hold of each of the seven festival days (except Shabat) and a brachah is said daily over them; after the first day of performing this mitzvah however, 'shehecheyanu' is not said.

'Netilat lulav' is a Torah commandment: 'And you shall take you on the first day, the fruit of the tree 'hadar', and branches of palm trees, and a bough of the tree 'avot,' and willows of the brook, and you shall rejoice before the Lord your God seven days' (Vayikra 23).

Fruit of the tree hadar — is the 'etrog.'
Branches of palm trees — is the 'lulav.'
A bough of the tree avot — is the 'hadas.'
Willows of the brook — is the 'aravah' which usually grows at the river edge.

The taking of the four species all seven days, is prescribed by the Torah only in the Sanctuary, whereas everywhere else, only the first day. As it is written: 'And you shall take for yourselves' — i. e., in all your dwellings — 'on the first day...,' 'and you shall rejoice before the Lord your God' — i. e., in the Sanctuary, 'seven days.' However, after the destruction of the Sanctuary, Rabi Yochanan Ben

Zakai ordained that the lulav be taken everywhere all seven days, as a memorial to the Sanctuary. The four species together comprise one mitzvah and if anyone of them be missing, the mitzvah is not fulfilled.

Eating is forbidden before performing the mitzvah of netilat lulav. If one forgot, and began to eat before netilat lulav — on the first day — he should interrupt his meal and perform the mitzvah. On the other days — if enough time remains during the day to perform the mitzvah of the lulav after the completion of his meal, he may finish his meal, and then perform it; if not, he should interrupt his meal and perform the mitzvah immediately.

It is forbidden to derive pleasure from the fragrance of the 'hadasim' all seven festival days since they have been designated for the mitzvah. In the case of the 'etrog', its fragrance is permissible, but it is forbidden for food; the difference being between the 'hadas' and the 'etrog', that the essence of the hadas is its fragrance, while the essence of the etrog is its taste.

THE ORDER OF NETILAT LULAV AND THE BRACHAH

One etrog is taken; one lulav; three hadasim; two aravot. The etrog is held separately, and the lulav, the hadasim, and the aravot are bound together. The stem of the lulav faces the holder; the hadasim are to the right of the lulav; the aravot are to the left, and are placed somewhat lower than the hadasim. The lulav, hadasim, and aravot are bound together with two knots made of two strips of leaf from the lulav. In addition, the lulav is bound together at three spots (above the knots which bind the species together) in order that the leaves of the lulav might not come apart during its 'na'anu'im' (Wavings).

The lulav should be bound together on Erev Yom Tov. But, if one failed to bind the lulav on Erev Yom Tov, or if the knots opened during Yom Tov, he may only make a knot that will not last, since the making of a lasting knot is prohibited on Yom Tov.

Since two other species are bound together with the lulav, and since the lulav is the one species mentioned in the brachah ('al netilat lulav'), the lulav is taken with the right hand, while the etrog, is taken with the left. Before the brachah both hands are brought together, but, till the brachah is made, the etrog is held with its 'pitma' down and its 'oketz' (by which it is attached to the tree) up. After the brachah, the 'etrog' is inverted to the direction of its growth, with its 'pitma' up, and its 'oketz' down. The holder then shakes the lulav and etrog towards the four sides of the heavens, and up and down.

The reason for initially holding the etrog inverted is that the brachah over a mitzvah must be recited before the performance of the mitzvah; so that, if one holds the four species in the direction of their growth, he has already fulfilled the mitzvah, before having recited the brachah. The etrog is therefore initially held inverted from the direction of its growth, so that the mitzvah is not yet fulfilled; the brachah is said; the etrog is again inverted to its proper direction of growth, and then the mitzvah has been properly fulfilled.

The same also applies to the other species. If any of them is held not in the direction of its growth, the mitzvah is not fulfilled. For the Torah has revealed elsewhere that, if any object which grows from the earth is used for a mitzvah, it should be held or placed in the direction of its growth.

Where is the matter alluded to?

With reference to the boards of the 'Mishkan'

(the Sanctuary-tent). For it is the way of the world that when a house is built of wood, the boards are placed lying down, one over the other. Of the boards of the mishkan however, it is written: 'And you shall make the boards for the mishkan of acacia wood standing up,' so that the boards might be placed in the mishkan in the direction of their growth. For this reason, it is the custom of the Sephardim not to take the etrog in one's hand till after the brachah. It is first placed on a chair or table; the brachah is said; the etrog is then taken in the left hand, joined to the lulav, and both are shaken together.

Some are stringent, and they make certain that there be no foreign body intervening between the hand and the four species, and they therefore remove any rings from their fingers.

The mitzvah of lulav applies only by day, and not by night.

The Sages have decreed that the mitzvah of the four species should not be performed on Shabat, even if the first day of the festival falls on Shabat, lest one come thereby, to violate the prohibition of carrying in a public domain on Shabat. (This Rabbinic decree is similar to the one prohibiting the sounding of shofar on Shabat.)

A minor should not recite the brachah over the lulav before the adults, on the first day of Yom Tov. (The minor can legally acquire ownership, but he cannot bestow ownership on others, which would cause the lulav to remain the property of the minor, and thus render it invalid for the performance of the mitzvah by adults, since the Torah prescribes: 'And you shall take you on the first day' — you shall take what is yours.

HIDUR AND THE FOUR SPECIES

The mitzvah of the four species is unique in that *hidur* (the enhancement of the mitzvah) is an essential aspect of its performance. It is written: 'This is my God, and I will worship Him with beauty.' And the Rabis expound: 'Beautify yourself before Him in mitzvot.' That is, any mitzvah which is performed for the sake of God, should be performed in the most aesthetically attractive and excellent manner possible. Nevertheless, in the case of this particular mitzvah, the Torah explicitly calls the etrog, 'a fruit of the tree *hadar*' *(beautiful, majestic)*. The Sages state further that the term *hadar* used here, refers not only to the etrog, but to all the four species as well.

What kind of an etrog is hadar?

One that is exceedingly clean and without the slightest spots;

that has many protrusions and depressions and is not smooth like a lemon;

whose peduncle is somewhat depressed into the bottom of the etrog;

whose form is like a tower — i.e., broad at the bottom on the side of the peduncle and growing narrower towards the pestle;

the flower of the pestle should be whole on all sides, with the entire pestle in the exact center of the top of the etrog, and over against the peduncle at the bottom of the etrog.

What kind of a lulav is hadar?

One that is moist and green from head to end without any dryness;

whose form is straight like a rod, without any twists or bends on any of its sides;

whose top is not broken or nipped in the slightest;

whose central leaf and those adjacent to it are not open at all, but are whole till their points;

whose leaves are not separated from each other at all, but are seen as one whole, and which separate only during the shaking of the lulav;

whose upper point should consist of only one leaf rising from its stem;

the number of whose leaves is sixty-eight, corresponding to the numerical value of lulav, and not less than sixty, corresponding to the numerical value of the letters in the blessings of the 'cohanim.'

What kind of hadas is hadar?

One whose leaves are all moist and green, without any dryness;

which is 'three-leaved' — i.e., which has three leaves in one even row on each stem, with none higher or lower than the other, and with the rows on each stem close enough to each other for the top of the leaves growing from the lower row to reach the bottoms of the leaves of the next upper row — for a length of three handbreadths till the top.

whose leaves are neither excessively large or small, but are approximately the size of an average person's thumb nail;

whose leaves are upright and cover the stem;

whose stem and leaves are whole and not nipped at their tops;

whose branch twigs are not more numerous than the leaves;

between whose leaves there do not grow branches over a span of more than one and a half handbreadths;

whose length is somewhat longer than the minimal three handbreadths, so that if any of its leaves fall off, there will still remain three whole handbreadths.

What kind of aravah is hadar?

One whose stem is red, whose leaf is narrow and

long, and the head of whose leaf is smooth and whole;

whose stem is not nipped at the top, and whose uppermost leaf is whole at the top;

whose leaves are green and moist, without any dryness at all;

which has all its leaves.

And if one can obtain an aravah which grows at the edge of a river, that too is an aspect of hidur.

There is one aspect of hidur which applies to all four species; namely, that there be no suspicion that any of their trees had been grafted, and that they might have grown in a pot having no orifice.

WHEN THE FOUR SPECIES ARE INVALID

Although hidur is essential in the mitzvah of the four species, nevertheless not all the above conditions render the four species invalid. The following do:

Dryness — without any remaining moisture invalidates any of the four species for the mitzvah; for dryness is like death and 'the dead shall not praise God.'

Theft — if obtained through stealing, the four species are invalid for the mitzvah since it would then be a mitzvah which comes through a transgression, and Scripture states: 'I, the Lord, hate robbery in a whole-offering.'

A broken head invalidates them all.

The following invalidates only the etrog:

An etrog of 'orlah' (the first three years' produce of a tree is 'orlah' — forbidden); one smaller than an egg; one that is pierced till the place of the seeds (even if it is not reduced in substance); one lacking even a minute part of its substance; a peeled etrog whose substance was reduced; an etrog on which warts have risen in two or three places (or, the minutest wart at the top of the etrog); if its color is radically changed (red or brown); if the 'pitma' or 'oketz', are removed; if it be shriveled, pickled swollen or malodorous.

The following make the lulav invalid:

If it be shorter than four handbreadths; if most of its leaves are detached from each other; if the top leaf is split the length of a handbreadth; if the stem is split, and the lulav has the appearance of two lulavim; if there are 'thorns' in the stem; if it is warped; if the stem is bent at the top.

The following make the hadas invalid:

If no three leaves grow on a parallel line, over most of its length; if it be shorter than three handbreadths; if the leaves have fallen off over most of its length; if its branches are more numerous than its leaves; and if the branches are red or black.

The following make the aravah invalid:

If it is shorter than three handbreadths; if its leaves are rough, or completely round (even if they be smooth); if the leaves hang downwards, are split, or if most of them have fallen off.

Just as theft invalidates the four species, similarly, the mitzvah cannot be fulfilled with borrowed ones, but only with those given as an outright gift. After the first day of Yom Tov, however, (outside the Land of Israel, after the second day) borrowed species are permitted, and we are likewise lenient with reference to most of the other requirements.

NA'ANU'IM (the waving of the four species)

The essence of mitzvat lulav is to take the four species and hold them in the hand. Nevertheless, the preferred manner of performing the mitzvah is to wave the lulav in all six directions: the four horizontal ones, upwards and downwards; with each waving of the lulav consisting of three movements to and fro.

The meaning of these na'anu'im is given in the Talmud as follows; 'One waves them to and fro to Him who owns the four directions; up and down, to Him who owns Heaven and Earth. That is to say: the four species are an allusion to God's having created all of existence, and that there is naught besides Him' (Tractate Sukah 37).

The Talmud also states: 'One waves them to and fro in order to restrain harmful winds; up and down, in order to restrain harmful dews.' For, Sukot, is the time of judgment for water and rain for the entire year. The four species give symbolic expression to our prayers for the blessing of water: the etrog needs more water than other fruits of the tree; palm branches grow in valleys which have an abundance of water; myrtles and willows grow near water. In waving the four species in all six directions, we therefore symbolically say to Him who sustains the whole world: Just as these four species cannot exist without water, so can the world not exist without water. And when You give us water, let no harmful winds or harmful dew undo Your blessing.

The *na'anu'im* are made once when the mitzvah of holding the four species is performed, and four times during Halel, at the places indicated in the *sidur* (prayer book).

Concerning the order of the *na'anu'im,* there are two accepted customs: Eastwards, southwards, westwards, northwards, upwards, downwards or southwards, northwards, eastwards, upwards, downwards, westwards.

THE PRECIOUSNESS OF THE MITZVAH

The Sages have said: 'For the sake of *hidur mitzvah* (the enhancement of a mitzvah) one should spend as much as a third more than the cost of the mitzvah.' Nevertheless, Jews have customarily spent profusely on the mitzvah of the four species, even if doing so entailed self denial, out of love for this particular mitzvah.

Their reason for going to such lengths was that the Torah explicitly relates the matter of hidur to this mitzvah. It is further written, concerning this mitzvah: 'And you shall rejoice before the Lord, your God, for seven days.' Now, wherever there is joy there is love, and where there is love, a person does not say: thus far I feel obligated, but further not. Rather, would a person give his all, for love of God and His mitzvot.

In Tractate Sukah, we have learned: 'It once happened that Raban Gamliel, Rabi Yehoshua, Rabi Elazar Ben Azarya, and Rabi Akiva embarked on a boat. The only one among them who had a lulav was Raban Gamliel, who had purchased it for a thousand zuz. Raban Gamliel took it in order to fulfill the mitzvah and then gave it to Rabi Yehoshua as a gift. Rabi Yehoshua performed the mitzvah and gave (the lulav) to Rabi Elazar Ben Azarya as a a gift. Rabi Elazar Ben Azarya did the same and gave (the lulav) to Rabi Akiva as a gift. Rabi Akiva performed the mitzvah and returned (the lulav) to Raban Gamliel. Why was it necessary to relate that Raban Gamliel had purchased (the lulav) for a thousand zuz? To make known how precious mitzvot were to them.'

These four Elders were travelling on 'a mitzvah mission.' For the sake of their people and their land, they had left their homes long before the Festival, and they were unable to acquire the four species. When the Festival came, they were aboard the ship, and were totally free of the mitzvah. For love of the mitzvah alone they exerted themselves to find a lulav. Raban Gamliel, the *Nasi* (Prince), acquired one at a cost of a thousand zuz. We learn thereby how beloved mitzvot were to them.

Further, those who practice a mitzvah with love, find it difficult to part from it:

'We have learned — Rabi Elazar Ben Tzadok says: It was the custom of the Jerusalemites, for a person to leave his home with a lulav in hand; to go to the synagogue with his lulav in hand; to read the *Shema* and to pray while holding the lulav; to place it on the ground while reading the Torah or reciting the blessings of the cohanim; to visit the sick, and to console mourners, while holding the lulav; and, on entering the *Beit Hamidrash* (for study) to hand it over to his son, or servant, or messenger. What do we learn from this ? How diligent they were in the practice of mitzvot.'

Even if a person spends profuse sums on mitzvot — beyond what is required — he suffers no loss. In the words of the Sages: 'Till one third — the expense is his; from here on — it is God's. That is, one is reimbursed providentially from above for spending in excess of one third of the normal cost of a mitzvah — for *hidur mitzvah.*

The more is this true of the mitzvah of etrog, which is expressly called *hadar* (beautiful) by the Torah. Further, the Sages have stated: 'One who is commanded and does is greater than one who is not commanded and does.' And the reward of one who is commanded is likewise greater than that of one who is not commanded.

HIDUR OF THE MITZVAH — NOT OF SELF

Since the mitzvah of lulav is so greatly cherished, and its reward is great in this world and the next, one should take care to perform it properly, and for the sake of God alone. One ought not indulge in vainglory, by saying or thinking. 'See how much more beautiful my etrog and lulav are than yours.'

One who does so exchanges an enduring world for a passing one. He forsakes God's glory, for his own imaginary glory, and thereby comes to conceit and arrogance. And of him the Torah says: 'One who is haughty at heart is abhorred by God.' Better that one's etrog be less beautiful, but let his intention be for the sake of the mitzvah alone.

Whoever turns away from hidur mitzvah and thinks only of 'hidur' for himself, is likened to a person who is given a testimonial which — if he uses it properly — may enable him to see the king. On seeing some artistic illustrations on the script, he decorates his window with it for show, and forgets its contents. Not only will he no longer be welcome to visit the king; he will have aroused royal anger, and will be subject to shame and penalty. And people will then say of him: 'Woe to this one, whose glory became his shame.'

Rather should one learn from the story of an impoverished tzadik (a pious man), who lacked even a few meager coins for the needs of the festival, but who saw a beautiful etrog on Erev Sukot, which he very much wanted to buy. Whereupon the tzadik sold a precious pair of inherited *tefilin,* thinking: the mitzvah of tefilin will not be obligatory again for nine days, while the mitzvah of lulav will be obligatory tomorrow. He thereupon sold his tefilin, and for their money he bought the beautiful etrog. On hearing what he had done, his wife felt intense anguish; and her anguish turned to anger against her husband, for having failed to provide her with at least the bare means of preparing for the festival. She threw the etrog to the ground, and made it invalid. Whereupon the tzadik said: 'The tefilin I have sold, the etrog I have lost; should I also fall into the pit of anger ?

What then is the measure of *lishmah* (proper intention) in the performance of a mitzvah ? The intention is proper if it does not lead to pride, anger, or any other negative trait, but only to joy as well as to any positive trait of character.

THE END DOES NOT JUSTIFY THE MEANS

A mitzvah which is performed through proper means is a mitzvah; it leads to other mitzvot and to rewards. A mitzvah which comes through sin is a sin, and not a mitzvah; it condemns the doer, and leads him to other sins.

A person should therefore take great care not to commit wrong in order to perform the mitzvah of etrog; not to lie, or hurt someone else in its behalf; not to borrow for its sake, if he knows that he will be unable to repay his debt; and certainly not to steal or rob any of the four species.

THE FOUR SPECIES CORRESPOND TO FOUR TYPES OF JEWS

Whoever performs the mitzvah as prescribed and with proper intention brings about peace and harmony among Jews, as well as a greater nearness between God and Israel. For, thus did the Sages expound: 'A fruit of a *hadar* tree' — this refers to Israel. Just as this etrog has taste and fragrance, likewise are there among Israel some who possess Torah and good deeds.

'Branches of a palm tree' — this refers to Israel. Just as this palm has taste but no fragrance, so are there among Israel some who possess Torah, but lack good deeds.'

'And twigs of an *avot* tree (the myrtle)' — this refers to Israel. Just as the *hadas* (the myrtle) has fragrance, but no taste, likewise are there among Jews some who practice good deeds, but lack Torah.

'And willows of the brook' — this refers to Israel. Just as the *aravah* (the willow) has neither taste nor fragrance, likewise are there among Israel some who have neither Torah nor good deeds.

'What does God do with them? To destroy them is impossible. God therefore says: 'Let them be bound together in one bond, and these will atone for those!' (Vayikra Raba 30).

PURIFICATION FROM SIN LEADS TO UNITY

The prophet speaks of God's remembrance of Israel's self sacrifice: 'I remember unto you the lovingkindness of your youth, the love of your betrothals, when you went after Me in the wilderness, in a land that was not sown' (Irmeyahu 2).

Were not this trait of devotion to God through self-abnegation implanted in Israel's soul in every generation, they would not constantly be reminded that they had once possessed it. Nevertheless, God knows that this merit of the past is characteristic of Israel at all times whenever they are united. 'I remember unto you... *ahavat kelulotayich*' (the love of your betrothals'— of your getting united); the people of Israel find in themselves wells of complete dedication to God when every individual Jew is included in the nation as a whole (*hitkalelut*). Thus it is also written of the time of the giving of the Torah: 'And Israel encamped there, beneath the mountain' — in the singular form — as one man with one heart.

In truth, a sense of unity and mutual love would be found always within Jewish hearts, were it not for their sins which separate them from their Maker, and one Jew from another. For it is their sins which are the root of discord among Jews. After they attain purification on Yom Kipur, they are again capable of inner unity and harmony. Then the days of Sukot come and they are again drawn after God in love, as they enter His sukah.

ALL MY BONES SHALL SAY

The four species also allude to a person's limbs, and when a person says a brachah over them for the sake of God it is as if he were subjecting his heart and limbs, his powers of sight and speech to God alone. And it is as if he were saying to God: All of me is given to You alone, and all my joy in this Festival is in You alone.

Every trace of sin and transgression remaining in a person's limbs, senses and powers, is atoned for through the performance of this mitzvah in love and fear of God.

'All my bones shall say: Lord, who is like You?' This verse refers to the mitzvah of lulav. The spine of the lulav, is similar to man's spine. The (leaf of the) hadas (the myrtle) is similar to the eye. The aravah (the willow) is similar to the mouth. The etrog is similar to the heart. David said: Among the limbs none is of greater importance than those, and they are like the entire body — 'All my bones shall say.'

It has also been said on this theme: 'Why the etrog? It

is similar to the heart and atones for the heart's evil thoughts.

'Why the hadas? It is similar to the eyes, and atones for the evil sights which the eye seeks; as it is said: 'And you shall not go about after your hearts and after your eyes.'

'Why the aravah? It is similar to the lips, and atones for the expressions of the lips.

'Why the lulav? As this lulav has only one heart, so does Israel have only one heart — for their Father in Heaven' (Anaf Yosef quoting Midrash Agadah).

NISUCH HAMAYIM (The Libation of Water)

Every sacrifice brought in the Temple, was accompanied by a flour-offering and the pouring of a prescribed measure of wine on the altar. During the seven days of the Festival of Sukot, a libation of water was added to that of wine, together with each of the daily morning offerings.

This water libation is not explicitly mentioned in the Torah, but it is a 'law revealed to Moshe on Sinai,' to which the Sages have found allusions in the Torah.

WITH GREAT JOY

All the observances of Sukot are performed with joy, for the Torah mentions joy with reference to Sukot more frequently than to any other festival. Thus, no explicit reference is made to joy with regard to Pesach; one such reference is made with regard to Shavuot, while in the case of Sukot, joy is mentioned three times: 'And you shall rejoice before the Lord your God' (Vayikra 23); 'And you shall rejoice in your festival (Dvarim 15); 'And you shall be only joyous' (ibid).

The most intense joy was however reserved for *nisuch hamayim* (the libation of water). In the pouring of these three measures of the 'waters of creation' — waters which had not been affected by human effort — there were engaged cohanim, levi'im, Israelites, elders, men of piety and a large multitude of men, women and children — for a period of fifteen and a half consecutive hours, every festival day excepting Shabat and the first day of Yom Tov (when the nisuch hamayim was not accompanied by music and song).

BEIT HASHO'EVAH (The Place of the Water-Drawing)

The festivities accompanying the water-libation ceremony were called, *simchat beit hashoe'vah* since the waters that were used for the libation on the altar were drawn from the pool of Siloan or Shiloach in the city of David (outside the present wall of Jerusalem). The proof text for this is: 'And you shall draw waters with joy from the wells of salvation' (Yeshayahu 2). The waters of Shiloach are called 'The well of salvation,' since the kings of the House of David were anointed over the Shiloach, and through them salvation came to Israel.

But there was more to it than the drawing of water. Whoever saw the joy which accompanied the pouring of the water, drew happiness for the soul and salvation from travail. It was thus said in the Jerusalem Talmud: '*Beit hasho'evah* (the place of the water-drawing) — there the spirit of holiness was drawn.' It was further told: 'Yonah Ben Amitai used to go up for the pilgrim festivals. When he participated in the rejoicing over the drawing of water, the Holy Spirit rested upon him and he became a Prophet)... To teach you that the spirit of holiness rests only on a heart filled with joy' (Yerushalmi Sukah, chapter 5).

SIMCHAT BEIT HASHO'EVAH
(The Rejoicing at the Place of the Water-Drawing)

It is written in Tractate Sukah: 'He who has not seen the rejoicing at the place of the water-drawing has never seen rejoicing in his life.'

The festivities were held in the *Ezrat Nashim* (the outer Temple-courtyard) which was no more than 187 ells in length and 135 ells in width. Yet, in a miraculous way, many tens of thousands were crowded therein.

There were three golden lamps with four golden bowls on the top of each of them and four ladders led to each. Four youths of the cohanim went up each ladder and poured oil into the bowls.

'From the worn-out drawers and girdles of the cohanim they made wicks and with them they kindled the lamps; and there was not a courtyard in Jerusalem that was not illuminated by the light of the place of the water-drawing.

'Men of piety and good deeds used to dance before them with lighted torches in their hands, and sing songs and praises. And Levites without number with harps, lyres, cymbals and trumpets and other musical instruments were there upon the fifteen steps leading down from the court of the Israelites to the court of the women, corresponding to the fifteen songs of ascents in their Psalms. It was upon these that the Levites stood with their instruments of music and sang their songs. Two cohanim stood by the upper gate which led down from the court of the Israelites to the court of the women, with two trumpets in their hands. When the cock crowed they sounded a *teki'ah* (long drawn-out blast), a *tru'ah* (tremulous note) and again a teki'ah. When they reached the tenth step they sounded a teki'ah, a tru'ah and again a teki'ah. When they reached the court they sounded a teki'ah, a tru'ah and again a teki'ah. And when they reached the ground they sounded a teki'ah, a tru'ah, and again a teki'ah. They proceeded sounding their trumpets, until they reached the gate which led out at the East; they turned their faces from East to West and proclaimed, 'Our Fathers who were in this place (stood) with their backs toward the Temple of the Lord, and their faces toward the East, and they worshipped the sun toward the East, but as for us, our eyes are turned to the Lord.' Rabi Yehudah stated, they used to repeat (the last words) and say 'we are the Lord's and our eyes are turned to the Lord.'

'...Our Rabis have taught... Some of them, used to say, 'Happy our youth that has not disgraced our old age.' These were the men of piety and good deeds. Others used to say, 'Happy our old age which has atoned for our youth.' These were the penitents. The former and the latter, however, said, 'Happy he who hath not sinned, but let him who hath sinned return and He will pardon him.'

'It was taught: Rabi Yehoshua Ben Hanania stated, 'When we used to rejoice at the place of the Water-Drawing, our eyes saw no sleep. How was this ? The first hour was occupied with the daily morning sacrifice; from there we proceeded to prayers; from the prayers to the additional sacrifice; then to the House of Study; then the eating and drinking; then the afternoon prayer; then the daily evening sacrifice; and after that the Rejoicing at the place of the Water-Drawing all night' (Tractate Sukah 53).

HAPPINESS AND GLORY

One should always run to attain the joy of a *mitzvah,* for there is nothing greater than such joy, and it is indeed more highly regarded by God, than the mitzvah itself. One who performs a mitzvah without joy, does so not out of love, but only out of fear, or habit, or the desire to impress others. If however, one rejoices in a mitzvah, he is certainly prompted by love of God and His commandments.

Let not a person say: I am wise; I am a prince; I am respected by people, and it is therefore not fitting for me, to dance joyously in the presence of the people. For King David was the most eminent of his people, and he disregarded his own honor, but rather accorded honor to God alone; which in turn redounded to his honor and to the honor of his descendants till the end of generations.

We likewise find that — at simchat beit hasho'evah in the Temple — the most eminent of the people disregarded their own honor, and not only accorded all honor to God, but made themselves subservient, and undertook to arouse the people towards joy in the performance of even so light a mitzvah as that of the water-drawing — which was the lightest of the mitzvot performed in the Temple; since it is unmentioned in the Torah, and the Sadducees denied it. It was taught thereby: there is no wisdom, no greatness, no glory before God. For God alone is the King of Glory, and His commandments and edicts, as well as the allusions discovered by the Sages in the Torah, are more weighty than all the glory of one of flesh and blood — even if he be the greatest of kings, as were David and Shlomo in their respective times.

In the Rambam's words in Hilchot Lulav, chapter 8:

'The joy experienced by a person, in the perfomance of mitzvot and the love of God who commanded them — is a great act of worship. And whoever refrains from such joy, deserves punishment. As it was said: 'Since you did not serve the Lord, your God, with joy and goodness of heart.' And whoever is coarse in mind, and accords honor to himself... in such instances... is a sinner and a fool. Concerning this (matter) Shlomo forewarned and said: 'Do not show pride before a king.' And whoever humbles himself... in such instances, is great, honored, and regarded as one who acts out of love. King David likewise said: 'And I shall be yet more shamed than this, and I shall be humble in my eyes.' And there is no greatness and honor other than in rejoicing before the Lord. As it was said: 'And she saw King David leaping and dancing before the Lord...'

THE JOY OF 'DVEKUT' (Cleavage to God)

Why was the water-libation ordained particularly for Sukot ?

Why was the festival joy associated with the water-libation ?

Why do the pious rejoice the more at simchat beit hasho'evah ?

These matters may be explained as follows:

A person knows perfect joy only when he cleaves to the root of his life; and this is especially so, if one returns to his root after having been separated from it for a time. The very life of Israel consists in their cleaving to their root — the source of the life of the universe. They know that they possess nothing which is their own, but that God alone bestows life and goodness upon them; that even their Torah, mitzvot, and good deeds, are a gift from Him.

As long as the people of Israel remember this, they are attached to their root. If they become arrogant at heart — Heaven forbid: if the simple among them say, my strength has wrought all this; if the pious say, righteousness is mine, for I have merited it; if the learned say, wisdom is mine, for I have acquired understanding — then, their very existence is in danger, for they have separated themselves from their root of life. At such an hour even their Torah and mitzvot do not avail them, since their very study and pious actions are steeped in arrogance. And conceit of heart is an abomination to God. Further, wherever there is arrogance, there is strife: one shows himself superior to another, and the other shows his friend as inferior to him. But God hates strife, and loves only harmony.

All year round, the evil inclination seeks to enter man's heart; to blemish even his service of God; to plant conceit even in the hearts of those who worship God and study His Torah; to cause every person to stumble over sin, in accord with their respective natures; and thereby to cause dissension among Jews, and separation between Israel and God.

When Yom Kipur comes and the people of Israel attain purification, and the evil inclination loses dominion over them, love and harmony return between Jew and Jew, and the barriers separating the Jews and their Father in Heaven are likewise removed.

When Sukot comes, every Jew — whether great or small — enters the Sukah to come under the shadow of the

Shechinah (Divine Presence). The following morning, the elders and Torah scholars, the pious and those lacking in any distinction — all perform the mitzvah of the 'four species' — thereby forming a unified band to do God's will wholeheartedly. Further, though the etrog is the most beautiful of all the species, 'he stands aside' and appears more lowly than them all. At that time Israel is completely liberated from the evil inclination, and they cleave wholly to their 'root' — the Life of the Universe... They then say to God: 'You have chosen us from all the peoples, You have loved us and desired us.'

Not because we were more numerous than all other peoples; not because of our righteousness or wisdom, did You choose us, but only because of Your love for us — a love which is beyond our capacity to deserve. For, what can a man of flesh and blood attain with his own strength, and if he is just — what does it avail God ? Since however, God desired us — not because of our merits, we are equal recipients of Your love, and we all equally love one another unto eternity.

God too answers Israel through the symbol of the 'water-libation.'

All the offerings you bring Me throughout the year are precious to Me, but this offering of the water which you pour on the altar during this festival — is especially precious. This offering requires neither planting nor reaping; neither pressing nor purifying... it is pure of the slightest taint of conceit. Let it be joined to the 'wine-libation' which does require all those activities. Both together are regarded by Me as if you had offered Me your all. For My love for you is unconditional, and your wine and water are equal in My eyes; the fruit of your physical efforts are equal to those unaccompanied by physical efforts, provided that you rejoice in Me, as I do in you — without the admixture of any alien thought.

The men of piety; the elders and the great; all of whose

lives are an altar of atonement, know no greater joy than that of *nisuch hamayim.* For through this joy, they know that all their exertion in the service of God throughout the entire year, rises to be accepted by Him.

Further, at that hour, all rises with them; not only their Jewish brethren but every living being and all existence as well. For wine can be blemished by gentile contact, but water remains eternally pure for all Mankind. The waters preceded the Earth, and when the Earth was destroyed, the waters were not — they remained eternally pure.

Therefore — 'Pour water for Me, so that you should be blessed with water.' As it was said: 'On the Festival (Sukot) there is judgment over water.' And when the Earth is blessed with water — all the world's inhabitants are blessed — Israel, as well as the nations of the world. 'I have made you,' says God to Israel — 'a kingdom of priests for all the nations on Earth — bring Me an offering from the 'root of Creation,' and let every creature receive its blessing thereby.'

THE SEVENTY FESTIVAL OXEN

When the people of Israel rejoice, their hearts go out to the whole world.

When dawn rose on the first day of the Festival, they brought the regular daily sacrificial offering and poured its libations; the wine-libation and the water-libation, and all the world was blessed with an abundance of good for the entire year.

After the regular daily offering, they brought a number of 'Additional-Offerings.' Each day there was a different number of these Additional-Offerings to be brought. All together seventy oxen were to be brought in the course of the entire festival.

These seventy oxen corresponded to the seventy original nations of the world who descended from the sons of Noah, and who were the ancestors of all the nations till this day. Israel brought these sacrifices as an atonement for the nations of the world and in prayer for their well-being as well as for universal peace and harmony between them.

The Sages have said:

'In place of my love they hate me, and I pray (for them)' (Tehilim 109): You find that during the Festival, Israel offers You seventy oxen for the seventy nations. Israel says: Master of the Universe! Behold, we offer You seventy oxen in their behalf, and they should have loved us... instead — 'in the place of my love they hate me' (Bamidbar Raba 21).

The Sages have further said in this matter:

'Rabi Yehoshua Ben Levi said: If the nations of the world would have known the value of the Temple for them, they would have surrounded it with fortresses in order to protect it. For it was of greater value for them than for Israel. Thus, when King Shlomo prayed concerning the gentile nations, at the time of the building of the Temple, he said: 'And you shall do according to all that the stranger shall call unto you' (First Melachim 8). With reference however, to Israel, Shlomo prayed, 'And you shall give to a man in accordance with all his ways that you know his heart.' If he was worthy — his prayer was granted; if he was not worthy — his prayer was not granted... and do not say that the Temple (caused this), but rather — were it not for Israel, rain would not descend and the sun would not shine. For by their merit God grants respite for the world' (Bamidbar Raba 1).

ISHMAEL AND ESAV

The Sages have said that the power which was given to Noah's sons to become the founders of the seventy original nations, was later vested in the descendants of Avraham, to whom it was said: 'for I have made you the father of a multitude of nations.' Henceforward all the seventy nations were to 'draw their sustenance' through Avraham's descendants. First, Ishmael was made head of the seventy nations, but after the birth of Esav to Itzchak, the flow of Divine sustenance for the nations was divided between Ishmael and Esav, each of whom became the head of thirty five of the nations. Likewise, when Ya'akov and his sons went down to Egypt, and founded the Jewish nation, they numbered seventy souls. They however became a people which was to stand alone in the midst of the other seventy nations, and their seventy souls corresponded to the seventy nations who were under the dominion of the other descendants of Avraham and Itzchak.

God appointed Israel a kingdom of priests to atone for all the other nations, and Jerusalem — a house of prayer for all the peoples. Therefore, when Israel came to sacrifice seventy oxen during the seven days of Sukot as an atonement for the seventy nations of the world, they sacrificed thirty five oxen in behalf of the nations under Ishmael's dominion, and thirty five in behalf of those under Esav's dominion.

These seventy oxen were sacrificed in the following order: On the first day, thirteen, and on each successive day one less; twelve, eleven, ten, nine, eight, seven. To teach us that, although they all exist by Israel's merit, Israel alone is eternal, as are those who will in the future become attached to Israel; whereas, all the others, are destined to decrease more and more.

The Gaon of Vilna has discovered a striking allusion in the Torah to the above division of the seventy nations between Ishmael and Esav:

In the chapter which recounts the additional-festival-offering, the following outline emerges (the tradition of the Sages should be noted that the term, 'kid of goats,' refers to Ishmael, while the term, 'kid,' refers to Esav):

On the 1st day 13 oxen	and 1 'kid of goats' (Ishmael) for a sin offering
On the 2nd day 12 oxen	and 1 'kid of goats' (Ishmael) for a sin offering

On the 3rd day 11 oxen	and 1 'kid' (Esav) for a sin offering
On the 4th day 10 oxen	and 1 'kid of goats' (Ishmael) for a sin offering
On the 5th day 9 oxen	and 1 'kid' (Esav) for a sin offering
On the 6th day 8 oxen	and 1 'kid' (Esav) for a sin offering
On the 7th day 7 oxen	and 1 'kid' (Esav) for a sin offering

It will be noted that thirty five oxen were sacrificed together with thirty five 'kids of goats' (Ishmael), while the other thirty five were brought together with thirty five 'kids' (Esav).

By rights Ishmael, who was a son to Avraham, should have preceded Esav who was Itzchak's son. If the first three days had been given, however, to Ishmael, thirty six of the oxen would have been brought in behalf of the nations under his dominion. He is therefore omitted on the third day (which is given to the Esav-nations) so that the atonements for both might be exactly equal. For this reason, 'kids of goats,' are mentioned on the first, second and fourth days; while 'kids,' are mentioned on the third, fifth, sixth and seventh days.

'AND YOU SHALL REJOICE ON YOUR FESTIVAL'

When the Temple stood, simchat beit hasho'evah was marked by great public festivity. Now that the Temple is in ruins, through our sins, we have neither altar nor sacrifices, nor wine-libations, nor water-libations. Nevertheless we still rejoice greatly during the festival of Sukot. The bringing of sacrifices has ceased, but the Torah prescribes: 'And you shall rejoice in your Festival.'

Therefore, it is customary in many Jewish communities for groups to gather during the nights of the Festival in Synagogues and Houses of Study to rejoice together through song and praise in memory of simchat beit hasho'evah.

It is customary to sing the fifteen 'Songs of Ascent' in

Tehilim (Chapters 120—134), which correspond to the fifteen steps in the Sanctuary between the men's courtyard and the women's courtyard. On these steps the Levites stood as they sang and played during simchat beit hasho'evah.

YOM TOV OBSERVANCE

A person is obligated to invest Yom Tov with joy, honor, and pleasure.

What is the joy of Yom Tov? When the Temple still stood, the essence of festival joy consisted in the special peace offerings, of which parts were offered on the altar, parts were eaten by the owners in a spirit of holiness and joy; and were shared with the Levite, the stranger, the orphan and the widow. Now that the Temple no longer stands, and there are no festival pilgrimages nor peace-offerings, the essence of the joy of Yom Tov consists in festival meals containing meat and wine; in rejoicing one's wife, one's household and companions. Ornaments and handsome clothes are bought for one's wife in honor of Yom Tov; nuts and candies are given to the children; and the poor are provided with the means of celebrating the festival joyously.

It is customary to eat more sumptuously on Yom Tov than on Shabat, as well as to dress more festively, since the Torah enjoins joy on Yom Tov, but not on Shabat.

The study of the Lord's Torah is part of the joy of Yom Tov, as is is said: 'The commandments of the Lord are upright, they rejoice the heart.'

A mourner does not observe the practices of mourning on Yom Tov.

What is 'the honor of Yom Tov?'

To recall Yom Tov and to prepare oneself for it before it arrives. A person is obligated to cut his hair on Erev Yom Tov in honor of the festival; to bathe, to cut his nails and to change his clothes for clean Yom Tov garments.

The Sages have said: 'A person is obligated to purify himself for the festival.'

It is therefore proper for a person to immerse himself in a 'mikvah' (ritual bath) or river on Erev Yom Tov.

It is likewise a mitzvah to prepare fine foods on Erev Yom Tov in honor of the festival.

Even if one has many servants at home, it is proper — in honor of Yom Tov — to make every effort on Erev Yom Tov, to personally participate in the preparations for Yom Tov.

It is prohibited to eat a meal on Erev Yom Tov during the last two and a half hours before the appearance of the stars, so that one might eat the evening festival meal with good appetite.

What is the pleasure of Yom Tov ?

The eating of two regular meals daily; one at night, and one during the day: the lighting of candles at the advent of the festival, in order to derive pleasure from their light during the night of Yom Tov.

A meal is regarded as a regular meal only if it contains chalah or bread, and two whole loaves are required. Wine is drunk during the meal, in addition to the wine over which one makes 'kidush' before the meal. Meat and other delicacies are partaken plentifully for 'the pleasure of Yom Tov.'

The prescribed blessing is recited over the candles ('l'hadlik ner shel Yom Tov'). It is customary for the woman who recites the blessing over the candles to pronounce the 'shehecheyanu,' with the exception of the last nights of Pesach, when 'shehecheyanu' is not said.

When Yom Tov candles are lit, the blessing is

said before the lighting, since the brachah over a mitzvah precedes the performance of the mitzvah. On Shabat, however, the lighting precedes the blessing since the blessing constitutes an acceptance of Shabat, after which it is no longer permitted to kindle fire.

It is proper for a person not to be parsimonious in spending whatever is necessary for Yom Tov, even if one's means are limited. For one loses nothing through any expense incurred in honor of Yom Tov. On the contrary, he obtains blessing thereby. A person's sustenance and expenses are fixed on Rosh Hashanah for the duration of the year, with the exception of whatever he spends for Shabat and Yom Tov, and to enable his children to study Torah. In these instances if he diminishes, he is granted less from above, and if he adds he is granted more.

THE JOY OF THE MITZVAH RATHER THAN THE JOY OF THE BODY

When one eats and drinks, he is obligated to feed the stranger, the orphan, the widow, together with the other unfortunate poor. One who closes his doors however, and eats and drinks together with his children and wife, but does not give food and drink to the poor and the embittered of soul, his joy is not the joy of a mitzvah but rather the joy of his stomach... and this joy is a mark of shame...

When a person eats and drinks and rejoices in the festival, he should not be drawn through wine to frivolity and levity, and he should not say that whoever does so, adds to the mitzvah of festival joy. For intoxication and undue levity, are not joy but mere foolishness. And it is not these experiences that we are commanded to seek, but only the joy involved in the service of the Creator. The Torah states: 'Since you did not serve the Lord your God in joy, and in goodness of heart, out of an abundance of all things.' You learn thereby that the service of God requires joy. It is impossible to worship God in frivolity, in levity, or in intoxication.

THE DIFFERENCE BETWEEN YOM TOV AND SHABAT

Only the preparation of food distinguishes between Yom Tov and Shabat. That is, every act of labor which is forbidden on Shabat is also forbidden on Yom Tov, with the exception of a number of labors which the Torah permitted for the sake of food and the joy of the Festival: kneading, baking, slaughtering, cooking, carrying from one domain to another, and the use of fire (by lighting one fire with another, but not igniting new fire).

Our Sages have received the tradition, that just as carrying and the use of fire are permitted when needed for food, they are equally permitted for pleasure. Cooking is likewise permitted also for the purpose of heating water for washing one's face, hands and feet. Reaping, uprooting from the ground, threshing, winnowing, grinding, sifting — are all prohibited. Only kneading and the activities which follow it, are permitted, as are also the above mentioned activities of slaughtering, cooking, carrying from one domain to another, and the use of fire. The last four, are permitted since it is either not possible to perform them Erev Yom Tov, or some loss or spoilage would occur if they were done before Yom Tov.

If flour was sifted on Erev Yom Tov and some foreign particles fell into the flour on Yom Tov, it is permissible to sift the flour again.

Although Yom Tov is like Shabat with reference to forbidden activities, it is not like Shabat with reference to penalties. For one who does a forbidden activity on Shabat deliberately, incurs the penalty of excision of the soul, and if there were witnesses and forewarning, a death penalty; while on Yom Tov he would be subject to the penalty of malkot (lashing). If one does a forbidden act unintentionally on Shabat, he is obligated to bring a sin-offering, while on Yom Tov he is not subject to any penalty.

It is permitted to carry one's 'talit' as well as any utensils or objects needed for food, from one domain to another; if possible, however, one should refrain from carrying heavy burdens in his accustomed manner during weekdays, but only through some variation.

Most of the laws of 'muktzeh' are alike for Yom Tov and Shabat, but in some cases, the laws of 'muktzeh' are more stringent on Yom Tov than on Shabat, so that Yom Tov might not be held in light regard.

It is forbidden to tell a gentile to do a forbidden act on Yom Tov, as is the case on Shabat.

The activities which were permitted on Yom Tov, were permitted only for the sake of another Jew.

It is likewise forbidden to perform those acts for the sake of one's livestock.

The lighting (not ignition) of a fire, is permitted, but the extinguishing of a fire is prohibited. And even to cause the extinguishing of a fire — unless loss would be sustained — is forbidden. It is therefore prohibited to place a lighted lamp where a wind could extinguish it — even if there is no wind when the lamp is put there.

If a flame is too high, and would therefore burn or spoil the food, it is permissible to reduce it; if, however, one can place his pot on another flame, he may not diminish the first flame.

It is forbidden to put a candle over a fire in order

to melt its bottom, and thereby to cause it to stick to the candelabra.

Those who regard smoking as permissible on Yom Tov, should be careful not to extinguish their cigarettes, and they should likewise be careful not to drop ashes which still contain fire.

The preparation of food is only permitted in the case of objects already in existence before the advent of Yom Tov. Something which was 'born' on Yom Tov — such as an egg laid on Yom Tov — may not be cooked on Yom Tov or even swallowed raw. Even handling it is prohibited. One may however, cover it with a utensil, to prevent its breakage.

It is permissible to kindle one light from another which is already burning, either for light, or warmth on a cold day. But it is prohibited to ignite new fire on Yom Tov. A match is not lit therefore by striking it; nor are two stones rubbed together to produce fire; nor is a glass used to concentrate sun rays for the production of fire.

The lighting of electricity is regarded by most authorities as an act of ignition of new fire, and the general practice therefore is not to light electricity on Yom Tov. It is certainly prohibited to put out electric lights on Yom Tov.

Only dishes needed the same day may be washed on Yom Tov.

CHOL HAMO'ED (The Weekdays of the Festival)

There are six days between the first festival day of Sukot and 'Shmini Atzeret' (outside the Land of Israel there are five days). And there are five days between the first festival day of Pesach and the last (in Exile there are four days.) These days are called 'Chol Hamo'ed.'

The Rabis deduced from various verses in the Torah the prohibition of labor on Chol Hamo'ed. The specific character of the activities prohibited on Chol Hamo'ed is not however explicitly stated in the Torah — as is the case with reference to Yom Tov — but was rather handed over to the Sages for determination.

Any labor performed in the preparation of food — whether for oneself or another — is permissible on Chol Hamo'ed.

Any labor in a matter where loss would be sustained, if the act were not done at the time — is permitted.

However, even where loss would be sustained by delay — if the particular labor could have been done before Yom Tov, but was deliberately not done, with the thought that it could still be done on Yom Tov — it is prohibited.

If one had a certain prohibited labor to be done, and a poor man asked to do it, in order to be able to provide for the needs of Yom Tov with the wages he would earn — it is permitted, provided it be done in privacy.

With the exception of watering, or the plucking of fruit needed during Chol Hamo'ed, all the labors of the field are prohibited — unless excessively great loss be incurred thereby.

It is forbidden to cut one's hair during Chol Hamo'ed, but if one could not cut his hair before Yom Tov (a mourner, or a prisoner) — he may do so during Chol Hamo'ed.

If one cut his nails Erev Yom Tov and they grew excessively he may cut them during Chol Hamo'ed. Otherwise, he may not.

The washing of clothes is prohibited, other than if they are greatly needed for the forthcoming Yom

Tov, and it was completely impossible for them to be washed Erev Yom Tov. The washing of baby diapers is permitted.

Anything needed for medical purposes — whether for man or animal — is permitted.

Business matters may not be written down, except if one fears that he might otherwise forget such details as would cause him a loss.

Friendly letters, which contain no reference to business matters may be written — but not in one's customary manner.

If one borrows money from his friend — even if the money is not needed till after Yom Tov — he may write a debtor's note. If however, he is certain to be able to obtain the loan he needs after Yom Tov, he may not write a debtor's note on Chol Hamo'ed.

One may not move from one residence to another unless the new apartment is in the same courtyard as the old. If one has been living in a rented apartment and wishes to move to a residence of his own, he is permitted to do so. For it is a joy to a person to live in a residence that is his own.

If one does an act of labor on Chol Hamo'ed — even if it be permitted — he should try to do it privately.

The buying and selling of merchandise is prohibited on Chol Hamo'ed unless one of the following conditions applies:

1. One needs to earn a sum in order to provide for the festival;

2. he has an opportunity to earn a much larger profit than usual, and if he could obtain it, he would spend more than he originally intended, in honor of Yom Tov;

3. if he should fail to sell now, he would lose

even the principal. However, the loss of profit is not considered a loss.

A person should take exceeding care not to perform any forbidden labor on Chol Hamo'ed. For the Sages have said: 'whoever treats Chol Hamo'ed lightly, is as if he worshipped idols.' They have also said: 'whoever treats Chol Hamo'ed lightly — though he possesses Torah and good deeds — has no portion in the world to come.' Rather, is one required to honor Chol Hamo'ed, and to sanctify it through cessation of labor, good food and drink, and proper clothes.

THE SHABAT OF CHOL HAMO'ED

Joy is added to the Shabat of Chol Hamo'ed, more than is usual every Shabat, because of the joy of Yom Tov. Some have the custom of preparing two 'kuglen,' one for Shabat and one for Chol Hamo'ed.

The shacharit prayers on Shabat-Chol-Hamo'ed follow the general order of a regular 'Shabat,' with the exception of the addition of 'ya'aleh veyavo,' and the recitation of 'Halel.' The 'musaf' prayer follows the order of musaf on Yom Tov with the exception of the prescribed references to Shabat, which are inserted where indicated in the prayer books. The Torah-Reading, relates entirely to the Festival.

On 'Shabat' of Chol Hamo'ed Sukot, or when the first day of Sukot falls on Shabat it is the custom of the Ashkenazim to read 'Kohelet' before the Torah-Reading. The authorities hold differing views with reference to the reading of Kohelet. Some say that each person should read it individually from a printed book, and that no blessing should be recited over its reading. Others hold that it should be read publicly from a hand written parchment scroll, and that two blessings should be recited before it is read; 'al mikra megilah,' and, shehecheyanu.'

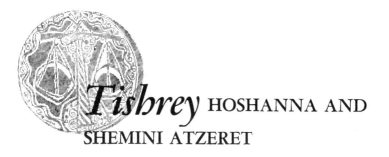

Tishrey HOSHANNA AND SHEMINI ATZERET

HOSHANA ◆ HOSHANA RABA ◆ THE NATURE OF THE DAY ◆ ONLY PRAYER ◆ 'ANI VA'HO HOSHI'A NA' ◆ THE ARAVAH ◆ BEFORE DARK ◆ SHMINI ATZERET ◆ A UNIQUE OFFERING ◆ THE PRAYER FOR RAIN ◆ GEVUROT GESHAMIM ◆ MASHIV HARUACH UMORID HAGESHEM ◆ SIMCHAT TORAH ◆ SIYUM HATORAH ◆ NOTHING REMAINS EXCEPT THIS TORAH ◆ BEYOND TIME ◆ BETWEEN ME AND YOU ◆ SIMCHAT TORAH CUSTOMS ◆ A TORAH WHICH IS ALWAYS NEW ◆ ISRU CHAG ◆ BIRKAT HACHODESH ◆ SHABAT BEREISHIT.

CHAPTER FOUR

HOSHANA

After *Halel* is said during the days of *Sukot* or after *musaf* — depending on local custom — a Torah scroll is taken out of the Ark and brought to the *bimah* (pulpit). The cantor and the congregation say aloud: '*Hoshana*,' four times, as indicated in the prayer books. Afterwards, a prescribed prayer is said each day; each of these prayers follows the alphabetical order. Each phrase is accompanied by the word, '*Hoshana*.' Simultaneously, the entire congregation circles the *bimah* with *etrog* and *lulav* in hand: During the first six festival days, there is one *hakafah* (circling) each day; while on *Hoshana Raba* (the last day of Sukot) there are seven *hakafot*.

This custom is a memorial to the Sanctuary, in which the *cohanim* encircled the altar with praise and joy once each day, and seven times on *Hoshana Raba* — which was then called 'the day of beating the *aravah* (willow).'

'How was the precept of the willow-branch carried out? There was a place below Jerusalem called Motza. They went down there and gathered thence young willow-branches and then came and fixed them at the sides of the altar so that their tops bent over the altar. They then sounded a *teki'ah* (long shofar blast), *tru'ah* (tremulous blast) and again a *teki'ah*. Every day they went round the altar once, saying, 'We beseech Thee, O Lord, save now, we beseech Thee, O Lord, make us now to prosper.' Rabi Yehudah said they were saying '*ani vaho* save now.' But on the day of Hoshana Raba they went round the altar seven times. When they departed, what did they say? 'Thine, o altar, is the beauty! Thine, o altar, is the beauty!'

'As was its performance on a weekday, so was its performance on the Shabat, save that they gather them on the eve (of the Shabat), and placed them in golden basins that they might not become mildewed...' (Mishnah, Sukah Chapter 4).

'Why was the rite of the *aravah* prescribed for Hoshana Raba ? The *aravah* grows on water, and then mankind is judged for water' (Rokeach).

In memory of these *hakafot*, we encircle the Torah scroll at the bimah; for nothing remains to us except the Torah, and it serves us as an altar of atonement. Prayers are said that God might grant us the blessings of rain and dew.

These prayers which we say on encircling the bimah are called 'Hoshana,' or 'Hoshanot' (the plural). Since the word 'Hoshana' is a contraction of the two words, '*Hosha na*' (help us), it is repeated with every verse of the prayers that are said as the bimah is encircled.

HOSHANA RABA

'Hoshana Raba' is the last day for the 'mitzvot' of 'the four species' and sukah (in the Diaspora customs vary with reference to the mitzvah of sukah also on 'Shmini Atzeret'). It is called Hoshana Raba ('raba' — many, numerous), since more 'hoshanot' are said on this day than on all the previous days of the festival. On Hoshana Raba the rite of the 'aravah' (willow branches) is performed, and the aravah is also called by the name 'hoshana,' after the name of the hoshana prayers of the day.

Although Hoshana Raba was not accorded any different status by the Torah than the other festival days, the people of Israel have observed many particular customs on this day, and they have invested it with a solemn character.

It was a custom of the Prophets (Chagai, Zechariah and Malachi) to take an aravah, to recite a special prayer over it, and then beat it on the ground. Unlike other Rabbinic commandments, over which a blessing is recited, no blessing is recited over the aravah. For when the 'holding of the aravah' was enacted, it was enacted merely as a custom.

It is customary to stay awake all night and to say 'Tikun;' to read from the book of Dvarim, to recite the entire Book of Tehilim, and to 'unite' the night and the day through Torah and prayer. The pious practice immersion before dawn.

Festival clothes are worn and some follow the custom of wearing white garments as on Yom Kipur, as well as to light the leftover lamps from Yom Kipur.

In most Sephardi communities the prayers are the same on Hoshana Raba as on Chol Hamo'ed (the weekdays of the festival). In the Ashkenazi communities however, there are minor differences, as indicated in the 'sidurim' (prayer books).

After 'Halel,' or after 'musaf' (depending on the local custom), hoshanot are said in the prescribed order; the bimah is encircled seven times; and when 'ta'aneh emunim' is reached, the 'lulav' and 'etrog' are put aside, the aravah is taken and the order of hoshanot is completed.

During musaf the complete 'kedushah' is said as on a regular Yom Tov, rather than the abbreviated version which is said on the previous days of Chol Hamo'ed.

A festive meal is taken, and even such activities as are permissible during Chol Hamo'ed are avoided, till the morning prayers are over.

THE NATURE OF THE DAY

On Hoshana Raba there takes place the final 'sealing of judgment' which begins on Rosh Hashanah. At the beginning of judgment, on Rosh Hashanah and Yom Kipur, all the world's inhabitants pass in review before God for judgment. During the festival of Sukot the world as a whole is judged for water, and for the blessings of the fruit and the crops. The seventh day of the festival — Hoshana Raba — is the day of the final 'sealing of judgment.' And since human life depends on water, and the end of a matter is decisive, Hoshana Raba is somewhat similar to Yom Kipur. There is profuse prayer and the quest for repentance, as on Yom Kipur.

The ancient Sages have also coined a parable on this matter: 'The Kingdom of Heaven is like the kingdom on earth.' And the modes of judgment in both are similar. In the kingdom on earth, when a merciful and just king sits in judgment, he decides it immediately, on finding merit. If not, he suspends judgment till the defender might discover merit for the accused. After a time he issues judgment. If he decides for mercy, he informs the accused immediately; if not — he keeps the decision to himself, lest the accused finds some merit, in which case the decree of judgment could be torn up and transformed to mercy. In the end he hands over his written judgments to his messengers whether for death or life. The messengers then leave to discharge their tasks; whether to dispense harsh judgments or mercy. If the written decisions were merciful, they cannot again change to harsh judgment. If they bespeak judgment, they may still be transformed into mercy at the last moment.

How? If a harsh decree went forth against so-and-so who had rebelled against the king, and the king's emissaries arrive to the place of the condemned, and find him happily and loyally fulfilling all the king's decrees, they say: this is not the one against whom such-and-such was decreed; the person who now appears to us is another man! They return to the king, and he also agrees with them. They tear up the royal decree and 'seal' him for a good life.

In the Heavenly Kingdom it is also thus. On Rosh Hashanah all the world's inhabitants pass before God: The perfect *tzadikim* (the just) are immediately inscribed and sealed for life; the intermediate ones are suspended till Yom Kipur and their judgment is sealed on Yom Kipur. The conclusion of their 'sealing,' however, is on Hoshana Raba, and it extends till dawn on Shmini Atzeret. Therefore, there is profuse prayer and supplication on Hoshana Raba; and an awakening towards *teshuvah* and Divine mercy. Even if a harsh decree had already been rendered, it is torn up, and in heaven new 'notes' (of acquittal) are written.

The eighth day is an *atzeret* (a solemn assembly) for all Israel and they say before God: It is difficult for us to separate ourselves from your commandments. Although the mitzvot of sukah and lulav, the festival sacrifice and the water-libation, are concluded — we linger before you and rejoice in you. Messengers from above then come and find all Israel rejoicing before God with the happiness of Love. And even if there were among them such as had been condemned, harm does not strike them. They are now different people, they love God, and rejoice in Him and His commandments.

The Sages have said:

'God said to Avraham: I am one and you are one — I shall give your sons a single day to atone for their sins — Hoshana Raba. God said to Avraham: If Rosh Hashanah will not atone for your sons, let Yom Kipur do so. If not, let Hoshana Raba do so.'

Why did God address this promise particularly to Avraham? Just as Avraham's light began to shine in the world after twenty-one generations (counting from Adam), so will the light of his sons not delay more than twenty-one days after the beginning of judgment on Rosh Hashanah (Hoshana Raba is the twenty-first day of the year). The essential character of the day is therefore seen to consist of: prayer, and the awakening of mercy when Divine judgment is sealed and the notes of decision go forth.

This is the source of the Jewish custom to extend mutual blessing on this day for a *pitka tava* (a good note).

ONLY PRAYER

On Hoshana Raba the people of Israel leave aside all their righteousness and all their merits of the entire year; nor do they even turn to the merit of their Fathers. They ask life for themselves and the entire world only through the merit of prayer, and they say before the Master of the Universe:

Lord of the Universe, we have come before You poor and empty handed. We possess neither Torah, nor mitzvot, nor good deeds, nor the merit of the fathers. We have only our mouths alone with which to pray to You. Answer us only through the merit of this prayer, which we address to You with broken and contrite hearts.

All the actions of the day allude to prayer: The many *hakafot* and the hoshanot, the taking of the aravah, the *ushpizin* (guests) of each day, the last of the seven loyal shepherds — David, King of Israel.

Each of the festival days the bimah is circled once during hoshanot; on this day — seven times. And after the seven *hakafot* (encircling of the bimah) many *piyutim* and supplications are said, all of them accompanied by the expression 'Hoshana' like one who has no claim at all, but pleads only for help.

The aravah which is taken on that day after the etrog and lulav are set aside, also alludes to prayer. It has already been mentioned above, that the aravah is similar to the mouth and lips, and it corresponds to those among Israel who possess neither Torah, nor mitzvot, nor good deeds. Now we put aside the entire band in which the four types of Jews were united though the symbolism of the four species, and we say: We possess neither the taste of Torah, nor the fragrance of mitzvah, neither the etrog nor the lulav, nor the hadas — we are all like this aravah. What then do we have? Only mouths with which to pray; like this aravah which is similar to a mouth.

Further, the head of the *ushpizin* on Hoshana Raba — King David, the sweet singer of Israel is the very symbol and embodiment of the strength of prayer. And the psalms of Tehilim which David said, were wellsprings of prayers for all the world's inhabitants through all the generations.

'ANI VA'HO HOSHI'A NA'

At the end of hoshanot each day including Hoshana Raba, after the hakafot, the cantor and congregation say the following verse out loud: *'Ani va'ho hoshi'a na!'* The saying of this verse is a memorial to the Sanctuary, in which — after the encircling of the altar with the aravah — a *teki'ah, tru'ah,* and a *teki'ah* were sounded and this verse was said.

The Sages differ in the Mishnah as to how this verse was said in the Temple: *'Ana Hashem hoshi'a na'* ('we beseech Thee, O Lord, Save'); or, *'Ani va'ho hoshi'a na'* ('I and He — God — share Israel's troubles, therefore — we beseech Thee, Help').

THE ARAVAH

It was 'a law given to Moshe on Sinai' that the aravah should be taken in the Sanctuary all the seven festival days (Tractate Sukah 45). This aravah was a separate mitzvah from the aravah which was part of the four species.

With this aravah one daily hakafah was made about the altar, while on the last day of the festival, the altar was circled seven times with the aravah. This tradition that was given to Moshe on Sinai applied only to the Sanctuary, but not anywhere else within Israel's boundaries.

However, Chagai, Zechariah, and Malachi prescribed the taking of the aravah as a custom everywhere (but without a blessing as indicated above) for the last day of the festival

— Hoshana Raba; and this custom is accompanied by prayer for the blessings of water.

Five aravah branches are taken, like those which are used for the four species, and they are bound together. And although we are not as stringent concerning this aravah as we are concerning the aravah of the lulav, nevertheless we take the most beautiful ones that are available, in fulfillment of: 'This is my God and I shall worship Him with beauty' — through the enhancement of mitzvot. After the hakafot are concluded and the lulav and etrog are put aside, the aravah is taken and we recite all the *piyutim* beginning with '*ta'aneh emunim*' till after '*kol mevaser*' (till the middle of kadish in the Chassidic custom or the end of the entire service in the Sephardi custom). Then the aravah is beaten five times on the ground and is put away in a place where it will not be trodden underfoot, since it is improper to cast it away as worthless even after it has been used.

This custom of beating the aravah on the ground contains profound esoteric significance, and only the Great of Israel merit the knowledge of those secrets. The uninitiated should intend merely to abide by the custom of the Prophets and the Sages of all the generations. Their reward for emulating their actions, will be regarded by God as if they had indeed had their profound intentions.

BEFORE DARK

On Hoshana Raba before dark (and in the Diaspora on Shmini Atzeret) it is customary to enter the sukah for a snack, in order to fulfill the mitzvah of sukah the last time. On leaving the sukah the following prayer is recited:

'May it be Your will, Lord our God and the God of our fathers, just as I merited and sat in this sukah, so may I merit the coming year, to sit in the sukah of the skin of Leviathan.' And we conclude: 'Next year in Jerusalem.'

For the Sages have said that at the time of the final redemption, God will make one sukah in which all Israel will sit and it will be made of Leviathan's skin, while its flesh will be food for the righteous.

It is customary to remove afterwards any ornaments or utensils which one might need in his home for the forthcoming festival (Shmini Atzeret).

SHMINI ATZERET

Shmini Atzeret is a separate festival, and is not tied to the Festival of Sukot, but is only adjacent to it. For this reason *shehecheyanu* is said both by the woman, when she lights the *Yom Tov* candles, and by the man, during *Kidush.* The festival is called, 'Shmini Atzeret' after its designation in the Torah (Bamidbar 29): 'On the eighth day it shall be an *atzeret* to you...' And this term *atzeret* is an expression of affection, as would be used by a father to sons who are departing from him. The father would say: 'Your departure is difficult for me, tarry yet another day' (Rashi ibid.)'

'Another interpretation: why were they kept back yet another day? Rav said that the matter may be likened to a king who celebrated a holiday. His servants came and honored him; the members of his household came and honored him. A matron hinted to them: while he is engaged with you — ask your needs of the king. So does the Torah hint to Israel: Ask your needs... (during the festival, the people of Israel had prayed exclusively for the life and happiness of the seventy nations of the world, while asking nothing for themselves.) For this purpose the Torah kept them back one more day — the eighth day' (Yalkut Pinchas 782).

Rabi Levi said: during every one of the summer months God desired to give Israel a festival. During Nisan, He gave them Pesach; during Iyar, He gave them Pesach Katan (whoever could not bring the Paschal lamb in its proper time because of defilement, could bring it a month later, on the 14th of Iyar); during Sivan, He gave them Shavuot; during Tamuz He wanted to give them a major festival, but they made the golden calf, and He anulled Tamuz, Av, Elul. When Tishrey came — He repaid them with Rosh Hashanah, Yom Kipur, and Sukot. God said: Tishrey repays others, shall he not take for himself? He gave Tishrey one day — 'on the eighth day it shall be an *atzeret* to you' (Pesikta d'Rav Kahana).

The observance of the day with reference to the prohibition of labor and the activities permitted for the preparation of food, is the same as that prescribed for every Yom Tov.

A UNIQUE OFFERING

Although Shmini Atzeret is an independent festival, of equal status with each of the other festivals, its sacrificial offering when the Sanctuary stood differed from those of the other festivals (Pesach, Shavuot and Sukot). During the seven days of the festival of Sukot which preceded it, the number of sacrifices exceeded those of all the other festivals. On the other hand, there is no other festival besides Shmini Atzeret on which the *musaf* offering consisted of only one ox.

Why?

The Sages have said in the Midrash (Bamidbar Raba 21):

'The matter may be compared to a king who held a festival for seven days and invited all of the country's inhabitants to the seven days of feasting. When the seven days of feasting were over, he said to his friend: we have already given all the inhabitants of the country their due. Let us now relax together, you and I, with whatever can be found — a *litra* of meat, fish, or vegetable. Thus did God say to Israel: 'On the eighth day it shall be an atzeret unto you.' Relax with whatever you find — with one ox and one ram.'

Indeed, the sacrifice of Shmini Atzeret is not like those of the other three pilgrim festivals, but it is like the musaf sacrifice of Rosh Hashanah and Yom Kipur which also consisted of one ox, one ram and seven sheep.

This is an allusion to the teaching of the Sages that Shmini Atzeret also comprises the theme of atonement and that it is the 'final sealing' for the days of the year — as mentioned above.

THE PRAYER FOR RAIN

'During the Festival (Sukot) there is judgment over water.' It would have been proper therefore to mention rain during the prayers on the first day of the festival, just as we pray for dew on the first day of Pesach (since the crops need dew and during Pesach there is judgment over the produce of the land). Nevertheless we do not explicitly pray for rain before Shmini Atzeret. During all the days of Sukot it is as if we were hinting to God that He should give us rain in the proper times, through the symbolism of the four species which grow near water, the water-libation on the altar, the circling of the altar with the aravah which grows near a river. During prayer, however, we do not explicitly mention rain.

The Sages have given the following reason: The dew for which we pray on Pesach, is always a mark of blessing for the world, and we therefore pray that the dew may fall even during the festival. With reference to rain, however. we pray that they might fall in their proper time and not during the days of Sukot. For the fall of rain during the festival — is the mark of a curse, since it prevents the fulfilment of the mitzvah of sukah. And it is as if the people of Israel were shown from above that their mitzvah is not acceptable before God... And thus did the Rabis say in the Mishnah (Tr. Sukah 28):

'The matter was likened to a servant who came to pour a cup for his master — and the master poured a pitcher over his face.'

For this reason rain is not mentioned in the prayers till

Shmini Atzeret. When the people of Israel have left their Sukot and reentered their homes, and they come to their Synagogues the next morning to pray, they address a prayer to God, that He might open the treasure of His heavens in order to fructify the earth and to bless its produce.

And although the prayer for rain is included in the prayers on Shmini Atzeret, nevertheless, we still do not ask for immediate rainfall but we merely mention rain by way of praise to God. Nor do we directly ask for rain in any of our prayers till the seventh of Cheshvan (the next month), so that there might be time for the pilgrims who had gone up to Yerushalayim for the festivals to return home before the rains would fall heavily.

GEVUROT GESHAMIM (The Power of Rain)

To the second of the eighteen benedictions (in the *amidah* prayer which is said thrice daily) the Rabis added a formula of praise to God for His gift of rain. That benediction contains the theme of the resurrection of the dead. It is called *Gevurot*, since it recounts the power of God in His world. He 'sustains life, revives the dead, supports the falling, heals the sick, frees the bound and keeps His faithfulness to those who sleep in the dust.' Rains are among those powers of God which all the world's creatures constantly see. At the head of all the above mentioned Divine powers, the Sages placed the reference to God's gift of rain: 'He causes the wind to blow and the rain to fall' — as if to indicate thereby that the power of rain is still greater than His other powers. For through rain the earth's produce grows and life comes to the world. The rains vivify the plants. If trees become parched and they are about to die, the rains come, and new life enters them. The falling are sustained and the sick are healed. Further, rain is like the revival of the dead — for the seeds are buried in the ground and through the rains they sprout and rise.

MASHIV HARUACH UMORID HAGESHEM
(He Causes the Wind to Blow and the Rain to Fall)

During 'musaf' of Shmini Atzeret we begin to say, 'mashiv haruach umorid hageshem.' Where it is customary to say 'tefilat geshem' during the cantor's repetition of musaf, custom varies: If an announcement was made before the silent musaf, 'mashiv haruach' is said by the congregation in the silent prayer. Otherwise, the congregation begins to say 'mashiv haruach' in the afternoon 'minchah' service.

A sick person who prays alone at home, or villagers who have no 'minyan' (a gathering of at least ten adult men for congregational prayer) wait with their musaf prayers till the time when they are certain that the city congregation has already prayed musaf, and then they include 'mashiv haruach' in their own individual musaf prayers.

The Sephardi custom is to say a particular 'piyut' whose theme is a prayer for rain, after the Torah-Reading, and before musaf. After the 'piyut' the Sephardim include 'mashiv haruach' in their prayers regularly.

'Mashiv haruach' is included in every service till musaf on the first day of the following Pesach inclusive — till the cantor pronounces 'morid hatal' (He causes the dew to fall). If one forgets to say 'mashiv haruach' in its proper place, but remembers before the conclusion of the benediction (Blessed are You, O Lord Who revives the dead), he says 'mashiv haruach' and concludes the blessing. If he remembers after having concluded the brachah but before he began the next benediction ('Ata Kadosh' — You are holy) — he says 'mashiv haruach' and does not have to begin anew. If he

remembers after having begun 'Ata Kadosh' he is required to begin the prayer anew.

If one concludes his prayer and does not remember whether he said 'mashiv haruach' or not, he abides by the following principle: if more than thirty days have passed from Shmini Atzeret, the presumption is that he did say 'mashiv haruach.' If less than thirty days, the presumption is that he did not say it.

If one erred and said 'morid hatal' either during 'ma'ariv' 'shacharit' or the silent 'musaf' of the first day of Pesach he does not have to repeat his prayer, despite the fact that 'mashiv haruach' is still said during those three services — since 'tal' is mentioned on the same day in the cantor's repetition of 'musaf' and during 'minchah.'

Those who follow the custom of saying either 'morid hatal' or 'mashiv haruach umorid hatal,' throughout the summer do not have to repeat their entire prayers if they erred and said 'mashiv haruach umorid hatal' during the winter.

SIMCHAT TORAH

Simchat Torah and *Shmini Atzeret* are one day, except that in the Diaspora, where all the festivals are observed for two days, the first day is reserved for the joy of the festival and the prayer for rain (and some make *hakafot* during the night of Shmini Atzeret as a prelude to Simchat Torah) — while the second day is essentially reserved for rejoicing over the conclusion of the Torah. In the Land of Israel, however, where there is no second festival day, and all the festivals consist of only one day — the order of Simchat Torah is performed entirely on the day of Shmini Atzeret, together with all else that relates to the day.

Shmini Atzeret is to the Festival of Sukot, as the Festival of Shavuot (which is also called *atzeret*) is to the Festival of Pesach.

On Pesach Israel achieved freedom: They saw God's wonders and the awesome penalties He inflicted upon the Egyptians and they believed in Him and in His servant Moshe. Afterwards, they waited fifty days till the fear of Heaven grew firm in their hearts — and they entered into the covenant of the Torah with God — with thunder and lightning — so that fear of God might always be upon them.

During the Festival of Sukot the people of Israel achieve freedom of the soul from the evil inclination. After having emerged pure and cleansed from their sins through Yom Kipur, they cleave to God and come under the wings of His faithfulness through the mitzvah of sukah. As joy in God and love for Him are awakened in them through the mitzvah of sukah they extend that love to the Torah; and they strike a covenant of love and joy with the Torah which will not depart from them for the duration of the year, whenever they study Torah. This covenant which they now make with the Torah is not made with thunder and lightning, nor with fear and trembling, but with joy, song, and dancing.

The people of Israel have therefore adopted the custom of observing *Simchat Torah* (the joy of the Torah) on Shmini Atzeret — which follows the Festival of Sukot. And this *atzeret* corresponds to the other *atzeret*. Just as the first *atzeret* comprises the covenant of the Torah, so does this *atzeret* comprise the covenant of the Torah: except that the first one comes through the freedom of the body and through awe and fear, while this one comes through freedom of soul, and joy and love. Fear of God is not perfect unless it be accompanied by love. And love of God is not perfect unless it be accompanied also by fear. Where both are found they complement each other. As it is written in Tehilim: 'and you shall rejoice in trembling' — where there is joy, there should also be trembling.

'It would have been proper for this *atzeret* to come fifty days after the festival, just as the *atzeret* of Pesach comes fifty days after Pesach. God however said: 'It is winter, and they will be unable to leave their homes to come here; rather, while they are yet with Me — let them observe *atzeret*' (Tanchuma Pinchas 15).

Nevertheless, they sustain no loss because of this nearness between the atzeret and Sukot. Were the first atzeret to have been made adjacent to Pesach, the covenant might not have succeeded, for fear of God was not yet firmly established in their hearts. During Sukot however — since the covenant which they now strike with the Torah is one of love, and it comes after their repentance during the days of awe — it does become firmly established in their hearts. For the strength of the repentant is greater than of the righteous. And what the righteous achieve in seven weeks, those who repent can achieve in seven days. And during the Festival of Sukot — all Israel have the status of having repented.

SIYUM HATORAH (The Conclusion of the Torah)

Moshe enacted that the people of Israel should read the Torah every Shabat. And the Sages of the generations who followed Moshe Rabenu prescribed which portions were to be read each Shabat, when to begin the Torah and when to conclude it. The prevalent custom among all Israel, is to conclude the Torah in one year, and to divide its *parshiyot* into fifty-four portions *(sedarim)*, corresponding to the number of Sabbaths in an intercalated year. In a regular year, which contains either fifty or fifty one Sabbaths, two weekly portions are combined and read as one on several Sabbaths. Since, even during an intercalated year several Sabbaths fall during the Festivals — in which case the Festival Torah-Readings take the place of the regular weekly portions — those portions are also combined with other portions during several other Sabbaths.

The Sidra Bereishit is read on the first Sabbath after the Festival, and the Torah is concluded, in the Land of

Israel — on Shmini Atzeret, and in the Diaspora — on the second Festival day which is called Simchat Torah. A sumptuous feast is held; there is rejoicing, dancing, song and praise in honor of the Torah. It is written of King Shlomoh (First Melachim 3): 'And Shlomoh awoke and behold it was a dream (the Holy Spirit had rested upon him), and he came to Yerushalayim, and he stood before the ark of the covenant of the Lord and he brought up whole-offerings, and he made peace-offerings, and he made a feast for all his servants.' The Sages commented (Midrash Kohelet 1): 'from here we learn that a feast is held and there is rejoicing when the Torah is concluded.'

NOTHING REMAINS EXCEPT THIS TORAH

The later Sages have expounded various insights relating to Simchat Torah and Shmini Atzeret:

During the seven festival days the people of Israel rejoiced with the festival commandments; sukah, the four species, the water-libation, the aravah with which the altar was circled. Upon the advent of Shmini Atzeret the people of Israel say before God: Today we have neither sukah, nor lulav, nor the water-libation, nor the aravah — we have left only this Torah with which we rejoice.

And this joy is greater than all other joys, for it is constant, and it never ceases or is diminished in the least. Though the Sanctuary was destroyed and Yerushalayim was destroyed; though Israel was enslaved among the nations, this rejoicing over the Torah never ceased from them or became diminshed. And thus did the Sages say (Tractate Brachot 8): 'Since the day when the Sanctuary was destroyed, God has only the four *ells* of the *halachah* (the place where Torah is studied). The Destruction affected everything in the world except the Torah and the four *ells* of the *halachah.* The joy aroused by them remains perfect and whole as it was before the Destruction; therefore the

Divine Presence continues to dwell upon the Torah, and it rejoices together with the people of Israel on Simchat Torah.

BEYOND TIME

In referring to Sukot the Torah uses the term, *year*: 'And the festival of ingathering — the season of the *year*' (Shmot 34), 'and you shall celebrate it as a festival to the Lord — seven days in the *year*.' The Torah did not however, mention 'year' in referring to the other festivals. We are taught thereby: all that is under the rule of time moves in seven day cycles, like the seven days of creation. Every additional, new week is no more than a repetition of the week that has already passed. There is one week however, which comprises all the other weeks within itself — the seven days of the festival. The entire flow of blessing which is found throughout the whole year — all comes from these seven days, and draws sustenance from them. For this reason it is written of this festival: 'seven days in the year,' and, 'the season of the *year*.'

The number 'eight' however, symbolizes what is beyond time. And if it were asked: what is it that stands above time, and its time should therefore correspond to the symbolism of 'eight'? — the answer would be — the Torah is above time. Let Israel — who are also above time — come and rejoice with the Torah which is beyond time, on a day which is above time. For this reason it is said: on the eighth day it shall be an atzeret to you.

BETWEEN ME AND YOU

It has been mentioned before in the name of the Sages concerning the one ox, which is brought as an offering on Shmini Atzeret, that God regarded it as an intimate light meal between Him and His beloved people of Israel alone. This 'light meal' is an allusion to the Torah of which it is written: 'Moshe commanded us the Torah — *morashah* (an inheritance) for the congregation of Ya'akov' — do not read *morashah* (inheritance) but rather *me'orasa* (betrothed).' For the Torah is betrothed to Israel as a wife to her husband and they rejoice with her as a groom rejoices with his bride. No other nation has any portion in the Torah. They have already taken their portion in the form of the dew of the heavens and the fat of the land — in return for the sacrifices offered by Israel in their behalf during the seven festival days... Now the people of Israel enter within to rejoice with the joy of the Torah which is hidden within the treasure house of God.

SIMCHAT TORAH CUSTOMS

After 'ma'ariv' all the Torah scrolls are taken out of the ark. Seven 'hakafot' (encirclings) are made with them around the 'bimah' (synagogue pulpit), and all the people dance before the Torah scrolls with intense joy. They pray that God may remember unto us the merit of the Seven Loyal Shepherds and that our prayers may pierce all the heavens to rise before the Throne of Glory. The same is done the following morning after Shacharit. And in many Sephardi communities it is customary to hold 'hakafot' also during minchah and ma'ariv at the departure of the festival.

Some have the custom of placing a lighted candle in the Ark after the Torah scrolls are removed, so that the Ark might not completely lack light; and so that the light of the candle might symbolize the light of the Torah which is constantly found there. In many Jewish communities, it is customary to read the Torah on the night of Simchat Torah which is not done on any other night. Customs vary with reference to the portion read, and each community follows its own tradition.

The Torah-Reading of shacharit consists of the last Sidra in the Torah, 'vezot habrachah.' Since everybody is called to the Torah on this day, the portion is repeated many times so that it might suffice for the entire congregation. The Reading concludes with the calling of three persons to the Torah for 'aliyot' which are unique to Simchat Torah. One goes up to the Torah for 'kol hane'arim' ('all the children'), which is one reading before the conclusion of the Torah. An adult (over Bar-Mitzvah) recites the blessings over the Torah, with all the boys under Bar-Mitzvah in the Synagogue standing by his side, and a covering stretched over their heads. They recite the blessings word by word, in unison with the adult called. After the concluding blessing, all the adults say together: 'hamalach hago'el...'

For the last 'aliyah,' the Rabbi or the most distinguished person in the Synagogue is called. The person called to this concluding portion of the Torah is called, 'Chatan Torah' (the groom of the Torah), as if the Torah were betrothed to him and he were its groom. The entire congregation proclaims aloud in response to him: 'Be strong, be strong, and let us strengthen ourselves.' After him the 'Chatan Bereishit' (the groom of the beginning of the Torah) is called to a Reading in another scroll, which consists of the first passage in the Torah, from the beginning till, 'which God created and made.' After him the 'maftir' is called, and it is customary to call him also the 'Chatan Maftir.' His portion is read from Pinchas in a third Torah scroll, and it recounts the special sacrifice for the day.

It is customary for the 'Chatan Torah' to invite the entire congregation to a feast on Simchat Torah.

A TORAH WHICH IS ALWAYS NEW

Why do we begin with Bereishit on Simchat Torah ? The Sages have said (Sifri Va'etchanan): In order to show that 'the Torah is beloved to us like a new object and not like an old command which a person does not submit to. It is like a new one towards which everyone runs.'

It is also written in the name of the Midrash: 'When Israel concludes the Torah the Accuser comes before God to contend against them, and he says: 'The people of Israel study the Torah but they do not conclude it.' When they do conclude it God says to him: 'Have they not concluded it?' And he answers: 'though they have concluded it, they do not begin it anew.' And when they again begin it with 'Bereishit' God answers him, have they not begun it anew?' As a result he is unable to contend against them.'

ISRU CHAG (Bind the Festival!)

The day after each of the three Pilgrim festivals, Pesach, Shavuot and Sukot, is called *isru chag* ('bind the festival!') As it is written (Tehilim 118): 'Bind the festival (offering) with thick (cords) to the horns of the altar.' The Sages have expounded this verse as follows:

'Bind the festival' — bind an additional day to the festival — add a day to the festival.

'With thick (cords)' — with fattened cattle for a feast.

'To the horns of the altar' — The virtue of doing so is as lofty as the virtue of the offerings that are sacrificed on the altar. And it was therefore said (Tr. Sukah 45): Whoever extends the festival another day for eating and drinking, Scripture accounts it to him, as if he had built an altar and sacrificed an offering on it.'

It is therefore customary to hold a partially festive meal on *isru chag*, and to invest it with something of a Yom Tov character. Eulogies and fasting are avoided, and *tachanun* is not said. If it falls on Shabat, *tzidkat'cha tzedek* is not said during minchah.

When the Temple still stood, and many Jews brought whole-offerings and peace-offerings as individual sacrifices, these individual offerings were sacrificed on *isru chag*: The reason being, according to some — that there was not enough time on Yom Tov for all the individual sacrifices; and according to others, because it is forbidden to sacrifice individual offerings on Yom Tov. For whichever reason, most of the individual offerings were brought on isru chag, and especially so on isru chag Shavuot which lacks a Chol Hamo'ed period when some of the offering could have been brought. The day was therefore invested with a Yom Tov atmosphere, but not with regard to the prohibition of labor.

Whoever acts joyously on isru chag is rewarded for fulfilling the words of the Sages. Further, he bears witness that the festival prescribed by the Torah is beloved to him, and that he finds it difficult to part from it all at once. And this is the way of the holy people of Israel, that they love the mitzvot, they eagerly await their arrival and are loathe to part from them.

BIRKAT HACHODESH (The Blessing of the New Month)

On the Shabat which precedes *Rosh Chodesh* (New Moon), a blessing is recited over the new month, and the day on which it falls is announced in the synagogue between the Torah-Reading and *musaf*: 'Rosh Chodesh such-and-such will fall on such-and-such a day.' This announcement together with the prayers which precede and follow it, are called *birkat hachodesh*. And the Shabat on which the new month is announced is called, *Shabat mevarchim* (The Sabbath-on-which-the- blessing-is-said).

The reason for saying this blessing on the Shabbat is that then all Israel are assembled in the synagogue, among them many who do not habitually attend during the week-days. They are all informed on which day of the forthcoming week Rosh Chodesh will fall, so that they might know the proper order of prayer in accord with the laws of Rosh Chodesh, and so that the women refrain from those activities which they customarily avoid on Rosh Chodesh.

Further, this public blessing also serves as a memorial to

the public act of sanctifying the new month which was performed monthly by the *Sanhedrin* (the High Court in Jerusalem).

This sanctification was of dramatic character and was accompanied by blessing and praise. The elders of the *Sanhedrin* and the most prominent men of Yerushalayim were seated, and awaited the witnesses who had seen the new moon. If witnesses came — they were examined, and if their testimony met the requirements — the *Beit Din* declared: 'The new month is sanctified — it is sanctified!' They then recited three blessings over a cup of wine. The first, over the wine itself, the second in thanksgiving for God's revelation to Israel of the principles on which our calendar is based; the third in prayer for the coming of Eliyahu, the appearance of the Messiah and the rebuilding of the Temple... (Tractate Sofrim 19).

Since the mitzvah of *kidush hachodesh* (the sanctification of the new month), was the first mitzvah given to Israel upon its first redemption from Egypt; and since the time of all the festivals and all that relates to them, is dependent on this mitzvah — the *Sanhedrin* performed the mitzvah in a spirit of thanksgiving and blessing.

Now that we have no Sanhedrin to sanctify the new months and to intercalate years, our blessing over the new month on the Sabbath which precedes it, serves as a memorial to the sanctification of the month.

The blessing over the new month is said only eleven times during the year, and in an intercalated year, twelve times; it is not however said at the advent of the month of Tishrey, as explained above.

In the prayer (*yehi ratzon*), which is said in Ashkenazi communities before the announcement of the day on which Rosh Chodesh will fall, there are eleven expressions of prayer which correspond to each of the eleven months when *birkat hachodesh* is said. As for the month of Tishrey it does not require inclusion in this prayer since the very essence of Tishrey — is the prayer for life. (And in an intercalated year — Adar II is included in the blessing for Adar I.).

It is proper to know the *molad* (the exact hour and minute of the appearance of the moon) when the blessing over the new month is said.

Just as the mitzvah of *kidush hachodesh* was performed standing, the blessing over the new month is also said standing.

After the announcement concerning the day of Rosh Chodesh, a prayer is said which implores Divine redemption for Israel, equally as our forefathers were redeemed miraculously from Egyptian bondage. The reason for this reference to our original redemption is that this mitzvah was originally given at the time of our redemption from Egypt. We therefore pray that we might again be able to perform it in a state of redemption and the ingathering of our exiled from the four corners of the earth.

On 'Shabat mevarchim' the souls of the deceased are not recalled, and 'av harachamim' is not said — since this Shabat is marked by additional joy. However, on Shabat mevarchim which falls during the 'sefirah' days, it should be said as well as on Shabat mevarchim of the month of Av — because of the spirit of mourning which prevails then. Those who abide by the customs of the Gaon of Vilna never say av harachamim on Shabat mevarchim with the exception of Shabat mevarchim of the month of Av.

The first 'Shabat mevarchim' of the year is: Shabat Bereishit,' on which the forthcoming month of Cheshvan is blessed.

SHABAT BEREISHIT (The Sabbath on which Bereishit Is Read)

The first Sabbath after the festival is called *Shabat Bereishit,* after its Torah-Reading, which consists of the first Sidra in the Torah — Bereishit.

After minchah of Shabat Bereishit it is the Ashkenazi custom to begin to say the Psalm, *barchi nafshi* (My soul, bless the Lord), and the fifteen 'Songs of ascent' in Tehilim. These Psalms are recited all the winter Sabbaths till Shabat Hagadol before Pesasch — on which the Ashkenazim read part of the Pesach Hagadah in the place of *barchi nafshi.*

The reason for the saying of *barchi nafshi* beginning with Shabat Bereishit is, that this entire Psalm treats of the theme of creation, the power of the Creator, and the wonders of Creation. Likewise, the fifteen 'Songs of ascent' that are said following *barchi nafshi,* also contain the same theme (Tractate Sukah 53).

It would have been proper to say these Psalms on all the Sabbaths of the year, for the Sabbath is a memorial to the works of creation, except that during the summer months, they are replaced by *pirkey avot* (The Ethics of the Fathers).

Rosh Chodesh

ROSH CHODESH ◆ A LAW UNTO MOSHE FROM SINAI ◆ THE FIRST SANCTIFICATION ◆ 'THIS MONTH SHALL BE UNTO YOU' ◆ WORK ON ROSH CHODESH ◆ ROSH CHODESH OBSERVANCE ◆ THE TORAH-READING AND MUSAF ◆ A BRIEF SUMMARY OF OUR MOLAD CALCULATION ◆ THE NINETEEN YEAR CYCLE ◆ TWO DAYS OF ROSH CHODESH ◆ FULL MONTHS AND INCOMPLETE ONES ◆ ROSH CHODESH AND THE PEOPLE OF ISRAEL.

CHAPTER FIVE

ROSH CHODESH

The day on which the new moon appears, or the following day is designated as *Rosh Chodesh* (new moon). At times Rosh Chodesh consists of one day; and at times of two. Rosh Chodesh of: Shevat, Nisan, Sivan, Av — always consist of only one day. Rosh Chodesh of: Cheshvan, Adar, Iyar, Tamuz, Elul — always consist of two days. In an intercalated year Rosh Chodesh Adar II also consists of two days. Rosh Chodesh of: Kislev and Tevet — at times both consist of two days; at times they both consist of one day; and at times one consists of one day, and the other of two. And Rosh Chodesh of Tishrey coincides with Rosh Hashanah.

The fixing of the new months does not merely depend on the calculation of the *molad* (the appearance of the new moon); and not everyone who knows these calendar calculations may fix the new months and the festivals. For this involves a mitzvah and only those authorized to perform this mitzvah in accord with the *halachah*, may do so.

Rosh Chodesh may be fixed only by a *Beit Din* (court) of *semuchim* (ordained Rabbis), and the members of a *Beit Din* are called *semuchim* only if their *semichah* (ordination) extends from master to disciple in uninterrupted succession from Moshe Rabenu. Only such a Beit Din may fix the new month upon the testimony of witnesses that they saw the new moon.

Afterwards, the Beit Din proclaimed the sanctification of the new month and uttered blessing to God. Special additional-offerings were brought, and the Levites sang. Nowadays, we recite *musaf*, and add *ya'aleh ve'yavo* to each

Rosh Chodesh service in place of the sacrifice. We say Halel, and abide by the prescribed observances and customs which mark the special sanctity of Rosh Chodesh over other days.

Nowadays, we possess no *Sanhedrin* (ordained high court), and there are no *semuchim*, and we do not sanctify the new months through the testimony of witnesses. We offer no Rosh Chodesh sacrifice and the song of the Levites has ceased. Nevertheless, the sanctity of Rosh Chodesh endures just the same as when the Temple stood, since an ancient Beit Din of *semuchim* has already sanctified every Rosh Chodesh till the coming of the Messiah, at which time *semichah* will be renewed, a Sanhedrin will again be appointed, and the new months will again be sanctified through testimony.

When Hillel, the Nasi (prince), the grandson of Rabi Yehudah the Nasi, who compiled the Mishnah, saw the ever more frequent and intense persecutions to which the gentile governments subjected Israel; and when he saw that the number of disciples worthy of *semichah* was diminishing more and more, he feared lest the government prohibit any further sanctification of the months, and put to death the few remaining semuchim — which would utterly confuse the determining of the festival dates. He and his Beit Din — all of them ordained in an unbroken chain from Moshe at Sinai — arose and adopted a standard system for calculating the new months and festivals till the time of our final redemption. They sanctified in advance all the new months to be observed in accord with their calculation, and the sanctity of Rosh Chodesh therefore adheres to every Rosh Chodesh, when it arrives in accord with our calendar. The sanctity of Rosh Chodesh thus never ceased from the people of Israel, from the days of Moshe Rabenu till today.

A LAW UNTO MOSHE FROM SINAI

The calendar calculation compiled by Hillel for all the generations did not originate with Hillel. For, since the day when the Torah was given to Israel from Sinai, even a prophet is not authorized to originate any further additions to it. This calculation had been transmitted to the Sages in an unbroken chain from Moshe. They knew the precise moment of the molad of each new moon even without witnesses. They followed, however, the procedure prescribed by the mitzvah of the Torah — which required that the new moon be sanctified upon the testimony of witnesses.

When witnesses came to Beit Din and testified that they had seen the new mon at such-and-such an hour, from such-and-such a place, on such-and-such a side, at such-and-such a width, and at such-and-such a height — the Beit Din knew perfectly well whether their words were correct; and if not, whether the witnesses had ground for making the error which they did.

It is not within the power of Man, or within the bounds of human knowledge, to know the movement of the constellations so precisely as to be able to calculate those movements within a tiny fraction of even a single second. There never were instruments capable of measuring the movement of the constellations unto a hairbreadth. The astronomers among the nations knew only how to measure time in accord with the movement of the constellations, through the observation and experimentation of generations. At first they adopted one hypothesis; with the passage of time, when they saw that their hypothesis was not tenable, they refined their calculations and adopted a more precise hypothesis than the first. They never however, arrived at an utterly final measurement.

If Moshe Rabenu had been an astronomer, and had based his calendar calculation on the science of astronomy alone, it would have been impossible for him to avoid some minute error. If he had erred, Heaven forbid, even to the extent of a fraction of a second, the differences would have added up in the course of the 3270 years which have elapsed from the days of Moshe till our time — which comprise approximately 40,500 lunar months — to a difference of many hours, and by now, all would have been able to observe the magnitude of the error.

Indeed, human knowledge is incapable of the utterly precise measurement of the limitless expanses of the universe.

These calculations however were given from the Creator of all the worlds to Moshe, who transmitted them to Yehoshua, through whom they were transmitted in turn, to the Elders, the Prophets, the Men of the Great Synod, and the Sages of succeeding generations till Hillel II, the last Nasi of Israel of the House of David. As long as the new month was sanctified through evidence, the Sages of the generations kept those calculations private, so that the mitzvah of sanctifying the new month might be performed as prescribed; and when witnesses came — they examined the witnesses to see if their testimony coincided with the traditional calculations. When Hillel saw that it was no longer possible to sanctify the new months through evidence, he revealed the calendar calculations which had been transmitted from Moshe Rabenu through all the generations.

THE FIRST SANCTIFICATION

Since the sanctity of Rosh Chodesh is the foundation for all the festivals which distinguish the sanctity of Israel from the life of any other people, the mitzvah of sanctifying the new month was given before any of the other mitzvot.

The people of Israel were still in Egypt, and no mitzvah had as yet been addressed to them. Nevertheless, they were already given the mitzvah of 'Chodesh:' 'And the Lord said to Moshe and to Aharon in the land of Egypt saying: 'This month shall be to you the first of months, it shall be first to you of the months of the year' (Shmot 12).

'And the Lord said to Moshe and to Aharon' — Why did God speak to both Moshe and to Aharon? Since the sanctification of the new month — requires three. When God wanted to sanctify the new month, he said to Moshe and to Aharon: I and you shall sanctify the new month (Shmot Raba 15).

'*This* new month — Moshe was in doubt concerning the molad of the moon, as to its required size, for sanctifying the new month. God showed him with a finger as it were, the moon in the firmanent and said to him: when you see the likes of this, you shall sanctify...' (Rashi Shmot 12).

'This *new month*' — God showed him the moon in its renewal, and said to him: 'When the moon is renewed — it shall be to you a new month' (Rashi ibid.).

'Unto you' — God said to Israel: In the past, it was in My hands... now within your domain' (Shmot Raba 15).

'The ministering angels gather before God, and say to Him: Lord of the Universe, when is Rosh Hashanah ? And He answers: Do you then ask Me ? Let us both ask the Beit Din below' (Yalkut Bo 191).

'If the Beit Din below decreed and said: 'Today is Rosh Hashanah' — God says to the angels: erect a platform, designate Defenders, and let the Accusers rise, for the Beit Din below has decreed that today is Rosh Hashanah! If the witnesses did not come on time, or Beit Din took counsel and decided to regard the next day as Rosh Hashanah — God said to the angels: remove the platform, and let the Defenders and Accusers leave, for the Beit Din below have decreed that Rosh Hashanah shall be tomorrow' (Ibid. 190).

You may say then: the sanctification of the new month was the first sanctity given to Israel, while they were yet in Egypt, and through it they were sanctified for all generations. Even when they dwell in Exile, this sanctity never leaves them. And even if the evil among the nations issue harsh decrees against them and seek to annul this sanctity, they yet guard it with their very lives.

THE MONTH SHALL BE UNTO YOU

'Before God took Israel out of Egypt He hinted to them that their kingdom would not set for thirty generations...

The month consists of thirty days, and their kingdom would endure for thirty generations. On the first of the month the moon begins to shed light, and its light grows till the fifteenth to the thirtieth of the month, its light diminishes, till it is no longer seen on the thirtieth. Likewise Israel: Fifteen generations passed from Avraham till Shlomo... When Shlomo came, the disc of the moon was full. From then, the kings continuously diminished for another fifteen generations... When Tzidkiyahu came... the light of the moon was completely lacking' (Shmot Raba 15).

'For this reason it is said, *This month shall be unto you* — that it might be yours, for you correspond to it' (Ibid.).

The capacity for repeated renewal is unique to Israel. For this reason, the lunar month, which symbolizes constant renewal, was made the basis of Israel's calendar.

The nations of the world count by the sun, which has no regular pattern of renewal. The people of Israel, however count by the moon — which is diminished, and enlarged, again and again — but which is always renewed. The lunar month is a sign to Israel. Though their light may be dim in comparison to the light of the sun; though their light may at times seem completely lacking — nevertheless, they have the perpetual capacity for renewal.

This capacity is the secret of Israel's endurance and eternity. All the nations of the world rise on the rungs of the ladder of history till they reach a given height; having reached that height, they fall, and do not rise again — till they vanish completely.

Israel is different however;

Fifteen generations — from Avraham to Shlomo — rose: Fifteen generations — from Rechabe'am till Tzidkiyahu descended, till they reached the lowest rung. Israel's enemies tumultuously raised their heads and said: Let us destroy them as a people, and let not Israel's name be remembered. It seemed as if Israel's light had been completely extinguished.

But, behold! A new molad — like the molad of a new moon. Israel's light began to shine again. It shone again in exile; it shone again in its land; above all it was constantly renewed.

WORK ON ROSH CHODESH

Though there is no prohibition against work on Rosh Chodesh, it is similar to Yom Tov in various respects. When the Sanctuary stood, 'Additional-offering' (besides the regular daily ones), was brought only on the Sabbath, on Festivals and on Rosh Chodesh. The 'Additional-offering' of Rosh Chodesh corresponded to those of the Sabbath and festivals. As it is written in the Torah (Bamidbar 10) : 'And on the day of your rejoicing, and on your appointed-seasons, and on your Rosh Chodesh days...'

At one time it was customary not to work on Rosh Chodesh. Thus we find Jonathan saying to David (First Shmuel 20): 'And you shall come to the place where you hid, on the work day.' 'The-work-day' is translated by Jonathan Ben Uziel as, 'on the week-day' — that is, on Erev Rosh Chodesh which is a weekday, and on which work is done. We learn by implication, that Rosh Chodesh was not a work day then. Likewise, the Men of the Great Synod prescribed that four persons be called to the Torah on Rosh Chodesh as on Chol Hamo'ed, since both were not work days; unlike ordinary Mondays and Thursdays, when only three persons are called to the Torah, so as not to interfere with work activity.

It was also customary to visit the Prophet on Rosh Chodesh, as on the Sabbath. We thus find a man saying to the Shunamite woman (Second Melachim 4) : 'Why do you go to him today it is not Chodesh or Shabat.' In the future too, Rosh Chodesh will be a day of pilgrimage to Jerusalem, as the Prophet says (Yeshayahu 66) : 'And it shall be, every Chodesh in its time, and every Shabat in its time, all flesh will come to bow down before Me, said the Lord.'

Some of the authorities hold that even nowadays heavy labor (such as most of the work done on the fields) is prohibited, and only light work is permitted. Most of the authorities differ, and they permit all work on Rosh Chodesh. It is nevertheless, a mitzvah to distinguish Rosh Chodesh from other days by one's meal, by dressing well, and the like.

Women observe Rosh Chodesh with greater stringency than men, and they do only such work as is necessary. They do not weave, stitch, embroider or sew on Rosh Chodesh.

The reason for this is as follows:

It is written in Pirkey d'Rabi Eliezer (Chapter 45):

'When the men came to remove their wives' gold earrings for the golden calf — the women refused to hand them over. They said to their husbands: We will not obey you in order to make an abomination which has no power to save! God rewarded them in this world, in giving them a greater degree of observance on Rosh Chodesh. And He rewards them in the world to come in giving them the power of constant renewal, which characterizes Rosh Chodesh.'

ROSH CHODESH OBSERVANCE

It is a mitzvah to feast more sumptuously on Rosh Chodesh, since Halel is said on Rosh Chodesh, and in Halel it is written: 'This is the day which God has made, let us rejoice and be happy on it.' In many Sephardi communities it is customary to light a candle on the night of Rosh Chodesh.

Whoever spends more for a Rosh Chodesh meal is repaid from Heaven. As it is said in the Pesikta (quoted by the Tur, Hilchot Rosh Chodesh): 'A person's sustenance is fixed from Rosh Hashanah to Rosh Hashanah, with the exception of what one spends for the Sabbath, the Festivals, Rosh Chodesh and Chol Hamo'ed, as well as for tuition for children. If one spends more, he is given more; if he spends less, he is given less.' It is therefore customary to add one dish to one's regular meal in honor of Rosh Chodesh whether it falls on weekdays or Shabat.

Fasting is prohibited, with the exception of a groom, who fasts on Rosh Chodesh Nisan (some hold — also on Rosh Chodesh Elul). Eulogies for the dead are not delivered.

'Half-Halel' is said on Rosh Chodesh, since Rosh Chodesh does not have the full status of Yom Tov.

Halel is said standing.

'Ya'ale ve'yavo' is said in the Grace after meals as well as in all the prayers (with the exception of 'musaf').

One who forgets to say 'Ya'ale ve'yavo' in the Grace after meals, but has not yet begun its fourth benediction, says: 'Blessed are You, O Lord, King of the Universe, Who bequeathed Rosh Chodesh days to His people Israel for a memorial.' If however, he has already begun the fourth benediction, he concludes the Grace as usual, since the Rosh Chodesh meal is not obligatory.

If he forgets to say ya'ale ve'yavo during 'ma'ariv,' he does not have to repeat his prayer, since the Beit Din only sanctified the new month during the day.

If he forgets to say ya'ale ve'yavo during 'shacharit' or 'minchah,' but remembers before 'modim,' he says 'ya'ale ve'yavo' immediately. If he remembers after beginning 'modim,' but before 'yiheyu leratzon' — he returns to 'retzeh.' If he remembers after 'yiheyu leratzon' — he repeats the entire 'amidah' prayer (of the eighteen benedictions).

It is written in the Levush: It is a mitzvah to change clothes for Rosh Chodesh.

It is customary not to cut one's hair on Rosh Chodesh.

THE TORAH-READING AND MUSAF

On 'shacharit' of a weekday Rosh Chodesh one Torah scroll is taken out of the ark, and the reading is taken from the prescribed part of Pinchas (in the book of bamidbar). Four persons are called to the Torah, but there is no 'maftir.'

When Rosh Chodesh falls on the Sabbath, two Torah scrolls are taken out: In one the portion of the week is read, and seven persons are called; in the second the 'maftir' is read from Pinchas. The 'haftarah' is taken from Yeshayahu ('Thus said the Lord, the Heaven is My throne') and it prophesies the pilgrimage to Jerusalem on Rosh Chodesh in the future.

When Rosh Chodesh Tevet — which falls during Chanukah — also falls on the Shabat, three Torah scrolls are taken out: in one the weekly portion is read, and six persons are called; in the second, the sixth person is called and the reading recounts the special sacrifice for the day, and is taken from Pinchas; and in the third, a passage relating to the dedication of the Altar is read as 'maftir'. The 'haftarah' which follows, relates likewise to the theme of Chanukah rather than to Rosh Chodesh.

After the Torah-reading there is a special musaf for Rosh Chodesh, as well as one for Rosh Chodesh which falls on the Shabat.

When Rosh Chodesh consists of two days, the status of both is equal in all respects, and the Torah-reading and musaf are the same for both.

A BRIEF SUMMARY OF OUR MOLAD CALCULATION

The two great luminaries placed by God in the firmament of the heaven on the fourth day of creation, are the foundation for the calculation of days, months and years. As it is written: 'And they shall be for signs, for seasons, for days and years' (Bereishit 1).

The sun is the foundation for the counting of years, since in addition to its daily rotation, it also has a yearly rotation — which is completed once in 365 days and 6 hours.

The moon is the foundation only for the counting of months. The time that passes from one appearance of a new moon till its reappearance, constitutes one month.

The sun has no months since it reveals no differences from month to month. Likewise, the moon has no years, since all of its *moladot* (appearances) are alike, and the time which elapses between one *molad* and the next is always equal.

The nations of the world fix their months and years by convention and mutual agreement:

The Christians count their years by the sun, and they divide the 365 days and 6 hours in the solar year, into 12 subdivisions, each of which they call a month. Whether the beginning of one of their months corresponds to the lunar molad or not — they always count 31 days, or 30 days, 28 days, and at times even 29 days, and they call it a month. We find therefore, that the Christian month is based on convention, rather than on reality.

The Mohammedans count by the moon, and their months are lunar months. They multiply 12 such months, and they call every 12 month period a year. Whether their first month occurs in the spring or in the summer or in the autumn, or in winter their New Year always comes after 12 lunar months. We find therefore, that the Mohammedan year is a year based on convention, but not on reality.

If the time beween one lunar molad and the next corresponded exactly to 1/12 of the 365 days and 6 hours of the solar year, the calculation of the solar and lunar years would be identical, but the matter is not so. For the lunar month is less than a twelfth part of a solar year.

As indicated above the solar year consists of 365 days and 6 hours. The lunar month however, consists of 29 days, 12 hours, 44 minutes, and 3 and 1/3 seconds. Multiply the lunar month by 12, and you have 354 days, 8 hours, 48 minutes and 40 seconds. Hence, 12 lunar months add up to a period of time which is less than the solar year by 10 days, 21 hours, 11 minutes and 20 seconds.

To summarize, in the solar calendar, the months do not correspond to the cyclical reappearance of the moon. And in the lunar calendar the years do not correspond to the movement of the sun; hence the four seasons do not correspond with their proper times.

When the Torah commanded the people of Israel to sanctify the months (Shmot 12), it also commanded: 'Observe the month of spring and you shall make a Passover unto the Lord your God' (Dvarim 16). That is to say, simultaneously with our fixing of the months in accord with the lunar molad, we are also commanded to make certain that the month of Nisan should always occur in the spring season of the solar month. How then can we reconcile these two requirements ? If we were to calculate our years on the basis of 12 lunar months, we would fall behind each solar year to the extent of somewhat less than 11 days. If we were to base our year on 13 lunar months, we would be ahead of each solar year, by some 22 days. In any event we would not be making certain that Nisan should always correspond to a spring month.

It was therefore commanded as a 'law unto Moshe from Sinai,' that we should intercalate years: That some of our years should be regular years — consisting of 12 months; and that our intercalated years should consist of 13 months. After several regular years pass, and the differential of days between them and the solar years adds up to approximately one month, we add another month before Nisan in order that Nisan might always fall in the spring, and that it might never fall at a greater distance from its proper time than 20 odd days.

THE NINETEEN YEAR CYCLE

For the sake of correspondence between the lunar months and the solar year, we fix nineteen year cycles, in each of which the number of regular years and of intercalated years is constant.

Every nineteen year cycle has twelve regular years and seven intercalated years.

The order of intercalated years in each cycle is as follows: The 3rd, 6th, 8th, 11th, 14th, 17th, and 19th years are always intercalated and each contains two Adars.

These seven intercalated years, which we add to each nineteen year cycle equalize the differential between the solar years and the lunar months — with the exception of a period of one hour, 26 minutes, 56 and 2/3 seconds, by which the solar years still exceed the lunar calendar.

In the year 2448 of creation — which was the year of the exodus from Egypt, the Festival of Pesach occurred in its precisely appointed time — in the proper season for Nisan. As it is written (Shmot 12): 'This day you are going out, in the month of spring.' 172 nineteen year cycles have already passed since then, and the remaining differentials within each cycle (1 hour, 26 minutes, 56 2/3 seconds) have added up to ten days, nine hours, three minutes, and six and 2/3 seconds — by which the lunar calculation falls behind the solar calculation. This differential does not however extract the month of Nisan from its proper time in the spring season. For the sum total of our calendar consists of 6,000 years, so that it will not be necessary to alter our system of intercalation till the end of all the generations who will live within our 6,000 year calendar.

TWO DAYS OF ROSH CHODESH

In the Torah only one Rosh Chodesh day is prescribed — the first day of the new month. However, ever since ancient days, from the days of the first Prophets it was customary at times to celebrate Rosh Chodesh for two days. Thus it is written (First Shmuel 20): 'And it was on the morrow of the second New Moon.'

When was Rosh Chodesh observed for one day, and when for two days ?

After 29 days of the preceding month had passed, and the night of the 30th day had arrived, it was already regarded as Rosh Chodesh, and was celebrated with feasting, rejoicing and the cessation of labor. And the Beit Din in Jerusalem (the Sanhedrin) waited the entire night and all of the following day, for witnesses to come and testify that they had seen the new moon.

(In the first hours of its appearance the new moon is not seen equally everywhere, and then only for a minute period of time. And whoever saw it in its proper time that is, on the thirtieth day, would run to testify before the Sanhedrin, lest no one else had seen it, beside himself and one other person.)

If the witnesses came on the 30th day, the special *musaf* (additional) sacrifice was offered the same day and the next day was a weekday. If witnesses did not come the same day, they no longer waited for witnesses, and sanctified the new month the next day automatically. It emerged therefore that two days were celebrated as Rosh Chodesh. In places that were distant from Jerusalem, to which Beit Din messengers did not arrive, in order to inform them which day was designated as Rosh Chodesh — Rosh Chodesh was observed for two days every month.

Nowadays, although we sanctify Rosh Chodesh by calculation, and we know in advance when the first day of the new month will fall — nevertheless we still observe the custom of our fathers and sometimes observe a two day Rosh Chodesh.

And this matter too, is constant for all the years, as to which months are to have two days of Rosh Chodesh, and which months only one. Though there are many reasons for the order we follow, nevertheless the consideration which applies mostly, is as follows: If the molad occurs on the thirtieth day, we celebrate it as Rosh Chodesh despite the fact that in our fixed calendar calculation, Rosh Chodesh of the following month is fixed for the next day — since, if the Sanhedrin were to sanctify the new month through the testimony of witnesses, the thirtieth day would be observed as Rosh Chodesh.

Therefore, the two days of Rosh Chodesh are not like the days of Yom Tov that are observed in Exile. In the case of the two Yom Tov days of the Diaspora, the first day is essential, and the second is observed only because of doubt; while in the case of the two days of Rosh Chodesh, the second day is essential and the first is observed only because of our fathers' doubt, when they sanctified the new month through testimony. For this reason, the first day of Rosh Chodesh is counted with the previous month, and we begin to count the days of the new month only with the second day of Rosh Chodesh. With reference to all the other observances of Rosh Chodesh, the two days are alike.

FULL MONTHS AND INCOMPLETE ONES

During most years, one 'incomplete' month follows one 'full' month regularly. Each 'full' month consists of 30 days, and the Rosh Chodesh which follows it, consists of two days. Each 'incomplete' month consists of 29 days, and the Rosh Chodesh which follows consists of one day.

Tishrey is 'full', Cheshvan is 'incomplete'; Kislev is 'full', Tevet is 'incomplete'; Shevat is 'full', Adar is 'incomplete', Nisan is 'full' and Iyar is 'incomplete'; Sivan is 'full', Tamuz is 'incomplete'; Av is 'full,' and Elul is 'incomplete.'

Every month which contains a festival is 'full.' Tishrey contains many festivals; Kislev contains Chanukah; Shevat contains Rosh Hashanah of the Trees; Nisan contains Pesach (which is also the Rosh Hashanah of the Pilgrimage Festivals); Sivan contains Shavuot; Av contains the Ninth of Av which is destined to become a Festival in the future. Adar is 'incomplete', even though it contains Purim, since it comes between Shevat and Nisan, both of which are 'full', and three months are not made 'full' except for some great need. Further, Purim is essentially a Festival of the Diaspora and a Festival whose essential observance is in the Land of Israel is regarded with greater distinction in this instance.

Why do we make the months alternately 'full' and 'incomplete ?' As mentioned above, a period of 29 days, 12 hours, 44 minutes and 3 1/3 seconds passes between one molad and the next. And since Rosh Chodesh is observed for a whole day, and not for part of a day, it is found that if we divide the months equally into 'full' and 'incomplete' months, we provide for the 12 hours which exceed the 29 days of each month.

Further, since in addition to these 12 hours, there is also a differential of minutes, in the course of a number of months the time to which those minutes add up, is provided for by occasionally making Cheshvan and Kislev 'full.' For this reason, as well as for others, these two months are at times made to correspond to their regular order; at times they are both 'full;' and at times they are both 'incomplete.'

In an intercalated year which has two Adars, Adar I is always 'full,' and Adar II is always 'incomplete'. Therefore, Rosh Chodesh Adar II always consists of two days, and Rosh Chodesh Nisan always consists of one day.

ROSH CHODESH AND THE PEOPLE OF ISRAEL

The nations of the world are compared to the sun, while Israel is compared to the moon. And though Israel is the weakest and the least of the nations, they are destined to rule the world, after the dominion of evil will pass.

And thus did the Sages say in the Midrash: 'It is proper that the great should count by the great, and the small should count by the small. Esau counts by the sun which is great — just as the sun rules by day, but not by night, so does Esav have a portion in this world, but not in the world to come. Ya'akov counts by the moon which is small — just as the moon rules by day and night, so does Israel have a portion in this world and in the world to come. As long as the greater light shines in the world, the smaller light is not seen. When the greater light sets, the smaller light attains prominence. Likewise, as long as Esav's light shines in the world, Ya'akov's light does not become prominent. When Esav's light sets, Ya'akov's light becomes prominent. Of this it is written (Yeshayahu 60) : 'Arise, shine, for your light has come and the Glory of the Lord has shone upon you for, behold, the darkness covers the earth' (Bereishit Raba Chapter 6, and Yalkut Bereishit).

Mar Cheshvan

ROSH CHODESH CHESHVAN ◆ CHESHVAN — MAR-CHESHVAN ◆ A LACK WHICH WILL BE RESTORED ◆ KIDUSH LEVANAH ◆ WELCOMING THE SHECHINAH ◆ THE BLESSING OVER THE MOON ◆ THE FAST OF BAHAB ◆ THE PETITION FOR RAIN ◆ GEVUROT GESHAMIM ◆ AN OPEN TREASURE ◆ FAITH LEADS TO FAITH ◆ THE DEATH OF OUR MOTHER RACHEL ◆ YOM KIPUR KATAN.

CHAPTER SIX

ROSH CODESH CHESHVAN

Rosh Chodesh Cheshvan always consists of two days, since it follows Tishrey, which is a 'full' month. The first day of Rosh Chodesh is counted as the thirtieth day of Tishrey, and the second day is counted as the first of Cheshvan.

Some authorities hold that the *musaf* prayer of Rosh Chodesh Cheshvan differs from musaf on any other Rosh Chodesh, in the respect that it may not be said by heart, but must be read from a *sidur* (a prayer book). The reason for this is the prohibition of the Sages: 'Words of the written Torah you may not say by heart.' Now, a portion from the written Torah which relates to the theme of the day, is included in every musaf prayer: whether it be Shabat, Rosh Chodesh, or Yom Tov. However, the musaf of Shabat and Rosh Chodesh of all the other months are said regularly and may therefore be known perfectly by heart — for which reason it is permissible to say them by heart. Whereas in the case of the musaf of Rosh Chodesh Cheshvan, which is said after an interruption of two months (since Rosh Chodesh is not mentioned on Rosh Hashanah) there is ground for concern lest the portion of the day is no longer known perfectly by heart, and hence it is forbidden to say so.

For the same reason the musaf of Yom Tov should also not be said by heart, since they are not said regularly as are the musaf prayers of the Shabat and Rosh Chodesh.

CHESHVAN — MAR-CHESHVAN

Cheshvan is the second month in the year, and the eighth after the count of the months from Nisan. In Scripture this month is called by the name, 'Bul' (First Melachim 6) : 'And in the eleventh year, in the month Bul, which is the 8th month, the House (the Sanctuary) was completed...' It is called 'Bul,' since during this month the grass withers *(baleh)* in the fields and feed is mixed *(bolelin)* for the animal in the house (Rashi). Others derive the etymology of 'Bul' from *yevul* (produce), for during this month plowing and planting begin in the land of Israel (Radak). Some derive 'Bul' from *mabul* (flood), for during this month rains are plentiful.

In the Midrash it is stated, that a plentitude of rain was decreed for this month, since it marked the beginning of the Flood.

The accepted name of the month, however, is 'Cheshvan,' which came up with the Returnees from the Babylonian Exile. It is also called 'Mar-cheshvan' for two reasons: During this month there are no festival days or rejoicing, but much travail and suffering befell Israel then. On the fifteenth of Cheshvan Yerovam contrived a new festival and aroused Divine wrath against Israel. On the fifth of the month, the Chaldeans slaughtered the sons of King Tzidkiyahu in his presence, and blinded his eyes before putting him in chains and bringing him to Babylonia. During this month God exacted retribution from the generation of the Flood, and He inundated the entire world. For this reason the month is called 'Mar-cheshvan' — a month which was 'bitter' (*mar*). A second and more basic reason: The month is called Mar-cheshvan because of its bountiful rains — for which the world thirsts. In this view 'Mar' means a drop of water, as in: 'Behold the nations are like a drop of water (*Ke'mar*) from a bucket' (Yeshayahu 40).

A LACK WHICH WILL BE RESTORED

Although there is no festival in the month of Cheshvan, there should have been one during the days of King Shlomo (Solomon). After erecting the Sanctuary for seven years,

Shlomo finished it during this month (First Melachim 6): 'And in the eleventh in the month Bul, which was the eighth month, the House was completed... and he had built it seven years.' All Israel waited for the dedication of the Sanctuary; Shlomo waited for God's command concerning its dedication, but God did not so command. The Temple stood locked for 12 months till Tishrey came and he was commanded to celebrate the dedication of the Temple during Tishrey. You may say then: Cheshvan lost its Yom Tov and Tishrey gained it.

Nevertheless, though Cheshvan sustained the loss of its Yom Tov, it did have the merit that the Temple was concluded in it. For, during all those years from the Flood till the year when the Temple was completed, the world was always filled with fear from the 17th of Mar-cheshvan till the 27th of Kislev (the forty days of the Flood). When the Sanctuary was completed in Cheshvan, those forty days ceased casting their fear upon Man. Therefore, the letter *Mem* (whose numerical value is 40) was taken from 'Mabul' — and the name of the month became, 'bul.'

'...and Mar-cheshvan will be repaid by God for its loss (with a festival of its own).' (Yalkut, Melachim 184).

KIDUSH LEVANAH (Sanctification of the Moon)

The Rabis have said (Tractate Sanhedrin 42): 'Whoever welcomes the new moon with a blessing at the proper time, is as if he welcomed the *Shechinah.*'

Our Sages offered various explanations of this dictum: The Maharsha writes: 'While in exile, we are unable to go up to Jerusalem and to be seen in the presence of the Shechinah. Nevertheless, we have not ceased to yearn to do so. And whenever we see the moon renewed, we remember God's promise to renew us also — so that we might yet attain the merit of going up and being seen in the presence of the Shechinah. As our Sages have said: If one intended to perform a mitzvah, but was prevented by circumstances beyond his control from doing so, Scripture regards it as if he had done it. Now, when we go out to see the moon's renewal and to make a blessing over it, our inner thoughts dwell upon our own renewal and our return to the place of our Sancturay, where the Shechinah dwells — and Scripture regards it as if we had already welcomed the Shechinah this day.'

The Levush explains: 'Since we see in the moon God's power to greater extent than we see it in any of the stars — whose movements are not apparent to us...; it is to us akin to a monthly welcome to the Shechinah, when we go out to see God's actions and the greatness of His deeds. And there is also an esoteric significance in the renewal of the moon — which alludes to the Shechinah.'

The later Sages offer a further explanation: 'Shechinah' refers to the indwelling Presence of God and to the manifestation of His Glory in human action, and in the laws of nature, as in the verse: 'And I shall dwell in their midst' within their actions. So that even when a person eats and drinks and plows and plants and reaps, as all other people do — the Shechinah may dwell within all his actions; providing that he believes and knows and always thinks at heart, that all comes from God. If however, a person thinks at heart, Heaven forbid, it is my strength and the power of my hands which is the source of all I have; all comes from nature or the influence of the stars, then he drives away the Shechinah as it were. Therefore, when the people of Israel go out to bless God for the renewal of the moon they testify concerning themselves and the entire world that all of nature and all human action — are from God alone; thereby they merit that the Shechinah might dwell within all their actions.

The blessing recited over the renewal of the moon is called, *Kidush Levanah* (the sanctification of the moon), though the accepted wording of the blessing is, *mechadesh chodashim* ('Who renews the new moon'), and not, *mekadesh chodashim* ('Who sanctifies the new moon'). However, we refer to the blessing with the term *Kidush* in memorial to the sanctification of the new moon, which was performed through Beit Din. The Sephardim however, call it by the name, *Birkat Halevanah* ('The Blessing of the Moon').

WELCOMING THE SHECHINAH

Since the theme of the blessing over the new moon is that of welcoming the Shechinah, it is distinguished from other blessings in the requirement that it be said standing, at a time of joy, while properly dressed, and publicly — as one would do in welcoming a king.

'The blessing over the new moon is recited only upon the departure of the Shabat, when one's feelings are pleasurable, and he is well dressed; One then lifts up his eyes towards the moon while standing at attention, and he recites the blessing' (Tractate Sofrim 20). Nevertheless many follow the custom of reciting the 'brachah' any night, because of the principle of: 'the diligent perform mitzvot early.' Others take care to wait till 'Motza'ey Shabat' (the departure of the Shabat), unless they would thereby delay the 'brachah' till after the tenth of the month. Nevertheless, during the winter months, one should not wait till 'Motza'ey Shabat', lest the night be cloudy.

The blessing over the moon during the month of Sivan is said 'Motza'ey Shavuot' in order to extend the joy of the festival with a blessing.

Even if one sanctifies the moon during the week, it is proper for him to wear proper clothing in honor of the mitzvah, and to purify his spirit and heart towards the act of welcoming the Shechinah.

Because of the mourning which prevails then, the blessing over the moon is not said before the ninth of Av; nor before Yom Kipur because of one's anguish over his sins before they are forgiven. Instead, we wait till the fast is over, and say the blessing over the moon immediately upon emerging from the Synagogue and before the tasting of food. The Sephardi custom however, is to recite the blessing Yom Kipur in order to add merit to the Day of Judgment, and to taste a minute amount of food before saying the blessing at the termination of the Ninth of Av.

In accord with the view of the Gaon of Vilna, it is customary in many Jerusalem synagogues not to wait with the blessing till after Yom Kipur or after the ninth of Av, but rather to abide by the principle: 'the diligent perform mitzvot early' and therefore to say the 'brachah' as soon as possible.

In accord with the verse, 'A king's majesty is in a great multitude,' we make every effort to bless the moon in a minyan (a congregation of a least ten adult Jews).

The brachah should not be recited standing under a roof, nor looking through a window or an open door. The worshipper should rather go outside as is done when a king is welcomed. If however, he finds it difficult to leave his house, he is permitted to recite the brachah at home also, provided the door or window through which he sees the moon is open, and there is not anything intervening between his eyes and the moon. If the glass of his window is clean, and if vision through it is good, and he finds it difficult to open a window, because of cold or the like, he may say the brachah without opening the window.

The brachah is not recited over the moon till three full day and night periods have passed from the time of the molad. Others require seven full days. Its time extends for one half the month, that is, half the time between the molad and the next, since till half the month has passed, the moon is still in a process of renewal and attaining its fullness. If half the month has passed and he failed to bless the moon, he does not recite the blessing any more.

The moon is not sanctified either on Shabat nights or Yom Tov nights. If however, it will be impossible to sanctify it the next night, it may be sanctified also on the night of the Sabbath.

Women do not say the brachah over the moon.

When one says the blessing, he lifts up his eyes once, in order to see the moon at the time of the blessing, but he does not gaze at it further, since it is not to the moon that we turn our hearts, but only to the One Who created it.

It is proper to stand at attention and recite the 'brachah' in a spirit of reverence.

In some communities it is customary to sing and dance after the blessing.

THE BLESSING OVER THE MOON

The blessing begins with the first six verses of Tehilim 148, in which the sun and the moon, the heavens and all the heavenly creatures are summoned to praise their Creator. Afterwards one say the prescribed blessing.

The content of this blessing is as follows: One gives praise to God for having created the heavens and their hosts, and for having assigned them tasks from which they never deviate, but which they always rejoice in anew, though they constantly repeat the same activity. The moon is an exception to this constancy of nature in that God commanded it to renew itself constantly. And this is a sign to the people of Israel who are borne by God from their time of birth. Though they sometimes rise and sometime descend, they are not shamed thereby and do not lose hope. The renewal of the moon is a crown of glory to them, since it is a testimony unto Israel that in the end they will rise everlastingly, and that they are destined for enduring self-renewal, just as the moon renews itself after its diminution. And as the people of Israel gather to acknowledge God's power when the moon is renewed, so are all the nations of the world destined to bless God and to give praise to their creator when Israel will be renewed — at which time the Glory of God's Majesty will be manifest to the eyes of every living being.

Afterwards one says three times: 'Blessed is the One Who fashions you, Blessed is your Maker, Blessed is the One Who possesses you, Blessed is your Creator.' The first letters of the four Divine appelatives in this verse together form the word Ya'akov; For this verse alludes to Ya'akov, who was the 'smaller' of the two brothers, and whose sons count by the moon — the smaller luminary.

When the worshipper say, 'just as I dance towards you, and cannot touch you...,' he dwells on the thought of God's being unreachable by us, despite all our rejoicing in Him and dancing before Him. Likewise are we beyond the reach of the nations of the world, even when they favor us, for Israel is holy to the Lord and will always dwell alone.

The following verse is then said three times — alternatively forwards and backwards: 'Dread and fear shall fall upon them, when the strength of your arm shall become great, they will be silent like a stone.' For, in the Hebrew, the words of this verse can be read and explained both when read in their formal order, as well as when they are read backward. Two alternate meanings emerge thus: At times, God first reveals His power to His creatures, and then the power of the wicked is broken. At other times, it is the power of the wicked is first broken, and through their destruction God's power is revealed.

'David King of Israel lives and endures,' is said three times, since the renewal of the moon is an allusion to the renewal of the Kingdom of the House of David. For fifteen generations, from Rechav'am till Tzidkiyahu David's kingdom declined, till is 'vanished completely;' just as the moon however, seemingly vanishes after fifteen days of decline, only to be renewed, and to reappear again — so does David, King of Israel live and endure forever.

The greeting, *shalom aleichem* (peace be unto you), is then mutually exchanged three times, and those to whom it is addressed, answer, *aleichem shalom.* For God's tidings of redemption to Israel will be accompanied by peace (Yeshayahu 52). And in the future world the kingdom of the house of David will be called 'Shalom' (Yeshayahu 8). For this reason we exchange greetings for Shalom as we pray for the renewal of the kingdom of the House of David.

We then say the verses, 'The voice of my beloved, behold, it is coming...' in order to strengthen our faith in the advent of the Messiah.

The blessing over the new moon is concluded with Psalms and the 'B'raita dvey Rabi Yishmael' which relate to the same theme.

The allusions and symbolisms in the blessing over the moon bear similarity to those of Rosh Hashanah; for Rosh Chodesh is akin to a minor Rosh Hashanah.

THE FAST OF BAHAB (the Fast of Monday, Thursday and Monday)

The first Monday, Thursday and Monday which follow Rosh Chodesh Cheshvan are days of prayer and fasting. They are called 'BaHaB,' after the days on which they are observed: Since the numerical value respectively, of the three letters which comprise 'Ba Ha B,' is 2, 5 and 2 — 'Ba Ha B' stands for the second, fifth and again second days of the week which follow Rosh Chodesh Cheshvan.

The reason for the designation of these days as days of fasting and prayer is as follows: Since the festival days which preceded them were days of feasting and rejoicing, we fear lest the joy of the festival led to levity and wrong-doing; and we therefore fast in atonement. This idea is expressed by the text,: 'Serve the Lord in Joy, and rejoice in trembling' — where there is rejoicing, there should be trembling.

We likewise find it written of Job: 'And it was, when the days of feasting were over, Job sent and sanctified them (his sons) and he arose in the morning, and brought up whole-offerings in the number of all, for Job said, Perhaps my sons have sinned.'

This fast and prayer was designated after Sukot and Pesach, in both of which there were many days of rejoicing without work; so that there is ground to fear that the people might have fallen into levity. In the case of Shavuot however, which consists of only one day, we have no such fear.

Some say that these fasts are for rain and the blessing of the fields.

These fasts were designated particularly for the second and fifth of the week, because the Torah is read on them. And in the days of our ancient Sages, the Rabis decreed fasting for Mondays and Thursdays over three things: The destruction of the Temple, the burning of the Torah, and the destruction of God's Name which resulted from the destruction of Jerusalem and the exile of Israel.

On the Sabbath which precedes the first of these three fast days — a special blessing is pronounced after the Torah-Reading for all those in the congregation who volunteer to observe the *Ta'anit BaHaB*. Whoever answers 'Amen' after this blessing, and intends at heart to accept the Fast — it is as if he accepted the fact explicitly. (Whoever observes a private fast, is required to accept the Fast no later than the time of *minchah* the previous day.)

In the Sephardi communities it is not customary in our days to observe 'Bahab.'

THE PETITION FOR RAIN

In the Land of Israel a prayer for rain is included in the ninth benediction of *shmoneh esreh amidah*-prayer beginning with the seventh day of Cheshvan. From Shmini Atzeret till the seventh of Cheshvan we do not yet pray for rain, but we only mention *gevurot geshamim* (the revelation of God's power through rain) in the second benediction, by way of praise to God, 'Who causes the wind to blow and the rain to fall.' Beginning with the seventh of Cheshvan, after 'the last of the pilgrims had already managed to reach the Euphrates,' we begin also to pray and supplicate for rain.

In the Diaspora, where water is plentiful, and there is not so great a need for rain, *she'elat geshamim* (the prayer for rain) is begun sixty days after the beginning of 'the Tishrey-season.' (The four seasons of the Jewish year are called after their first months: the Tishrey-season; the Tevet-season; the Nisan-season; and the Tamuz-season.) Since we calculate our *tekufot* (seasons) by the solar year, *she'elat geshamim* in the diaspora has no fixed day in our calendar (which is based on the lunar months). It does however, have a fixed date in the non-Jewish solar calendar: in a regular year of theirs, in which February has 28 days it falls on December 5th; in their leap years, when February has 29 days, it falls on December 6th.

We pray for rain till Erev Pesach both in the Land of Israel and in the Diaspora.

Although there are countries which are as much in need of rain in the beginning of winter as the Land of Israel; and there are countries which need rain also after Pesach, *she'elat geshamim* is begun only on one of two dates — either the seventh of Cheshvan or sixty days after the *Tekufah;* and it ends on one date everywhere — Erev Pesach. Every country or city which needs rain outside these days, may observe special fast days, and may follow a special order of penitential prayers for the gift of rain, but they may not deviate from the fixed mode of prayer which the Sages prescribed for *shmoneh esreh.*

If one forgets to say, *veten tal umatar* ('and give dew and rain'), but he remembers before beginning the tenth benediction, he says it then. If he remembers after the beginning of the tenth benediction — he waits till reaching the sixteenth benediction (*Shome'a tefila* —'who hears prayer'), and he says: 'and give dew and rain for blessing, for You hear the prayer of every mouth...' If he remembers after the sixteenth benediction, but before beginning the seventeenth, he says it then. If he has begun the seventeenth benediction, but remembers before stepping backwards at the end of the prayer he returns to the beginning of the ninth benediction and repeats the remainder of the *shmoneh esreh.* If he remembers after stepping backwards — he is required to repeat the whole of *shmoneh esreh.*

If the rains fall in their proper time, the following blessing is said: 'Blessed are You, Lord our God, King of the Universe, Who is good and bestows good.' Nowadays however, it is not customary for everyone to say this blessing, since not everyone feels the good of rain, and they are unable to say the blessing with the intention of the heart.

However, one, who is truly sensitive to the public need, may express praise and thanksgiving to God for this *chesed* (lovingkindness) which is the greatest of God's kindnesses towards His creatures, and the greatest of Israel's ancient Sages observed it as a Yom Tov when they saw the rains falling; they recited this *brachah* with great joy of heart and they added to it a variety of praise and thanksgiving (Dvarim Raba 7 — Bereishit Raba 13).

GEVUROT GESHAMIM

It is customary for a hungry person to acknowledge a debt of gratitude and thanksgiving to one who gives him a single fig or date with which to sustain life even for a brief hour. On the other hand, if one receives all his sustenance from another person, who provides his needs constantly without being asked — he is not likely to remember his benefactor's kindness — because of the very regularity and plenitude of his benefactions. Nevertheless it is readily understood, that the good bestowed by the latter is a thousand times greater than that of the former. Come and see! There is no greater *chesed* than the rains which God brings down for us in their proper times. People sleep in their beds, while God opens His treasures for them, grants them dew and brings down rains, waters the fields and brings forth their produce — are we not required to thank Him?

However small this great *chesed* may seem in ordinary eyes — it is not at all small in the eyes of the Sages who know God's powers, and who never forget them.

AN OPEN TREASURE

'... There are three keys in God's hand, which were not given to a messenger: the key of rain, the key of giving birth, and the key of the revival of the dead...' (Ta'anit 2).

'The falling of rain is greater than the revival of the dead. For the revival of the dead is only for man, while rain is for man and animal; the revival of the dead is for Israel, but rain is for Israel and the nations' (Bereishit Raba 13).

'...Many drops did I create in the clouds, but I created each drop different than all others; for if any two drops were identical... the earth would not bring forth fruit' (Baba Batra 16).

'... Through rain everything is blessed; the conduct of business is blessed; the merchants profit; ... and even those who suffer from boils find respite... Even a precious stone is affected for the good (its colors shine more brightly)... even fish are affected (their weight increases).

'Three things are equal: Earth, Man and Rain... without earth — there is no rain; without rain — there is no earth; without both — there is no man' (Bereishit Raba 13).

'And I shall give your rains in their proper time' — Rabi Yochanan said: 'three gifts were given to the world: The Torah, the luminaries, and rain in their proper times — during the nights of Sabbath. In the days of Shimon Ben Shatach rains fell on the Shabat nights till the wheat and barley grew to immense size, and they preserved them for later generations so that it might be known what the effects of sin are' (Vayikra Raba 35).

The Sages have further said (Ta'anit 7):

'A day when rain falls is as great as the day when the Torah was given.

'A day when rain falls is as great as the day when heaven and earth were created.

'The rains fall if Israel's sins were forgiven.

'Great is the day of rain for even a small coin in one's pocket is blessed by it...' (ibid. 8).

'The day of rain is as great as the day of the ingathering of the exiles...' (ibid.)

The matter may be likened to a father who sends gifts to his sons. As long as the gifts are few, and he sends them with a messenger he only gives his sons what he promised to give them. If he wishes to give them a large gift, he does not send it with a messenger, but gives it himself. He calls his sons and opens his store house in order to give each one his intended gift. When the store house is open and they see all the treasures hidden there, the clever among them ask whatever their hearts desire, and their father gives it to them. For the treasure is open, and the hour is an hour of goodwill.

Likewise, all of God's kindnesses towards His creatures are done through His angels — who carry out His mission, without adding to it or diminishing from it. The gift of rain, however, God does not trust His messengers with, lest they be unforgiving towards the transgressions of His creatures, and withhold the rains — thus causing the world to become desolate.

The key of rain therefore remains in God's hand, and when He gives rain to His world — He gives it solely out of His treasure; without regard to strict judgment, or reward, or merit, but only with lovingkindness, for He is all good. When the treasure is open — it is a time of good-will for Israel to ask all the good that their soul desires. If at that time, they ask of their Father in heaven that He might put the Torah into their hearts, as when their fathers stood at Mount Sinai — He grants their request. If they ask for salvation, for forgiveness, for sustenance, for the ingathering of their exiles, for the cessation of war from their midst — the time is one of good will for the granting of their requests. For all their requests are contained in the good treasure which God opens when the rains fall. And the Torah testifies to this (Dvarim 28) : 'May the Lord open for you His good treasure, the heavens, to give rain for your land in its time... ;' and if you should say that good treasure is open only for the gift of rain, it is not so, but rather — 'and to bless all the deeds of your hand.'

We learn from this, how great is the *chesed* of rainfall, and how much devout intention one ought to have, when one asks of God: 'And give dew and rain for a blessing.'

FAITH LEADS TO FAITH

It is written (Job 41) : 'Who has preceded Me — that I should have to repay it; what is beneath all the heavens — is Mine.' Has a man ever performed a mitzvah before God gave him the strength and the ability to perform it ? How much more is this so with reference to the great *chesed* of rain — which no creature could have merited by some preceding act !

Before the first man was created, it is written: 'and a cloud rose up from the earth, and watered the face of earth.' And only afterwards — 'And the Lord God formed Man.' We see then, that rain comes through the Chesed of the Creator, and not through human merit. Nevertheless, the

Sages have said, that there is a merit, for whose sake Man may receive the gift of rain — faithfulness between Man and his fellow.

Thus did the Rabis say (Ta'anit 8) :

'Rains fall only for the sake of men of trust...'

Why is faithfulness the particular virtue, above all other good actions, through which the gift of rain is merited? But thus did God say: As long as there is faithfulness among men; an object is given to another for safekeeping without witnesses, and the other does not deny it; he finds a lost object and returns it to its owner, though no one saw him find it; he buys or sells an object without a bill, and he keeps his word; his measures and weights are honest; he does not mislead his fellow — of such persons God says: Even if they possess no other merit besides this one, I am obligated to give them rain. Let their toil not have been in vain; let not the soil be unfaithful to them, as they are not unfaithful to each other.

Heaven forbid, if there is no faithfulness between Man and his fellow, and they are guilty of robbing the poor, or stealing in general, or slander, or arrogance — then the heavens too are closed and they become like copper; and the earth becomes like iron and does not bring forth its produce.

Therefore the Sages said: 'For the sin of failure to give heave-offerings and tithes (theft from the Levites and the poor), the heavens are locked and do not give dew and rain; prices rise, profit is lost; and men pursue their livelihood without success' (Tractate Shabat 32).

'...The rains are withheld only because of those who bear slander...' (Ta'anit 7).

'...The rains are withheld only because of the arrogant...' (ibid.).

'...The rains are withheld only because of the sin of theft...' (ibid.).

'...The rains are withheld only because of those who

pledge charity publicly, but do not make good their pledge...' (Ta'anit 8).

'...The rains are withheld only because of cessation from the study of Torah...' (Ta'anit 7).

THE DEATH OF OUR MOTHER RACHEL

On the eleventh of Chesvan our mother Rachel died, and was buried on the road to Bethlehem.

The place of her grave in Bethlehem, southward of Jerusalem, is known to us by tradition.

A stone edifice was built over her grave, to which the inhabitants of the Land of Israel have always come to pour forth their hearts in prayer, and to awaken her merit in any time of travail, for the community as well as for individual. But mainly they come to her grave on the day of her death — the eleventh of Cheshvan.

Our mother Rachel was not buried in the cave of Machpelah, in Chevron, together with the Matriarchs and the Patriarchs of our people. She was buried on the road, where she died on coming from the House of Lavan with Ya'akov.

'Why did our Father Ya'akov bury Rachel on the road to Bethlehem ? He saw prophetically that the exiles would one day pass by on that way, and he therefore buried her there, so that she might seek mercy for them. When Nebuzaradan exiled them, and they passed her grave, Rachel emerged to weep and to ask for mercy in their behalf, as it is said (Irmeyahu 31) : 'Thus did the Lord say, a voice is heard on high, lamentation and bitter weeping, Rachel weeps for her children, she refuses to be consoled for her children, for they are not.' And God answers : 'Thus did the Lord say, refrain your voice from weeping and your eyes from tears, for there is reward for your labor, said the Lord, and the children shall return to their boundary' (Rashi Va'yechi, and Midrashim quoted by Radak, Irmeyahu 31).

Another Midrash relates : When the Patriarchs and Matriarchs went to intercede with God over the image which

Menasheh placed in the Temple, God was not reconciled. Rachel entered and said before Him: Lord of the universe! whose mercy is greater — Yours, or the mercy of a person of flesh and blood. Surely, Your mercy is greater. Have I not brought my rival (Lea) into my house? For all the work which Ya'akov did for my father, was done by him only for my sake. When I came to enter the *chupah* (to be wed to Ya'akov), my sister was brought in my place. And not only did I keep silent, but I even gave her my signs. You too — though Your children have brought Your enemy into Your House — be silent towards them! He said to her: You have defended them well, there is reward for your labor, and for your righteousness in having given your signs to your sister (Rashi Irmeyahu 31).

From the time when the People of Israel went into their first exile until Irmeyahu's prophecy of redemption ('and the children shall return to their boundary'), the grave of our mother Rachel has always been and will always remain a House of Prayer to Israel, for she is a mother to all Israel, and always awakens mercy in their behalf.

YOM KIPUR KATAN (A Small Yom Kipur)

The day before Rosh Chodesh, is called 'Yom Kipur Katan,' and men of piety fast either part of the day or the entire day. During *minchah* they say special penitential prayers and *vidui (confession of sins)*, and they also say 'the Great Vidui' which was authored by Rabenu Nisim. They utter profuse supplication for atonement, and for the rebuilding of the Sanctuary. If there is a *minyan* of fasters in the Synagogue, the Torah-Reading and the Prophetic portion which are read on every public fast, are also read on Yom Kipur Katan.

The reason for this custom is that Rosh Chodesh is a day of atonement for the sins of the preceding month, as it is said in the account of the special sacrifice for the day: 'and one kid of goat — a sin offering to the Lord.' And it surely would not enter the mind, that a person's sin might be forgiven, unless he completely forsakes it. Therefore, some fast the day before Rosh Chodesh — since on Rosh Chodesh fasting is prohibited — as an act of self judgment, and remorse over any previous wrong doing.

Although only rare individuals fast, all Israel are worthy of attaining forgiveness through the merit of those who do fast, since those who fast include themselves within the People of Israel, and all of Israel includes itself with them. And perhaps this is the reason for the phrase, 'All Israel are friends' (*chaverim kol Yisrael*) which is part of the blessing for the new month. It is as if we were saying that all Israel are worthy of atoning for each other. For any *mitzvah,* which is not obligatory upon all — if individuals perform it, they do so in behalf of all Israel, and their merit is the merit of all Israel.

When Rosh Chodesh falls on Sunday or on Shabat, Yom Kipur Katan is not observed the previous day, for *selichot* (penitential prayers) may not be said after *minchah* on Erev Shabat. It is likewise prohibited to fast the entire day on Erev Shabat (with the exception of the Tenth of Tevet); instead, Yom Kipur Katan is observed on Thursday.

Yom Kipur Katan is not observed on either Erev Rosh Chodesh Cheshvan or on Erev Rosh Chodesh Iyar, since fasting is prohibited at the end of Tishrey and during all of Nisan.

Kislev

KISLEV ❖ CHANUKAH ❖ WITH WHAT THE LIGHTS OF CHANUKAH MAY BE LIT ❖ HOW THE LIGHTS ARE TO BE LIT ❖ WHERE THE LIGHTS ARE PLACED ❖ THE TIME FOR KINDLING ❖ UPON WHOM THE OBLIGATION RESTS ❖ CHANUKAH OBSERVANCE ❖ CHANUKAH CUSTOMS ❖ A DAY PREPARED FOR INAUGURATION AND GREATNESS ❖ AN ALLUSION TO THE FESTIVAL OF CHANUKAH IN THE TORAH ❖ WHY CHANUKAH IS OBSERVED EIGHT DAYS ❖ PURE IN THE MIDST OF DEFILEMENT ❖ WHY IS ONLY THE MIRACLE OF THE OIL MENTIONED IN THE TALMUD ❖ THE LIGHTS OF CHANUKAH ARE BELOVED ❖ DIVINE JUDGMENT IS NOT ARBITRARY ❖ A WAR BETWEEN SANCTITY AND DEFILEMENT ❖ THE DOMINION OF GREECE ❖ WHEN DOES BEAUTY BECOME UGLINESS? ❖ HELLENISTS ❖ THE MIRACLE OF THE REVOLUTION ❖ MEASURE FOR MEASURE ❖ BETWEEN CHANUKAH AND PURIM ❖ INSIGHTS ❖ ZOT CHANUKAH ❖ THE CONCLUSION OF SUKOT ❖ ALL ISRAEL ARE EQUAL DURING CHANUKAH AND PURIM.

CHAPTER SEVEN

KISLEV

Kislev is the Babylonian name of the month. In Scripture it is called the ninth month, since it is ninth after Nisan — the first of months.

The first rainbow observed after the Flood was also seen in Kislev. 'And God said: this is the sign of the covenant which I set between Me and yourselves, and between every living being that is with you, unto eternal generations. I have given my bow in the cloud, and it shall be a sign of a covenant between Me and the Earth.' 'This is the sign of the covenant' — God showed Noah the bow and said to Him: 'This is the sign of which I spoke' (Bereishit 9). This passage was spoken to Noah at the beginning of the month of Kislev. On the 28th day of Cheshvan he had emerged from the ark, and afterwards, 'Noah built an altar to God and he took of every clean animal and of every clean bird and he brought up burnt offerings on the altar.' The month of Cheshvan then came to a close, and Kislev began. God blessed Noah; permitted him the use of meat for food; forbade him to shed human blood; struck a covenant for life with him: and showed him the rainbow.

Rosh Chodesh Kislev consists at times of one day, and at times of two. As has been indicated earlier the preceding month of Cheshvan sometimes consists of twenty nine days, and sometimes of thirty days. In the former instance Rosh Chodesh Kislev consists of one day; in the latter, of two, with the first day of Rosh Chodesh counting also as the 30th day of Cheshvan.

From the days of the Hasmoneans and later, as long as the Beit Din sanctified the month through the testimony of witnesses, messengers of the Beit Din went forth to places distant from Yerushalayim, to make known when the new month had been sanctified. They went forth however, only during months in which festivals occurred, in order that the date of the festivals should be known. When the Beit Din sanctified the month of Kislev, messengers went forth from Jerusalem, so that the people might know on which day Chanukah would fall, since Chanukah has the status of a festival, despite the fact that the *mitzvot* of Chanukah were only ordained by the Scribes.

CHANUKAH

On the 25th of Kislev the eight days of Chanukah begin, and lights are lit at the advent of each evening.

'What is Chanukah ? The Rabis have expounded: Beginning with the 25th of Kislev, eight days of Chanukah are observed, during which no eulogies are delivered, nor is fasting permitted. For when the Greeks entered the Sanctuary, they defiled all the oils, and when the Hasmonean house prevailed and vanquished them, they searched and found only one remaining jar of oil with the Cohen Gadol's seal. Although it contained only enough oil to burn one day, a miracle occurred, and the oil burned eight days. A year later they (the Rabis) designated these days as *Yamim Tovim* on which praise and thanksgiving were to be uttered' (Tractate Shabat 21).

'During the period of the Second Temple the Greek kings issued harsh decrees against Israel; outlawed their religion, forbade them to engage in the study of Torah and the practice of mitzvot, laid hands upon their money and their daughters, entered the Sanctuary and ravaged it, and defiled all that had been ritually pure. They caused Israel great anguish, till the God of our Fathers granted them mercy and delivered them from the hands of their enemies. The Hasmonai Cohanim Gedolim prevailed, slew them, and delivered Israel from their hands. They designated a king from among the *cohanim*, and the Kingdom of Israel was restored for more than 200 years, till the second Destruction.

'And Israel prevailed against their enemies and vanquished them, on the 25th day of the month of Kislev. They entered the Sanctuary and found only one jar of ritually pure oil that was sufficient to burn only one day; but they lit the lights of the *Menorah* from it for eight days, till they pressed olives and extracted pure oil' (Rambam, Hilchot Chanukah, Chapter 3).

The Sages of that generation therefore decreed, that the eight days beginning with the 25th Kislev should be days of rejoicing; that Halel be recited, and that lights be lit at the entrance to the homes, each of the eight nights, in order to publicize the miracle. And these days are called 'Chanukah' that is to say, *Chanu Kaf-Hay* (they rested on the 25th), for on the 25th of Kislev they rested from their enemies.'

The above expression of the Talmud: 'They made it a Yom Tov for praise and thanksgiving,' refers to the literal recitation of *Halel* (praise), and therefore, the complete Halel is said during *shacharit* all eight days of Chanukah. The term 'thanksgiving' refers to *al hanisim*, which is included in each *shmoneh esreh* during these days, as well as in *birkat hamazon*.

WITH WHAT THE LIGHTS OF CHANUKAH MAY BE LIT

The preferred way to perform the 'mitzvah' is to light the Chanukah lamps with pure olive oil and cottonwool wicks, since their light is pure, and it also recalls the light of the 'Menorah' which was lit with olive oil. All other oils and wicks are also permissible, if their light is pure and does not flicker. Lights made of wax or parafin are also permitted.

The holder in which the oil and the wick are placed should be aesthetically attractive, made of metal or glass, polished and clean. An earthenware holder is permissible for lighting only once, while it is yet new. After one use it becomes unclean and may not be used for kindling on the morrow.

A wick which was used one night may be used on succeeding nights as well. The same is true of the remaining oil or of the remainder of wax and paraffin candles.

HOW THE LIGHTS ARE TO BE LIT

On the first night one light is lit, and every successive night another light is added till the eighth night when eight lights are lit.

If one has a 'menorah' containing eight lights on the first night he lights the one on the extreme right. The following night he adds the one immediately to the left and kindles it first. He then turns to the right and kindles the light of the previous night. He follows the same procedure each night, always adding from right to left but always lighting from left to right.

The reason for this procedure is that the additional light always recalls the 'growth' of the miracle.

The lights are to be placed in a straight row; none higher or lower than the others, none receding or protruding out, and none in a circle. There should also be sufficient space between one light and the other, so that the flame of one might not be joined to that of the other; and so that the heat of one light might not melt wax of another.

The first night three 'brachot' are said before the lights are kindled:

'Baruch ata Hashem, Elokenu melech ha'olam, asher kidshanu b'mitzvotav v'tzivanu l'hadlik ner shel Chanukah.' (Blessed are You, Lord our God, King of the Universe, Who has sanctified us with His commandments, and has commanded us to light the Chanukah lamps.)

'Baruch ata Hashem, Elokenu melech ha'olam, she'asah nisim la'avotenu, bayamim hahem bazeman hazeh.' (Blessed are You, Lord our God, King of the Universe, Who has done miracles for our fathers in bygone days, at this time.)

'Baruch ata Hashem, Elokenu melech ha'olam, shehecheyanu, vekiyemanu vehigi'anu lazeman hazeh.' (Blessed are You, Lord our God, King of the Universe, Who has given us life, and has sustained us, and has brought us to this time.)

Then he kindles the light. The remaining nights he utters only the first two 'brachot' but omits 'shehecheyanu.' If he was prevented by accident from lighting the Chanukah light first night, he says 'shehecheyanu' the first time he kindles the Chanukah light.

It is customary to light one extra light in addition to the required number of lights for the given night. The extra light is called the 'shamash' (the 'servant'). The 'shamash' may be used for kindling other lights, and one may derive benefit from its light. The Chanukah lights themselves however, may not be used for any other purpose, while they burn in fulfillment of the mitzvah. It is proper to see to it, that there should be yet another light in addition to the shamash, in the house.

It is customary not to utilize a Chanukah light even for kindling another light in the same 'menorah.'

For that purpose only the shamash or another light may be used.

At the time of kindling, the entire household should gather so that 'the miracle might be publicized.'

After the first light is kindled, 'hanerot halalu' is said, the remaining lights are kindled. When the lighting is concluded, Chanukah hymns are sung, in accord with local custom.

WHERE THE LIGHTS ARE PLACED

The Sages have prescribed that the Chanukah lights are to be placed at the street entrance to one's home — on the left side of the entrance, so that the 'mezuzah' might be to the right and the Chanukah lights to the left. They are not to be placed at a lower height than three 'tefachim' (handbreadths) from the ground, nor at a greater height than ten 'tefachim' above the ground. If he places them at a greater height than ten 'tefachim', but less than twenty 'amot' (ells) he has still fulfilled his obligation. If he raises the lights however above twenty 'amot,' he has not fulfilled his obligation. The reason for these regulations is, that only the placement of the Chanukah lights within the prescribed confines could achieve the effect of 'pirsum hanes' (publicizing the miracle).

In recent generations most people place their Chanukah lights in a window facing the street. One should not however, place them on his table since no 'pirsum hanes' is achieved thus.

If one's residence is on an upper story and his windows are more than twenty ells above street level, it is preferable for him to place the Chanukah lights near the most heavily used entrance on the left side of the entry.

THE TIME FOR KINDLING

The Chanukah lights are to be lit immediately upon the appearance of the stars. If one has not however done so, he may still perform the mitzvah through the remainder of the night as long as the members of his household are still awake. If he is unable to light the Chanukah lights till an exceedingly late hour — when all are finally asleep — and 'pirsum hanes' could no longer be accomplished, he kindles the lights without a brachah. If the night has passed and he has failed to kindle the lights, he can no longer do so the remainder of the day and can only resume performance of the mitzvah the following night.

Eating or drinking intoxicating liquids is prohibited one half hour before the time for kindling the lights. Once the prescribed time has arrived, even the study of Torah is prohibited till the Chanukah lights are lit. Upon the appearance of the stars, 'ma'ariv' is said, and is followed immediately by the kindling of the lights. In Yerushalayim, many abide by the custom of the Gaon of Vilna and light the Chanukah lights at sunset, and prior to 'ma'ariv.'

The lights should burn half an hour. At the time of lighting there should therefore be sufficient oil in the menorah for the prescribed period of time. Those who kindle the lights at sunset are required to pour sufficient oil into the menorah for burning a minimum of 50 minutes, so that the lights might burn for the prescribed half hour period after the appearance of the stars. If, at the time of lighting, the lights have insufficient oil for burning half an hour, one may not add oil after the lights have been kindled, but he is required to extinguish the lights, to add oil, to recite the brachah and to kindle the light a second time; for the essential performance of the mitzvah takes place at the time of lighting.

If one has poured oil in excess of the required measure into the menorah, he may extinguish the lights after one half hour of burning, if he wishes to use the remaining oil for the Chanukah lights the following night. If it had been his original intention upon the lighting of the menorah, to derive any other benefit from the remaining oil, he may use that oil for any desired purpose. However, no use may be made of the remaining oil and wicks after the final night of Chanukah. They are to be disposed of by burning — unless one had originally intended to use their remainders for non-sacred purposes, at the very time of lighting.

If a Chanukah light accidentally goes out in the midst of its prescribed time for burning, it is to be kindled again, but without a brachah. After the fact however, if one fails to rekindle it, he is nevertheless considered as having fulfilled the obligation of the mitzvah. As long as the Chanukah lights burn — even after the prescribed half hour — their light may not be used for any personal benefit. Nor may they be moved from place to place. After the prescribed half hour — if one wishes to make use of them — they are first to be extinguished, and then reused.

Erev Shabat the Chanukah lights are lit first, and subsequently the Shabat lights. One is required to pour adequate oil into the menorah for burning half an hour after the appearance of the stars.

On the termination of Shabat, 'havdalah' is first recited over wine and then the Chanukah lights are lit. Others invert the order; each person should therefore abide by the custom of his fathers.

The custom of the Sephardim is to light the Cha-

nukah lights first, and then to recite 'havdalah' in the synagogue, whereas at home they recite 'havdalah' and then kindle the Chanukah lights.

ON WHOM THE OBLIGATION RESTS

All are obligated to light Chanukah lights — both men and women. A minor who has reached the age of nine is also obligated to light Chanukah lights unless others do so in his behalf.

As for a son residing in his father's home — if he has a separate room, he is required to kindle Chanukah lights himself. If not, his father may fulfill the obligation in his behalf. In Sephardi communities it is the custom for the head of the family to light the Chanukah lights for the entire family.

A guest in another home, who has a special place within the home for himself, lights for himself. If not, he shares the cost of the lights with the head of the house, and then fulfills his obligation through the lighting of the Chanukah lights by his host.

In the synagogue Chanukah lights are lit between 'minchah' and 'ma'ariv,' and a 'brachah' is recited over the lighting. If one has lit the lights at the synagogue and recited the brachah he is nevertheless required to recite a brachah again upon lighting his own Chanukah lights at home. (The lighting of Chanukah lights is also required in any regular place of gathering, for the sake of 'pirsum hanes.')

In the synagogue the Chanukah lights are placed at the southern wall.

In a place where a number of people light Chanukah lights, sufficient space should be left between the different 'menorot,' so that the number of lights lit by each individual may be distinguishable.

'The mitzvah of Chanukah lights is an exceedingly

beloved mitzvah. And a person ought to take special care in its performance, in order to publicize the miracle; and to increase praise of God and thanksgiving to Him over His miracle in our behalf. Even if one lacks food, other than through charity, he should borrow, or sell a garment in order to buy oil and lamps.

'If one has only one penny and he is faced by (the need of money for) 'kidush' (on Shabat) and the kindling of Chanukah lights, he first buys oil for the kindling of Chanukah lights, and secondly wine for 'kidush'; since both are prescribed by the Sofrim (the Scribes), the Chanukah lights are to be given precedence for they recall the miracle' (Rambam, Hilchot Chanukah).

CHANUKAH OBSERVANCE

All eight days of Chanukah full 'Halel' is recited after 'shacharit.' Likewise, 'al hanisim' is included in each service and in 'birkat hamazon.' If one forgets to say 'al hanisim' during 'shmoneh esreh' but remembers before uttering the Divine Name at the conclusion of 'modim,' he reverts to 'al hanisim.' If he has uttered the Divine Name, he concludes the 'shmoneh esreh' and does not recapitulate it.

In the synagogue the account of the 'Nesi'im' (which recounts the offerings brought by the heads of the 12 tribes of Israel upon the dedication of the altar in the Tabernacle) is read. Each day the 'parashah' (portion) of one 'nasi' (head of tribe) is read, and is not repeated the next day. On the eighth day the Torah-Reading begins with the passage on the eighth 'nasi' and continues through the conclusion of the entire passage on the 'nesi'im', till 'thus did he make the 'Menorah' in the 'sidra Beha'alotcha.'

When Rosh Chodesh Tevet falls on Shabat, three

passages are added to 'birkat hamazon': 'al hanisim' for Chanukah, 'retzeh' for Shabat, and 'ya'ale veyavo' for Rosh Chodesh — which makes it the longest 'birkat hamazon' ever to be recited. In the Synagogue three Torah Scrolls are taken out. Six people are called for the reading of the weekly 'sidra' in one scroll; in the second, a seventh person is called for the Rosh Chodesh reading; in the third the passage for the 'Nasi' of the respective day is read as the 'maftir'; the 'haftarah' is from the book of Zechariah, and is related to the theme of Chanukah.

Eulogies for the dead, and fasting, are prohibited during the eight days of Chanukah but work is permitted. If a scholar dies, he is eulogized even during Chanukah.

The Maharil writes: 'We have it as a tradition that one ought not to perform acts of labor during the prescribed time for the burning of the Chanukah lights. (An allusion to the matter: The first letters of Chanukah mean 'they rested.' They rested from their enemies — they rested from work.)

Women abide by the custom of not doing work as long as the lights burn, and they should not be lenient in the matter. (In some Sephardi communities women refrain from work all the days of Chanukah and some abide by this custom only the first and last days of Chanukah.)

The reason for the particular stress upon Chanukah observance on the part of the women, is that a harsh decree had then been issued against the daughters of Israel; upon marriage, a maiden was first to be brought to the ruler. In addition, a miracle was performed through a woman. The daughter of Yochanan Cohen Gadol was especially beautiful and the tyrant-king desired her. She seemingly acquiesced, came before him and fed him cheese foods till he became thirsty. She then gave him wine to drink till he became intoxicated and fell asleep, whereupon she severed his head and brought it to Yerushalayim. When the Syrian soldiers saw that the king had perished, they fled. Because of this reason also, some eat cheese foods during Chanukah.

It is likewise traditional to eat foods fried in oil, in memory of the jar of oil through which the miracle was performed.

CHANUKAH CUSTOMS

Though festive meals are not prescribed for the days of Chanukah, many Jews abide by the custom of investing the Chanukah meals with special rejoicing, by discoursing on Torah themes and recounting the miracles performed for Israel. The meals hence become *seudot mitzvah* (meals having the status of a mitzvah).

It is likewise customary among the Sephardi communities in Yerushalayim for joint meals to be arranged during the days of Chanukah. Friends who quarreled during the year, are reconciled at these meals.

It was also customary in many Jewish communities to focus public concern, during Chanukah, on matters affecting the education of the children. Community officials used to gather to prescribe ways and means for enhancing the study of Torah among the youth, as well as the masses of the people. For 'Chanukah' means both inauguration and education.

For this reason it is also traditional among most Jewish families for the father to give 'Chanukah-money' to the children — as if saying thereby: 'These gifts are given to you today so that you might accept the yoke of Torah constantly.'

Many Rabbis used to undertake trips during Chanukah to the small villages, in order to teach Torah and fear of God to the people. From this teaching Jews in the rural communities derived inspiration for the entire year.

The widespread practice among Jewish children of playing 'dreidel' games also reflects the theme of Chanukah. Since the children have ready money (gifts received from their parents), and since the lighting of Chanukah lights causes some *bitul Torah* (neglect of the study of Torah) during the winter nights, the little ones are told, as it were: 'Relax tonight and spend your hours happily, so that you might take upon yourselves the yoke of Torah, and the exertion required for the performance of mitzvot after Chanukah. And even now, as you play, do not forget the miracle and wonders wrought by God for us.'

On the *dreidels* the letters *nun, gimel, hay, shin,* are therefore inscribed. These letters are an abbreviation of the words, '*Nes Gadol, Haya Sham*' ('A great miracle happened there'). In the Land of Israel however the fourth letter is a *Peh* rather than a *Shin* — the letters thus stand for the words, *Nes Gadol Haya Po.* ('A great miracle happened here'). Thus even when the children are at play, the remembrance of the miracle is woven into their games.

The customs of Chanukah are hence seen to have an educational aim — for children as well as for adults — in recalling God's lovingkindness towards His people Israel, and evoking Israel's thanksgiving and praise before Him as they accept His Torah and mitzvot anew.

A DAY PREPARED FOR INAUGURATION AND GREATNESS

The very day of the 25th of *Kislev* which received the 'crown of inauguration' during the days of the Hasmoneans, had already been prepared for its greatness from the days of Moshe Rabenu — and had been reconfirmed in its special glory during the days of the prophet Hagai. But it was the merit of the Hasmoneans that the redemptive light of the day should be fully revealed in their days. And thus did the Sages say:

'Rabi Chanina said: On the twenty-fifth of Kislev the work of the *Mishkan* was concluded but it was kept folded till the first of Nisan, as it is written: 'On the day of the first month, on the first of the month, you shall erect the *Mishkan* of the tent of meeting.' And Israel murmured against Moshe saying: Why was it not erected immediately? Did some blemish affect it? God however intended to merge the rejoicing over the *Mishkan* into the month in which Itzchak was born *(Nisan)*... Kislev therefore missed the inauguration though the work had been concluded therein. God therefore said: It is for me to make restitution. How did God repay Kislev? With the Chanukah of the Hasmoneans' (Yalkut Melachim 184).

When the returnees from Babylonian Exile began to rebuild the Temple, their work was interrupted for twenty-two years because of enemy intrigue and opposition. When their work of rebuilding was resumed, they erected the foundation of the Sanctuary on the 24th day of Kislev. During the following night — the night of the 25th of Kislev — they celebrated the foundation laying.

AN ALLUSION TO THE FESTIVAL OF CHANUKAH IN THE TORAH

In *Emor* the Torah recounts all the festivals of the year: Shabat, Pesach, Shavuot, Rosh Hashanah, Yom Kipur and Sukot. The account of the festivals is followed by the commandment to maintain an eternal light in the Sanctuary. It has been suggested that the proximity between the two passages — that of the Eternal Light and that of the Festivals — anticipates a future day when the kindling of the Eternal Light would become a yearly Festival — a festival directly following Sukot, which is listed among the Torah-ordained holidays.

There is a similiar allusion to Chanukah in the proximity between the passage on the offerings of the *Nesi'im* (when the altar was dedicated), and the directly following passage on the Menorah. The Ramban writes in his commentary to the Torah (Beha'alotcha) : 'In the *Megilat Setarim* of Rabenu Nisim, I found the following statement: 'I saw in the Midrash that when the twelve tribes had each brought their offerings to the dedication of the altar, and the tribe of Levi had not been included in the altar offerings, God said to Moshe: Speak to Aharon and tell him that one day there will be another inauguration (Chanukah) with kindling of lights. Through your sons I will perform miracles and bring deliverance for Israel. I will give them another Chanukah to be called by their name: the Chanukah of the Hasmoneans. For this reason the present passage was placed in proximity to that of the altar dedication.

'I also saw in Midrash Yelamdenu, as well as in Midrash Raba: God said to Moshe: Go and say to Aharon: Have no fear. You are ordained for something greater than this. The altar offerings are only brought while the Sanctuary stands. The lights however will burn forever... and all the blessings which I gave you, that you might bestow them upon my children, will never cease. We know however, that in the absence of the Temple, and after the cessation of sacrificial offerings, the Menorah is likewise no longer lit. The reference of the Sages is accordingly, to the lamps of the Hasmonean Chanukah whose lighting remains binding even after the destruction of the Temple.' (Thus far the words of the Ramban.)

Still other allusions to Chanukah in the Torah:

The twenty-fifth word in the Torah is *or* (light).

The twenty-fifth place of encampment in the journeying of the children of Israel in the wilderness, was *Hasmonah.*

WHY CHANUKAH IS OBSERVED EIGHT DAYS

It is written in Megilat Ta'anit (Chapter 9) : 'What caused them (the Rabis) to designate the observance of Chanukah for eight days? Did not Moshe designate the Chanukah-dedication of the Tabernacle for only seven days?

'During the days of the Greek Kingdom, the Hasmoneans entered the Sanctuary, rebuilt the altar, repaired the walls of the Sanctuary, replaced the Sacred Vessels and were engaged in its rebuilding eight days.'

The Chanukah which we observe hence commemorates not only the dedication of the Menorah, but also the dedication of the altar and all the new Sacred Vessels. For the Hasmoneans hid the altar stones which the Greeks had defiled with pagan worship; and they erected a new altar and fashioned new Sacred Vessels.

In the Babylonian Talmud however, mention is made only of the miracle of the jar of oil, 'which had sufficient oil for burning only one day, but which miraculously burned eight days.' The above question therefore remains unanswered: Why do we observe Chanukah eight days, since the miracle of the oil occurred only for seven days, there having originally been sufficient oil for one day? Many of the great scholars have offered a variety of answers. The following are some of their explanations:

1. The first day of the festival commemorates the miracle of the military victory. 'On the 25th of Kislev the Jews rested from battle with their enemies.' They therefore celebrated the day, just as Purim celebrates the day when the Jews 'rested from their enemies.' The remaining seven days commemorate the miracle of the oil.
2. The very discovery of the one remaining jar of pure oil that was marked with the Cohen Gadol's seal, was itself a miracle.
3. The discovered oil was divided into eight portions to last the eight days required for the production of new oil. Till then the Menorah was to be lit for at least a brief hour every evening. Miraculously, the minute measure of oil poured into the Menorah each evening, burned the entire day.
4. After the Menorah was filled with all the available oil, the jar remained full as before.

5. All the oil was emptied into the Menorah, but after the lamps had burned all night, they were found next morning still filled with oil.

6. The Greeks prohibited circumcision, and this decree was the harshest of all the decrees they issued; its aim being to annul the covenant between God and Israel. When the Hasmoneans prevailed against their enemies, they rejoiced over the renewal of the covenant of circumcision, which is set for the eighth day in a child's life.

7. The first night they made thin wicks, which could only draw a minute measure of oil; they also apportioned the oil itself, of which they poured only a little into the Menorah. Miraculously, the lamps burned in full light all night, and the same occurred every remaining night. And therefore *hidur mitzvah* (the 'enhancement' of the mitzvah) is an essential aspect of the mitzvah of Chanukah lights — in contrast to other mitzvot, where hidur mitzvah is voluntary.

8. The jar itself absorbed some of the oil so that there did not remain even sufficient oil for one day.

9. The Greeks wanted to uproot faith in Divine Providence from the Jewish heart. They wanted to implant the belief that the events of nature occur only in accord with mechanical laws. Many Jews inclined to their view. Events however, convinced them that all existence reflected Divine Providence; that even when the world functioned in accord with natural law, it still remained totally dependent on the Hand of God and His Providence. From the miracle they understood that the natural function of oil is also a miracle.

10. The very fact that they did not despair from lighting the lamps even the first day, despite the knowledge that they would be unable on the morrow to fulfill the Torah's command to light 'a perpetual lamp,' was in itself a great miracle; a miracle which enables the people of Israel to endure through all generations and every exile.

Had they always tried to surmise what the future held in store for them, they would long since have lost the capacity to survive. The people of Israel have however placed their trust in God, and they have rejoiced whenever they were given the opportunity to abide by His Word.

PURE IN THE MIDST OF DEFILEMENT

The question is asked: The eight day period required for the production of the new oil resulted from the fact that the Jews had to wait seven days before they could press new oil, since they were defiled by contact with the dead in the war. But, it is an established principle in the Halachah that 'defilement is repealed for the community' (i.e., a community may perform the service of the Sanctuary even if its majority is in a state of defilement). Why then was it necessary for the Jews to wait seven days for their purification ?

The answer is: Although they were permitted to light the Menorah even with defiled oil, they were unwilling to do so, since this was to be the first lighting after an interruption; it was hence to be an act of dedication. And an act of dedication should be done in accord with the most stringent requirements of Purity.

WHY IS ONLY THE MIRACLE OF THE OIL MENTIONED IN THE TALMUD

Among the reasons mentioned above for the eight day observance of Chanukah, one was to the effect that the first day of Chanukah was originally designated in memory of the miracle of the military victory. This matter is mentioned in Megilat Ta'anit, which antedates the reaction of the Mishnah and the Talmud; whereas in the Talmud only the miracle of the lights is mentioned. Why the difference ?

The Scholars of later generations offer numerous explanations, of which the following is a partial summary:

At the time of the event — during the days of the Hasmoneans and shortly thereafter — the essential rejoicing of the Jews was over the military victory; over the destruction of the wicked and the nullification of their decrees against Shabat; against the sanctification of Rosh Chodesh (on which the dates of the festivals depended); and against circumcision. To later generations however the essential joy was over the miracle of the oil. For, the Hasmonean kingdom subsequently ceased to exist. Their descendants were annihilated while the Sanctuary still stood. The Sanctuary itself was destroyed and Israel reverted again to bondage among the nations. The miracle of the oil however, endured forever. And in commemoration of that miracle the people of Israel light the lamps of Chanukah every year in all their places of habitation.

Thus it is written in our sacred works: Wherever oil is mentioned in the Torah or in the words of the Sages, with reference to lighting the Menorah, an allusion is intended to the wisdom of the heart and the thoughts of the mind. When the Greeks entered the Sanctuary they defiled all the oils. That is to say, they blemished the thoughts and feelings of the majority of the people of Israel. For even among the Jews a majority began to be attracted to the wisdom of the Greeks, and began to believe that that wisdom contained enduring reality.

When the Hasmoneans returned to the Sanctuary victoriously, they found only one jar of pure oil; which was sufficient to light lamps for only one day. That is to say, despite all that the Greeks had done to mar the thoughts of the holy people of Israel, there still remained a light in their hearts, a minimal purity of thought and lone sparks of true wisdom. Some of them still retained the knowledge that they were sacred and chosen, among all other peoples; that the nations would one day walk by Israel's light, and not the opposite.

This remnant however, was incapable of lighting a perpetual lamp, since their thoughts were largely blemished and confused, through the impact of the Greek spirit. 'And a miracle occurred and they burned eight days.' That is to say, they received aid from above so that the sole surviving spark of true wisdom within them might be fanned into a flame, till it would illuminate them enduringly. (Each seven day period symbolizes a complete cycle of time. The eighth day represents the totality of time as well as what is beyond time.)

This miracle of purification is needed by Israel during all their generations, and especially during their times of bondage. For, as long as their faith and thoughts are pure, they are as if redeemed and upright, even in bondage. But when their inner faith and wisdom are 'blemished,' they are enslaved even in freedom. All the decrees which a non-Jewish world issues against Israel are subject to nullification, but when their faith is weakened, and their wisdom is falsified from within, they are liable — Heaven forbid — to be destroyed. They can then be saved only by Divine aid. The people of Israel is capable of escaping calamity only through miraculous Divine aid. Such aid comes while there is yet enough oil for one day.

The light kindled by the Hasmoneans from the lone jar of pure oil which burned eight days, lights up Israel's darkness eternally. Through its glow the sanctity of Israel and her unique identity among the nations are safeguarded. This miracle alone remained for the generations. The military miracle however, did not endure for the later generations. Therefore, the remembrance of the miracle of Chanukah unto later generations relates only to the lights of the Menorah.

THE LIGHTS OF CHANUKAH ARE BELOVED

Beloved are the lights of Chanukah for they are a memorial and a symbol of the Menorah in the Sanctuary. (We currently have no physical memorial of any other service in the Sanctuary). Beloved was the Menorah in the Sanctuary whose lights 'outweighed all sacrificial offerings.' What is the greatness of these lights ? They are a testimonial to Israel that all the light and rejoicing that a[illegible] come to them only from the light shed upon them [illegible] And even if this light seems small, and the light [illegible] by the nations of the world seems exceedingly larg[illegible] desires only the light which God sheds upon them, and no other light. The eyes of all Israel are lifted up to *Beit Hamikdash* (the Sanctuary), from which alone light emits to illuminate their world. When Shlomo built the *Beit Hamikdash,* 'he made for the House windows broad within and narrow without' (First Melachim 6), so that the light would radiate outwards from the Sanctuary and not into the Sanctuary from without. We are taught thereby that the Sanctuary was not in need of light coming from without, but rather that the whole world was sustained by the light which emits from it. The Menorah too, whose lamps the Cohen Gadol lit every evening, was not intended for casting light within the Beit Hamikdash, but rather for radiating light into the houses and the souls of Israel.

God too, greatly cherished this testimony of Israel's that they cleave to Him alone, and they seek His light more than that of all the works of creation. And He prefers this light, to the worship of all his hosts and ministering angels.

'To what may the thing be likened ? To a king who had a beloved friend. The king said to him : 'Be informed that I intend to dine with you; prepare a place for me.' The king's friend prepared a place according to his ability. When the king came, servants and attendants accompanied him, and there were golden lamps, on both sides. When the kings' friend saw all that glory, he was embarassed and hid all he had prepared. The king said to him : 'Did I not tell you that I would dine with you ? Why then did you fail to prepare anything for me ?' He answered : 'My lord the King ! I saw all the glory which accompanied you, and I felt ashamed, and hid all I had prepared. Said the king to him : 'By your life, I leave all that I have brought with me, and I will make use only of what is yours, for the sake of your love.'

'God himself is all light, but He commands Israel to light the lamp of the Menorah for Him perpetually. When Moshe erected the Tabernacle and the Menorah, and the Divine Presence entered the Tabernacle, it is written that, 'Moshe was unable to enter the Tent-of-Meeting, because the cloud dwelt upon it, and the glory of the Lord filled the Tabernacle.' Thereupon, 'And He called unto Moshe. And when Moshe came into the Tent-of-Meeting to speak with Him, he heard the voice speaking unto him.' And what was said to him? 'When you bring up (light up) the lamps...'

'Israel said: God has created the sun and the moon which shed light upon the entire world, but He desires that we should light lamps before Him!' (Midrash quoted by Rabenu Bechayey).

Israel's awareness that God desired their actions, elevated them above all other peoples, and lit up their path eternally.

The Greeks wanted only to uproot from Israel this exalted faith in what is above the laws of nature. They wanted Israel to act only in accord with natural laws; to honor the strong, to shame the weak, to negate themselves before the many, to disregard the few. Thus said Antiochus, the chief enemy of Israel, to his armies: 'They have one mitzvah. If you succeed in nullifying it, they are as if they had already perished. Which one? The lighting of the Menorah of which it is written that it is to be kept burning perpetually. As long as they light this lamp perpetually they will stand... They rose and defiled all the oils' (Be'er Chadash, Hilchot Chanukah).

Now that that one lamp was not extinguished, it rises ever higher and higher. It lights up all of Israel's houses, wherever they live eight days during the year. For Israel says before God: 'Your small lamp is better to us than the thousands of lamps of Your creatures!' And God answers them: 'I forsake all my legions, and I wish to use only what is yours. No law rules Israel, but only the Will of Him who fashions the laws of nature. If nature becomes an obstacle at times, nature will be cast aside, but the love between Israel and their Father in Heaven will not be cast aside. The miracle will come and will again light up the little lamp which 'devours' all the large luminaries.

DIVINE JUDGMENT IS NOT ARBITRARY

The *cohanim* of the house of Hasmonai were exalted in saintliness. Through them a great salvation was achieved for Israel at the time; and a miracle was revealed for all later generations till our time. Why then did their kingdom fail to endure? Why did the 'Attribute of Divine Judgement' strike them down so harshly, till they were all slain, and their seed was cut off from Israel?

Indeed, the matter was Divinely ordained, that all the generations of the house of Israel might learn thereby, not to violate God's oath to David that his kingdom would endure forever: and in order that not a word might fall from the testament of our father Ya'akov. For our father Ya'akov bade his sons before his death: 'A sceptre shall not depart from Yehudah, nor a lawgiver from between his feet, till *Shilo* will come, and to him peoples will gather' (Bereishit 49). That is to say, once sovereignty is given to Yehudah, it will not depart from him forever. Princes, judges, there could be among the other tribes, but not anointed kings.

The Hasmoneans were without peer in wisdom and piety among their brothers. They were righteous and saintly as angels on High, and they feared to entrust kingdom and dominion over the shattered people of Israel, to the hands of descendants of the royal house of David, who were not strong as they were, or pious as they were. The Hasmoneans feared that Israel might be harmed by them. They therefore took glory unto themselves for the sake of Heaven, and for the sake of their people and their land. The Lord, however, thought otherwise. 'Once did I swear by My Holiness, whether I would lie unto *David*.' This thought of theirs, to grasp the kingdom for themselves, was an unintentional wrong on their part; but Divine judgment is not arbitrary. And the merit of all their righteousness did not suffice to save them. Further, because they were righteous, God judged them stringently, unto a hairbreadth. For they struck at the House of David, and they anointed kings, who were not of the seed of David.

The Ramban writes in his commentary to the Torah, in *Va'yechi*: 'And this was the penalty of the Hasmoneans who reigned during the second house; though they were saintly, and if it were not for them, Torah and mitzvot would have been forgotten from Israel. Nevertheless, they suffered great punishment. For the four sons of the aged saint (Matityahu) reigned one after the other, and each in turn fell by the sword of their enemies, despite all their strength. In the end their punishment extended so far... that our Sages said: 'Whoever says, I am from the house of Hasmonai is a slave.' (For Herod first served them, then anihilated them, and then sat on their throne). They were all cut down for the sin of having reigned though they were not from the seed of Yehudah and the house of David; having removed the sceptre (from Yehudah) completely. They were penalized measure for measure. For God caused their servants to rule over them, and their servants cut them down.

'It is also possible that their sin consisted of their assumption of sovereignty despite the fact that they were *cohanim*. For the cohanim were bidden: 'You shall guard your kehunah unto every matter of the altar,...' It was not for them to reign, but only to be engaged in the Divine service. And I have seen in the Jerusalem Talmud: cohanim may not be anointed as kings... for it is written, 'in order that he might live long on his kingdom, he and his sons in the midst of Israel' (Dvarim 17). What is written immediately afterwards? 'There shall not be unto the Levite cohanim, the entire tribe of Levi, a portion or inheritance.' (Thus far the words of the Ramban.)

We may learn from this how awesome is Divine judgment against those who stretch forth hands against the sovereignty of the House of David.

WAR BETWEEN SANCTITY AND DEFILEMENT

The war waged by the Hasmoneans against Greek rule was not similiar to a typical revolt of the enslaved against their oppressors. Had it been Israel's aim to seek only freedom, they were able to achieve full national freedom even under Greek dominion.

The Greeks made no designs upon their bodily freedom. They desired only to enslave the Jews spiritually. More than this: The Greeks held that they were benefitting the Jews, in imposing upon them, Greek culture and wisdom. It was their aim to 'liberate' Israel from 'superstition and backwardness.'

The other peoples living under Greek domination willingly accepted Greek culture, and saw a great light in it. Among Israel too, there were many whose spirits were captivated by the enchantments of Greece. The Greeks wanted only to shed the spirit of their culture upon Israel, till the people of Israel would place their faith in Man's strength, in his aesthetic sense, and the ultimate reliability of human reason. The cardinal principles of Jewish faith — that God speaks to Man and prescribes specific commandments for him to observe — these were to be nullified and uprooted from the Jewish heart. The people of Israel of that generation, with the Hasmonean cohanim at their head, viewed this 'Torah' of the Greeks as the root of all evil, as the most abominable form of paganism. All idolatry is an abomination, but when Man himself becomes an idol, and all his faculties minister to the idol — he has then created an infinitely worse abomination. When wood and stone are worshipped, they inflict no greater harm or ruin than their worshippers do, because they have no spirit of their own. Whereas, if man is deified, and ultimate faith is placed in the superiority of his good taste and the truth of his reason, he is then capable of evil and destructiveness that are without limit.

The Hasmoneans saw this defilement strike root among their people and branch out among them more and more from day to day. Till the Sanctuary itself was defiled. They saw war with the Greeks as a 'war of obligation.' For the people of Israel had been invested with the task of safeguarding purity and sanctity in the world. As it is written: 'And you shall be unto me a kingdom of cohanim and a holy nation.' 'For all the land is Mine.' These teachings stood in fundamental opposition to the belief which the Greeks sought to impose. The two could not abide together. Sanctity stood arrayed in war against defilement.

THE DOMINION OF GREECE

Yefet, the son of Noah, had seven sons, of whom *Yavan* (Greece) was the fourth. For seventeen hundred years the family of Yavan played an insignificant role in the world, till her star rose, and she became the chief of kingdoms, in the days of Alexander of Macedonia. The earthly hosts are like the hosts of Heaven. Just as God ordained boundaries for the Heavenly hosts — one was given dominion over the day, while another was restricted to the night — likewise the hosts of the earth. Their Creator placed each of the nations and kingdoms within its set boundaries. To one He gave beauty, to another strength; to one wealth, to another wisdom, so that each might entrench himself within his own sphere, without needing to enter that of his fellow. Israel alone was ordained to be God's precious treasure among all the nations. All the good and the beautiful that was to be found among all the nations, could be acquired by Israel also. In one respect Israel was to rise above them all — in cleaving to God.

Yefet and his sons were given by God, the domain of beauty and wisdom. Their father Noah blessed them thus: 'God, you have given beauty to Yefet, and he shall dwell in the tents of Shem.' 'The beauty of Yefet, within the tents of Shem.' That is to say, it is fitting for the beauty of Yefet to enter the tents of Shem, and to find there its proper fulfillment.

After Alexander of Macedonia had lifted Greece to the pinnacle of power, and had conquered nations, one of his successors, King Ptolemy of the Egyptian segment of Alexander's empire, made his capital a center of learning and science. The Sages of Israel were then requested to translate the Torah into Greek, to enable the seekers of Greek wisdom to enter the outer gates of the Torah of Shem. The Jewish Sages relied upon the above interpretation of the blessing to Yefet, to confirm the propriety of their translation.

While Alexander lived, he showed reverence to the Sages of Israel and bowed his head before Shimon the Tzadik. Alexander's Greece, replaced Persia in preeminence. And Yehudah lived under Greek dominion as she had previously done under Persian dominion. As long as Alexander lived however, he inflicted no harm upon Yehudah, but rather showed her friendship.

After Alexander's death, his empire was divided in three. One of his generals achieved power in Egypt, one in Greece itself, and a third in Syria. The Syrian kingdom became known as the Selucidean kingdom after Selecus, who established its royal family. Yehudah fell under the dominion of the Syrian kingdom and from them, the people of Israel suffered ever harsher oppression.

The Syrian-Greeks resented the little Judean kingdom in their midst, which maintained its separateness despite its subjugation to them; which rejected all of Greece's culture and wisdom, and stubbornly resisted its spirit.

The competition was not one of strength, for physically Yehudah was subjugated to her conquerors. It was a contest only of the spirit. In the contest of strength the hand of Yavan had prevailed. In the contest of spirit, the hand of Yehudah had prevailed, to the bitter chagrin of the rulers.

After the Torah was translated into Greek, the rulers of Greece first delighted in it, and were even inclined to forgive the pride of those who adhered to the Torah. Later, that Torah became as thorns in the eyes of succeeding Greek rulers, and they resolved to uproot it from the hearts of those who were faithful to it, in order to subjugate them completely in body and spirit. Israel's Torah became a target for enemy arrows, and conflict erupted between mighty, conquering Greece, and weak, subjugated Yehudah.

WHEN DOES BEAUTY BECOME UGLINESS?

The Heavenly hosts and the Earthly hosts both have tasks. But they are not alike with reference to freedom of will. The Heavenly hosts can only perform their assigned tasks. Men however, are invested with freedom of will, and are capable of altering their tasks for evil to themselves and evil to all the world. When the beauty of Yefet dwells in the tents of Shem, and serves Shem, it is genuine beauty. When the maidservant seeks to replace the mistress; when the beauty of Yefet seeks to subjugate Shem's tents, and to make Shem serve her, there is nothing uglier.

Strength becomes transformed into brutal tyranny. Wisdom becomes cunning. Truth becomes distortion. Why ? For without tyranny, cunning and distortion, how could the mistress submit to the maidservant ? — What beauty remains for them ?

The rulers of Greece were prepared to consent to major portions of the Torah; to those of its practices which they imagined as capable of being 'poured into Greek utensils.' Three mitzvot alone, however, they wished to annul completely. If these could be annulled, the remaining mitzvot could be transformed into empty Greek ritual; to be forgotten from the heart in the end. The three are: Shabat, the consecration of the new month, and the covenant of circumcision.

Shabat recalls to its adherents, and all who see them, that the world has a ruler, through whose word naught turns into being, and being can be turned into naught. Shabat proclaims: 'Accord honor to your Creator, and let all the Earth bow down to Him.' It must be uprooted, and its memory forgotten. 'We are lords of the earth and all its inhabitants shall bow only unto us,' said the Greeks.

The consecration of the new month recalls to those who consecrate it, and to all who view them, that God's power acts in Time. Time does not have final dominion over those who live within its confines, but everything depends on the sanctity with which Time is invested by those who worship God. If the *Beit Din* sanctifies the new month, it is sanctified; its festivals are sanctified; and they become wellsprings of holiness and exaltation. for body and soul. If the Beit Din fails to sanctify the new month, it remains profane. Since it is the basis for the observance of the festivals, the consecration of the month also teaches the Presence of God and the fulfillment of His aims, within History. The consecration of the new month hence teaches both the holiness of time and the holiness of history. It must be uprooted from Israel, and its memory must be erased. 'We ordain festival times: we determine when to rejoice and when to grieve !'

The covenant of circumcision recalls to those who strike it, and to all who see them, that body and soul — both together — are hewn from one source. Just as the human soul has a grasp in the upper worlds, and is obligated to adhere to their laws. For, all the worlds together are one world — the world of the Creator. And all that is found in them serves Him and performs His will. This covenant is to be uprooted from Israel; let it not challenge the Wise Men of Greece who say: There are two worlds — the body rules without restraint in its world, and the soul rules without restraint in its world — with nothing standing in the way of its highest aspirations, its song and visions. The body is not subject to the soul, and the soul is not subject to the body. The body is pig-like; the soul is angelic.

A world without a Creator, a year without holiness, a body without restraint — is there anything uglier? Sights of external beauty in the place of the visions of God. Wild spectacles in the place of exaltation and holiness. A conflagration of instincts in the place of sanctifying the body. What value is there in such a life?

HELLENISTS

At first the Greeks thought that they would attract the people to their teachings with peaceful techniques. They therefore won over the light-minded among the people by giving them power in both the government and the Sanctuary. These were appointed as officials, Cohanim Gedolim, Elders and Judges. Together they formed a sect which came to be called, 'The Hellenists.' The Hellenists sought to spread Greek culture among the people. They incited the people to forsake God's Torah, and to embrace the Greek way of life, as they had done. They arranged evenings of lust and licentious dancing. They erected altars to the Greek idols, to which they brought offerings. All their days were filled with celebrations, enchanting entertainment and inflammatory pleasures.

The larger part of the people did not follow them and continued to adhere to the Torah of their fathers. They turned their backs on the traitors, and hated them in their hearts. They wept to their God over their traitorous brothers, and over the people of God who were handed over to enemies without, and to traitors within. The evil Antiochus saw that the Hellenists were not achieving their aim; and that they were as outcasts in the eyes of the majority of their people. Whereupon he sent his armies, under the leadership of relentless brutal commanders, either to force the Jews into submission or to subject them to slaughter.

These armies murdered, slaughtered and plundered. They spread desolation among the people, and afflicted them with all manner of persecution. They put to death tens of thousands of men, women, children and infants, who offered their lives for the Torah. Some of the people surrendered, bowed to the idols, and participated in the abominations. Some fled to the wilderness, or hid in caves. The Hellenists helped the enemy track down those who were in hiding; to torture those who had not fled, and to incite them to wanton transgression. And they handed over the daughters of Israel to the enemy tyrants for defilement.

They then came to the courtyard of the Sanctuary and defiled it. They suspended the daily offering. They defiled the oils and the Menorah. They built an altar and offered a pig on it, whose blood they then brought into the Holy of Holies. The people heard and trembled in outrage. It became apparent that there was no escape from open war with sword and spear, against both the enemy and the traitorous brothers.

THE MIRACLE OF THE REVOLUTION

The first miracle was performed through the daughters of Israel. If a child was born to the wife of one of those who had fled into hiding, the mother would circumcise the child on the eighth day. She would go up upon the wall of Yerushalayim carrying her child. She would hurl herself and her child from the wall to certain death — thereby saying to her husband, and all her brothers who had gone into hiding to escape war: 'If you will not go out to wage war against your enemies, you will have neither children nor wives, and your end will be total annihilation. We will observe what is holy to us, not in hiding, but publicly, before the eyes of all. If you intend to save us, emerge from your caves, and wage war against the enemy till you destroy him. God will be with you !'

Then Matityahu and his five sons arose like lions. They

gathered about them all who were faithful and valiant. They went out to slay the enemies of God, or to be slain. For many days they battled — the few against the many, the weak against the mighty — but the hand of God sustained them, till they vanquished their enemies, and cleansed the land from Antiochus' armies and their abominations. Then they came to the Temple Court, cleansed the altar, and rebuilt it. They made a new Menorah of wood and lit lamps for eight days. They kindled the lights of Torah, of joy, of faith and trust in God, in the homes of all Israel — in all their habitations, and for all generations.

MEASURE FOR MEASURE

The great salvation performed by God through his chosen *cohanim* in behalf of his chosen people opened the eyes of many of those who erred. Many of the peoples saw that God's name was called upon Israel; that He exacted vengeance in their behalf, and repaid their enemies measure for measure.

After the Greeks had conquered most of the peoples of the world and became masters over them, they arrogantly thought: We will rise above the clouds, and will subjugate the chosen people. We will remove its crown of glory, and will cast it down to the ground, as we have done with so many other peoples. After the Hasmonean victory over them, their penality was, to become the lowliest of nations. They intended to cause the Torah to be forgotten from Israel, and to extinguish Israel's light; instead they added yet another Yom Tov of remembrance and testimony that the Torah will never depart from Israel. An allusion to the matter is found in the saying of our Sages: 'The *mezuzah* is on the right, the light of the Chanukah is on the left, and the head of the house, whose *talit* contains *tzitzit*, is in the middle.' These three are safeguards against forgetfulness. *Mezuzah* causes us to remember His sovereignty — *tzitzit* is intended to be a remembrance. The Chanukah light is also a remembrance. (The later Sages have said that gazing at the Chanukah lights, causes one to remember the *mitzvot*, just as gazing upon *tzitzit* does.)

Thus did our ancient Sages say: 'And there was darkness upon the face of the abyss' — this refers to Greece which darkened the eyes of Israel. For this reason the lights of Chanukah were prescribed.

The Sages likewise interpreted the verse: 'And its side was that of a serpent,' as referring to Greece. For the serpent is without gratitude and the Greeks wished to uproot from Israel the sense of subjugation to God's will, and of gratitude to Him. For this reason, the people of Israel prescribed additional thanksgiving over the miracle.

The Greeks wanted to uproot the sanctification of the new month from Israel; that is to say, the power of perpetual self-renewal and God gave Israel an additional capacity for self-renewal. The mitzvah of Rosh Chodesh is the first renewal which God gave to Israel, and Chanukah is the final renewal, till the Messiah will come.

The Greeks took pride in their strength and numbers. But they fell by the hand of a people who were few in number, and who were poorly armed.

They took pride in their great wisdom, and in their well ordered government. But they were revealed before the eyes of the world, as predatory animals. Their disciples from among the Jews, the Hellenists, scoffed at Israel for placing its trust in God, and waiting for His salvation. They said: 'Learn the art of war from the Greeks; do not turn to your Torah and to your prayers. If you will rely on these, you will be trodden under the foot of any people who will attack you. And then salvation came; through the mighty heroism shown by the weak against those who were renowned for strength. Further, the war did not begin from the strong and the militant among the Jews. It rather began with cohanim who served in the Sanctuary — upon whom no hatchet could be raised. 'These with chariots, and those with horses, but the cohanim of the Lord proclaimed the Name of their God. The others kneeled and fell, but the servants of God rose and prevailed.' We learn thereby, that none are strong before God, or before the people of God; that the many are as naught, if they are defiled and evil; that victory is not theirs, but goes to the weak, and to the few who are pure and righteous. For real strength endures only if it is based on purity. And a genuine bond prevails only among the righteous. The bond of the wicked however, is without endurance.

BETWEEN CHANUKAH AND PURIM

When the wicked Haman decreed the annihilation of all the Jews, young and old, children and women, on one day, and the decree was sealed irrevocably with the king's ring, they fasted three days, and poured forth their hearts in prayer that God might rescind the evil decree. Why did they not originally band together to defend themselves on the day of the calamity ? The decree was for one day only, and even if they might not all have been saved through self defense, some might have been saved. Were there not many valorous men amongst them ? Were not many of them capable of hiding in caves, till the day of anger would pass ?

On the other hand, when the Greeks decreed the eradication of the Torah from Israel, and the decree struck at all that had been Divinely sanctified for them, they did go forth with sword and spear, and offered their lives in battle. Why did they not then proclaim days of fasting, prayer and repentance, so that the anger of God might recede from them ? Were there not among them exalted saints, cohanim of the Lord, who were erudite in Torah and knew the ways of prayer ? Why then did they all take only to sword and spear ?

Thus, however, did the people of Israel say: 'Your light — the Torah — is in our hands. Our light — our soul — is in Your hand. You have entrusted your Torah in our hands, and we entrust our lives in Your Hand. If we will guard Your light, You will guard ours. If we save Your light, You will save ours.

'As for the enemies of God, they hate both Your light and ours, and they desire always to extinguish both. But as long as one guards the other, they cannot prevail against either.'

The Holy One, Blessed is He, is always faithful, and never removes His protection from Israel even for a single hour. Israel is at times unfaithful, and does not guard God's light. At such an hour, Israel's enemies are given power to inflict harm. They rise then to extinguish Israel's light, so that God's light would, Heaven forbid, be extinguished at the same time. At times they rise to extinguish God's light, so that Israel's light might, Heaven forbid, be lit out simultaneously.

When enemies rise against Israel to destroy him bodily, it is a sign that the Divine Presence has withdrawn from Israel, and has ascended above. And though the enemies themselves have not seen it, they sense it intuitively. They are then not concerned with the Divine Presence — which has already withdrawn from Earth. But they devise schemes only to extinguish Israel's light. In such an hour, it is for us to seek strength and repentance, in prayer, and in Torah — in God's light — till the Divine Presence returns to dwell in our midst. When the Divine Presence descends again — God's light again sheds light over the earth — and our enemies no longer have dominion over our light; it is secure by itself.

When the wicked of the nations conspire to extinguish God's light — to cause Torah and mitzvot to be forgotten — it is a sign that a decree of annihilation has, Heaven forbid, been issued against Israel from above; but that the Divine Presence has not yet withdrawn, and still dwells on earth. And though the wicked have not seen it, they intuitively sense, that Israel's protection has been taken away. They therefore are not concerned with Israel during such an hour, but they devise all their schemes only against God's light on earth, and they seek to defile the Sanctuary; so that the Divine Presence might withdraw from earth, and His light might also, Heaven forbid, be extinguished.

In such an hour, it is for us to exert our physical strength; to commit our lives in military struggle, in order to again light our light. For, in the strength of physical battle for the sake of God and His Sanctuary, we show that our physical lives also have enduring substance, since they are servants to God's light. Divine compassion is then awakened unto us anew from Heaven; the decree of annihilation is rescinded: for, in rendering our lives holy to God, we ourselves become infused with a spirit of new life. And then, the wicked certainly no longer have the strength to extinguish God's light on earth.

It may hence be said: we save the light of our own lives with God's light, and God's light, with ours.

Since the ways of salvation during Chanukah differed from those of Purim, the memorials prescribed for these days also differed from one another. The days of Chanukah were not given for feasting, for the memorials are intended to reflect only the character of the festival; and since our striving in war was then for the sake of God's light, and physical salvation came as a secondary result, the days of Chanukah are not days of feasting and physical enjoyment, but rather days of praise for God's continued Presence.

The days of Purim are not 'days of praise,' since the essential aim of our prayer then, was for our own light. The days of Purim were rather given for feasting and rejoicing, to show that our aim was achieved, and God saved our physical lives from the hands of our enemies.

INSIGHTS

The Miracle of the Oil — What need was there for the entire miracle ? Does not the Torah free one from the obligation of a mitzvah, if he is prevented by circumstances beyond his control from performing it ? Furthermore, could not the miracle have provided oil for all eight days? The answer is that the miracle came to demonstrate how beloved Israel was before God; that He desires their actions and performs miracles for them, so that they might be able to fulfill His will. For this reason there is greater help from above during these days, for one who seeks strength in the service of God.

The lack of sufficient oil for the entire eight day period was an allusion to the lack of proper preparation and atonement on the part of those who were to light the Menorah for there was left in them only a minimal 'dot' of inner preparedness for the mitzvah — the 'dot' which is concealed within every Jew, and which God protects against all alien defilement. If this 'dot' is sought after, it is surely found, and with God's help it expands till it fills the entire person, similarly to the candle which originally had sufficient oil for only one day, but which miraculously burned eight days.

It is Forbidden to Make Use of the Chanukah Lights — Why were the Sages more stringent concerning this light, to the extent that they forbade all benefit from it? The Chanukah light is a memorial to the light which burned in the *Beit Hamikdash*, whose light also was not to be used for any personal benefit or pleasure.

'Mehadrin,' and 'Mehadrin Min Hamehadrin' — All the mitzvot require *hidur* (enhancement), in accord with the verse: 'This is my God and I shall worship Him with beauty.' One should beautify himself before Him, through the manner in which he performs mitzvot. Why then is the Chanukah light singled out among the other mitzvot to the extent that it is largely performed after the manner of those who are *mehadrin min hamehadrin* (applying more *hidur* than most)? As mentioned earlier, were it not for Israel's desire to reconsecrate the Menorah in keeping with the requirements of *hidur*, the entire miracle would not have been necessary. Further, at the time of the miracle, the people did not all rejoice alike. Those who performed the mitzvah only out of a sense of obligation did not rejoice greatly, since were it not for the miracle, they would have been free from the obligation. Those who performed the mitzvah lovingly however, rejoiced exceedingly, and without the miracle, they would have grieved. Similarly, those who performed the mitzvah with readiness to sacrifice themselves in its behalf, rejoiced still more. The *Halachah* thus remained fixed that three options be given in the performance of the mitzvah corresponding respectively to a sense of 'obligation,' *hidur*, or *hidur-min-hidur*.

The Chanukah Light Is Placed at the Left Side of the Entrance — It is written: 'There is length of days in its right hand; in its left there are wealth and honor.' Wealth and honor belonged to *Yavan* (Greece), the son of Yefet. But since the Greeks turned to evil, Israel merited their portion too. Hence, Israel requests of God also the wealth and honor which were 'with the left hand.'

The door serves for entry as well as departure. The mezuzah is placed to the right of the way of entry, and the Chanukah light is placed on the right of the way of departure. That is to say, this lamp sheds light upon us even when we are 'outside,' when we dwell in the midst of the nations. And even now that the *Beit Hamikdash* no longer exists, the light of the Chanukah lamp still shines constantly.

During Chanukah we read in the Torah from the passage recounting the offerings of the heads of the tribes when the altar was consecrated. As mentioned earlier, the altar was consecrated on the 25th day of Kislev — the same day on which Chanukah was later observed. The mitzvah of, 'And they shall make for Me a Sanctuary, and I shall dwell in their midst,' is a timeless one. Every Jewish person is obligated to yearn daily for the rebuilding of the Sanctuary. Now that we light Chanukah lamps in memory of the miracle which occurred in the sanctuary, we place the Chanukah lamps in the doorway of our homes facing outward — like a person who stands waiting at the door for one who will bring the tidings of our redeemer's arrival, speedily in our days, Amen.

The Door and the Mezuzah Shall Be Witnesses — The Sages prescribed the placing of the Chanukah lamps near the door and the mezuzah; that these might be witnesses that even if Israel be enslaved by tyrants, they yet remain the servants of God alone, and of no other master. And just as the ear of a slave is pierced, near the door and the mezuzah — if he refuses freedom when his time comes — likewise now, at a time of liberation from enslavement, and of yearning for a return to God's service — let the lamps of freedom and redemption burn before the door and the mezuzah. And let the door and the mezuzah testify that Israel desires no foreign yoke, but only the yoke of the Kingdom of Heaven. For they are His servants and not servants to servants.

In Those Days At This Time — Israel has many days — besides the festival ordained by the Torah — which commemorate spectacular miracles and acts of salvation. But of these days only Chanukah and Purim were ordained as fixed festivals every year. For a day of salvation becomes a fixed Yom Tov only if the salvation which it celebrates opened 'gates of Divine Mercy,' from which the same salvation flows year after year and generation after generation — on the very day on which the miracle occurred. If the salvation 'sheds light' in every generation on the same day, the day is ordained as a fixed Yom Tov; otherwise not. And judgment in this matter is entrusted to the Prophets and to the outstanding Sages of the time.

Chanukah and Purim are also similar to the festivals prescribed by the Torah, in the sense that they are capable of 'shedding their light' all year; just as Pesach with the light of freedom; Shavuot with the light of Torah, Sukot with the light of rejoicing and the Days of Awe with the light of forgiveness. We therefore say during Chanukah and Purim: 'That He made miracles for our fathers in those days at this time.' That is to say, those miracles shine for us during the days of Chanukah and Purim, even at this time.

'The Following Year They Established the Days of Chanukah with the Recitation of Halel and Thanksgiving — Why did the Sages fail to do so the same year? For prophecy no longer existed, and the Sages of the generation feared to establish a yearly Yom Tov, lest its mark might not be recognizable the succeeding year. When the Sages saw that these days shed light within them during the following year as during the previous one; when they inwardly felt true freedom and an ever growing desire to speak praise and thanksgiving before God, they then fixed the days, as days 'for the saying of Halel and thanksgiving' for every generation. It is for us to know that the tolerance which evil enemies have often shown towards Israel's observance of the Torah and mitzvot, comes largely from the effect of what transpired in that generation, and the mark of that salvation is recognizable every year during the days of Chanukah.

Another Allusion — 'They established them with *Halel* and Thanksgiving' — Because of the fact that the Sages prescribed the recitation of Halel and a specific Thanksgiving prayer during Chanukah, these days were 'established' within the souls of the Jews; who are able in those prayers to sense, during Chanukah, the light of the original days of Chanukah.

Halel and Thanksgiving — Halel and Thanksgiving relate to the soul and the body. Halel comes from the illumination of the soul. As it is written: 'Every soul shall praise God.' Thanksgiving reflects the submission of the body when it acquiesces to the soul. We therefore bend the knee during prayers of thanksgiving, but we do not bend the knee during Halel. Thanksgiving is done verbally, whereas Halel is also experienced in thought and desire.

Halel is said for redemption; Thanksgiving is said for the end of enslavement — it stems from the understanding that even the earlier oppression was also for the good.

Halel — for the miracle of the lamps, which was entirely spiritual. Thanksgiving — for the military miracle and the physical salvation. The miracle of the lights is therefore not mentioned in the prayer of thanksgiving (except for the general reference, 'and they lit lamps in the courtyard') because thanksgiving is essentially said for the military miracle.

ZOT CHANUKAH (The Last Day of Chanukah)

The last day of Chanukah is called 'Zot Chanukah' because of the closing portion of the Torah-Reading of the day: *'Zot Chanukat hamizbe'ach'* ('This was the dedication-offering of the altar...') The Sages have said *'Zot Chanukah* (This is Chanukah) — this eighth day is the essence of Chanukah.' The 'Eight' is always an allusion to eternity, to what is timeless. 'Seven' alludes to what is timebound.

This day corresponds to the 'eighth day of *atzeret*', which follows the seven days of Sukot. Just as Shmini Atzeret contains the essence of all the festivals which preceded it; the atonement of the Days of Awe and the rejoicing of Sukot — similarly, 'Zot Chanukah,' the eighth day of Chanukah, contains all the rejoicing and salvation of all the previous days.

THE CONCLUSION OF SUKOT

Three festivals are prescribed for Israel in the Torah: Pesach, Shavuot and Sukot. Corresponding to these three festivals authority was given to the Sages to establish three festivals deriving from the Oral Torah. The three festivals deriving from the Oral Torah are reflections of the light of the Written Torah, similar to the moon's reflection of the light of the sun. Through Israel's observance of the three God-given festivals, a mark is made upon the soul of the community of Israel by each of the festivals. From this inner effect, Israel is capable of deriving corresponding festivals which reflect the light of the original ones.

The light of the eight days of Chanukah reflects the light of Sukot and Shmini Atzeret — the time of our rejoicing. Through Israel's having walked after God in the wilderness; their having dwelt in the protection of His sukah; their having rejoiced before Him the 'one additional day' of Shmini Atzeret — there was inscribed in their souls a deep imprint on the light of Sukot. Therefore, even if all their enemies beset them, and seek to becloud their eyes, in order to separate between them and their Father in Heaven, they are nevertheless assured of emerging again from darkness to light; of returning to dwell in the shadow of trust in Him.

The light of Purim is a reflection of the light of Shavuot, the time of the giving of the Torah. Through Israel's declaration: 'We shall do and we shall obey,' beneath Mt. Sinai, a powerful imprint of the covenant-of-Torah was made upon their inner beings. And even though they were later enslaved under the hand of a harsh king, who intended to annihilate all the Jews, they again accepted upon themselves, lovingly and willingly, the original covenant: 'We shall do and we shall hear.' Further, at that time a new light was given to them, the light of the festival of Purim whose essential rejoicing is for their reconfirmation of Israel's original acceptance of the Torah.

At the time of the final redemption — may it come speedily in our days — a new light will shine upon Israel which will stem from the light of the first redemption, which occurred on Pesach. That new light will come to Israel through the merit of their having borne the yoke of exile; of their not having despaired of final redemption; of their having waited for it daily; of their having retained the joy of their first redemption, even in the depths of their later exile. Of that day the prophets foretold: 'As during the days of your departure from the land of Egypt, I will show them wonders.' 'Therefore, behold, days are coming, and it shall no longer be said: As the Lord lives, who brought up the children of Israel from the land of Egypt, but rather, as the Lord lives, who brought up the children of Israel from the land of the North and from all the lands whither He cast them away — and I will return them to their land which I gave to their fathers.'

The Sages have said: 'Even if all the other festivals will be annulled, Chanukah and Purim will not be annulled.' To what may the thing be likened? To one who was given money to invest in business. He did so and profited heavily. Later, even if what was originally given to him is taken from him, what he profited on his own, will not be taken.

Likewise, the festivals which were prescribed in the Torah were given to Israel without their own previous merit. Whereas Chanukah and Purim were given to Israel by the merit of their own deeds; through their having offered their lives in behalf of the purity of their faith — in the case of Chanukah; and through their having voluntarily accepted the covenant of the Torah at the time of Purim. Their merit was further enhanced because they accomplished all this when they were in a state of oppression and enslavement.

ALL ISRAEL ARE EQUAL DURING CHANUKAH AND PURIM

Since Chanukah and Purim were achieved by Israel through the merit of their own deeds, the sanctity of these festivals is therefore equally experienced by Jews wherever they live.

The later Sages have said that for this reason Chanukah and Purim are not observed for two days, outside the Land of Israel as is the case of the festivals written in the Torah. In addition to the doubt concerning the proper day for the observance of the festival, another reason has been suggested for the observance of a second day of Yom Tov outside the

Land of Israel: In exile we do not have the strength to enter into the sanctity of the festival in one day alone. In the Land of Israel, the holiness of the land helps us to absorb the holiness of the festival more quickly. Chanukah and Purim however — since the people of Israel merited them through their own deeds — are close to Israel's inner soul, and Jews therefore find it easier to enjoy their glow wherever they are — even outside the Land of Israel — without adding an additional day.

Tevet

THE MONTH OF TEVET ◆ A MONTH OF ANGUISH ◆ THE TRANSLATION OF THE SEVENTY ◆ AN ACT OF GOD ◆ A TROUBLED DAY ◆ SIX FAST DAYS ◆ THE TENTH OF TEVET ◆ UNDER SIEGE AND TRAVAIL ◆ FASTING IN ORDER TO RECTIFY OUR SINS ◆ EXPULSIONS BUT NOT SPITTING OUT ◆ THE OBSERVANCE OF THE FAST ◆ THE PUBLIC FAST AND THE INDIVIDUAL FAST ◆ DAYS ON WHICH MANY FAST ◆ SHOVAVIM TAT.

CHAPTER EIGHT

THE MONTH OF TEVET

The month of Tevet is the tenth in the number of months counting from Nisan. The name Tevet was acquired by the people of Israel in Babylonia, as is the case with the other names by which the Hebrew months are designated. In the Scroll of Esther (Chapter 2) the month is referred to as, 'the tenth month which is the month of Tevet.'

Rosh Chodesh Tevet is at times observed one day and at times two days. The month of Tevet itself always consists of 29 days, hence Rosh Chodesh Shevat which follows always consists of one day.

A MONTH OF ANGUISH

During the month of Tevet, three fast days are observed in commemoration of the three calamities which befell Israel on the 8th, 9th and 10th of the month. The fast days of the 8th and 9th of Tevet are called 'fast-days-for-the-righteous.' On these days, only individuals fast, whereas the fast of the 10th of Tevet is a public fast for the entire community.

On the 8th of Tevet the Torah was translated into Greek by the decree of King Ptolemy. The day was regarded as equally calamitous for Israel as the day on which the Golden Calf was made — since it was impossible to adequately translate the Torah.

On the 9th, there occurred the death of Ezra the Scribe and Nechemiah, who faithfully led Israel during the return from Babylonian captivity. And the eyes of all Israel were clouded by their death for their loss was irreplaceable.

On the 10th, Nebuchadnetzar, King of Babylonia, laid siege to Yerushalayim. He beleaguered the city three years till its walls were breached on the 9th of Tamuz during the third year of the siege.

On the 1st of Tevet, Yechoniah, King of Yehudah, was exiled together with the Sages and the nobles of Yerushalayim. The day was not however designated as a fixed fast day.

With the exception of the closing days of Chanukah, the month of Tevet contains no Yom Tov or festive day.

THE TRANSLATION OF THE SEVENTY

At the beginning of the period of the second *Beit Hamikdash,* the people of Israel lived under Persian dominion. After the fall of the Persian Empire, Greece inherited her place, and Israel was subjugated to Greece.

One of the Greek Kings who succeeded Alexander of Macedonia, Ptolemy of Egypt, bade the Jewish Sages to translate the Torah into Greek. That his motives were questionable is attested to by the fact that he did not assemble the Jewish scholars in one place so that they might execute their task in joint deliberation. He rather did differently. In the Talmud it is related:

'King Ptolemy once gathered 72 Elders. He placed them in 72 chambers; each of them in a separate one, without revealing to them why they were summoned. He entered each one's room and said: 'Write for me the Torah of Moshe, your teacher.' God put it in the heart of each one to translate identically as all the others did' (Tractate Megilah 9).

Ptolemy found no discrepancy between any of the individual translations. Even in a number of places where the Elders intentionally altered the literal translation, the results were identical; which in itself constituted a public sanctification of God's Name, as well as of the name of Israel and its Sages.

Ptolemy imposed a task on the 72 Elders, which was beyond human capacity. The Torah was written in such a way that its content might be open to great variety of possible interpretations, as a 'hammer cleaves a rock.' The Torah was given to Israel in the Holy tongue together with a prescribed method for interpreting its words, verses and letters; thereby eliciting the wide range of meaning which inheres in them. By contrast one who seeks to translate the Torah into a foreign tongue, will find that there is no language whose words are as rich in possible connotation, as is the holy language. What then does such a translator do ? He forsakes all the treasures of interpretation, allusion, and esoteric meaning contained in each word, and translates only the literal meaning. If one translates the Torah into another language, he is therefore like one who makes of the Torah an empty vessel; empty of its entire wealth of meaning which is the essence of Torah. He is left with literal meaning alone. How impossible is such an effort therefore, for those who love the Torah and know its greatness.

At times the literal meaning of a particular verse or word is also in doubt and allows for alternate meanings. Which is to be chosen ? If the translators are many, and they work separately without joint deliberation, the difficulty becomes manifold greater; it being highly unlikely that the path chosen by one, would also be chosen by the others. Is it indeed possible for any individual to reach identical conclusions with 71 other individuals in a multitude of details by surmise and conjecture alone ?

Further, there are many passages in the Torah which, if translated literally, would be misunderstood by the gentiles, and would cause them to deride our Torah's sanctity. It would therefore become necessary either to add explanatory phrase, or to render the intent of the Torah in translation, rather than its literal meaning. Would it then be possible for 72 Sages of differing personality, to perceive the identical intention ? If the interpretations of the Elders were to vary widely, it would not blemish either the Torah or its interpreters in our eyes, since we would say: 'These and those are the words of the living God.' As for the gentiles however, any dispute in interpreting the Torah, would cast blemish on the Torah, and on the Sages in their eyes. For they would say: 'Where there is dispute — there is a lack of truth.'

The very act of Ptolemy and his manner towards the Jewish Sages betray his desire to mislead them, and to find an opportunity for faulting their words.

The 72 Elders were however granted Divine assistance. And they all interpreted the meaning of the Torah identically, wherever the interpretation or even style were in doubt; thereby confirming the verse: 'The teeth of the wicked, you have broken' (Tehilim 2).

A TROUBLED DAY

The day on which the 72 Elders concluded their Greek translation of the Torah — the 8th of Tevet — was a day of sorrow for Israel, despite the fact that they all saw an awesome act of God in it. Although God's Providence in behalf of His people and the Divine protection accompanying his Sages were made manifest that day, and the matter evoked general wonder in non-Jewish eyes, the day was nevertheless as tragic a day for Israel as the day on which the golden calf was made. In Megilat Ta'anit, the Sages described the event as follows:

'On the 8th of Tevet, the Torah was rendered into Greek, during the days of King Ptolemy, and darkness descended upon the world for three days.'

To what may the matter be likened ? To a lion captured and imprisoned. Before his imprisonment, all feared him and fled from his presence. Then, all came to gaze at him and said, 'Where is this one's strength ?'

Likewise the Torah. As long as the Torah was in the hands of Israel and was interpreted by the Sages in its own language — the holy language — it evoked reverence, and many feared to cast blemish upon it. Even the gentile who was imbued with a desire to study the Torah, had no contact with the Torah till he had previously entered under the wings of the Divine Presence; till he had acquired a knowledge of the Holy tongue and the prescribed ways for understanding the Torah. Once the Torah was imprisoned in Greek translation, it was as if the Torah were divested of reverence. Whoever wished to could now come and gaze at her. Whoever wished to fault her, could now do so.

The Sages therefore likened the event of this day, to the day on which the golden calf was made; for just as the golden calf had no reality, and yet its servants regarded it as having real substance, likewise, was the translation devoid of the true substance of Torah; and yet the gentiles who see the translation, imagine that they already know the Torah.

The assertion of the Sages, 'and darkness came to the world for three days,' is therefore a possible allusion to the fact that the events of the 8th of Tevet themselves anticipate all the calamities which occurred respectively on the 8th, 9th, and 10th of Tevet: the translation of the seventy; the death of Ezra and Nechemiah; the siege around Yerushalayim.

The following is a partial list of the identical changes made by the Elders in their translation from the literal words of the Torah:

'God created in the beginning' instead of, 'In the beginning created God' — lest it be said: 'In-the-beginning was the Creator.'

'I will make Man' instead of 'We will make Man' . . . lest it be said that God is dual in nature.

'With an image and a likeness' instead of 'In our image

after our likeness' ... lest the creature be compared to the Creator.

'And God finished on the sixth day,' instead of, 'on the seventh day' ... lest it be said that God labored on the Sabbath day.

'Male and female He created him,' instead of, 'He created them' ... lest it be said that they were originally created with two bodies.

'Come, I shall go down and confuse their language,' instead of, 'Let us go down and confuse'... lest it be said God is dual in nature.

'For in their anger they killed a man, and with their will they uprooted a bucket' instead of 'They killed a man, and with their will they uprooted an ox' ... lest it be said that the sons of Ya'akov were murderers. (for having slain even animals indiscriminately).

'And the time that the children of Israel dwelt in Egypt and in other lands was 400 years'. .. they added the words, 'and in other lands,' and deleted the words, '30 years,' lest it be said that the Torah contains falsehoods. For the celebration of 400 years does not correspond with a literal reading of the Torah, but is in accord only with Rabbinic interpretation — which is not accepted by the gentiles.

'Not one desired object of theirs did I take up.' They wrote, *chemed* (desired object) instead of, *chamor* (mule)... lest it be said that Moshe did not take any mules from Israel, but he took some other objects.

'Which the Lord your God apportioned to them to shed light unto all the nations.' The word for, 'to shed light' was added ... lest it be said that the Torah permitted the nations to worship the sun and the moon.

They also wrote, 'The young of foot,' instead of, 'The *arnevet* (the hare) ... since Ptolemy's wife was named *Arneveth,* and he might say the Jews ridiculed him by inserting his wife's name in the Torah.

SIX FAST DAYS

There are six fast days during the year, on which all are obliged to fast: One is prescribed by the Torah; four were ordained by the later prophets... Hagai, Zechariah, Malachi, and one which was ordained by the Sages after the period of the prophets. The six fast days are: Yom Kipur, the Fast of Gedaliah, the Tenth of Tevet, the Seventeenth of Tamuz, the Ninth of Av, and the Fast of Esther.

Yom Kipur was prescribed by the Torah for the tenth of Tishrey as a day of repentance and atonement for transgression. 'And it shall be unto you as an eternal statute; in the seventh month on the tenth of the month, you shall afflict your souls.'

The four fast days prescribed by the prophets commemorate our grief after the destruction of the Sanctuary and the exile of the people of Israel from their land. In Zechariah reference is made to the Fast of the Fourth and the Fast of the Fifth, and the Fast of the Seventh, and the Fast of the Tenth...' (Zechariah 8).

On the Seventeenth of Tamuz ('the fast of the fourth'), the walls of Yerushalayim were breached at the time of the destruction of the second Temple, whereas during the time of the first Sanctuary, the city walls were breached on the Ninth of Tamuz. (Other calamities also occurred during the same day which will be discussed at the appropriate place.) On the Ninth of Av ('The Fast of the Fifth') both Sanctuaries were destroyed, and numerous other calamities occurred the same day.

On the Third of Tishrey ('The Fast of the Seventh') Gedaliah the son of Achikam, was slain, and Jewish autonomy was totally crushed, after the destruction of the first Sanctuary.

On the Tenth of Tevet ('The Fast of the Tenth'), the King of Babylonia laid siege to Yerushalayim and beleaguered it till its final conquest.

The Fast of Esther was adopted by the Sages and the people of Israel in memory of the Fast they observed during the time of Mordechai and Esther, when they gathered to defend themselves against their enemies, and also in memory of the fast observed in Shushan when the decree by Haman to annihilate Israel was made public.

The fast days of Yom Kipur, the Ninth of Av, and the Tenth of Tevet are observed on the fixed days prescribed by the Torah and the Prophets respectively.

The Fast of Esther was first observed not on the day on which the original fast occurred; the date of the original occurrence having been the 15th, 16th and 17th of Nisan, on which the Jews of Shushan fasted. At the time, the *Sanhedrin* in Shushan agreed to suspend the festival of Pesach and to fast on it because of the danger to the life of Israel. When however, they fixed the date of the fast for later generations, they chose the Thirteenth of Adar, which was the day when the Jews gathered to wage war against their enemies; with the following day to be observed as Purim, in commemoration of their victory. Our contemporary fast therefore, recalls both original fasts; that of Esther, Mordechai, and the Jews in Shushan, as well as the day of ingathering for war.

The 'Fast of the fourth month' was originally fixed for the ninth of Tamuz, on which day the walls of Yerushalayim were breached, at the time of the destruction of the first Temple. After the destruction of the second Temple however, Rabi Yochanan Ben Zakai and the Sages of his generation, agreed to move the observance of the day to the 17th of Tamuz; on which the walls of the city were breached, during the destruction of the second Temple. Their motive was that the destruction of the second Temple was a greater calamity than that of the first, since the first one was rebuilt, while the second has not yet been rebuilt, And since both dates occur within the same 'fourth month,' the fast day would still be observed in the month originally prescribed by the Prophets.

Concerning the Fast of Gedaliah, there is a dispute. Some say that it is observed on the day of occurrence; namely, that Gedaliah was slain on the third of Tishrey, Others hold that Gedaliah was slain on the first of Tishrey, but that the fast was not fixed for that day, because Rosh Hashanah falls on the first and second of Tishrey. Hence, they fixed it for the day following Rosh Hashanah the third of Tishrey.

THE TENTH OF TEVET

From the day they entered the land under the leadership of Yehoshua, the people of Israel inhabited their land for a period of eight hundred and fifty years; and twenty generations of children and grandchildren were born to them, till the evil Nebuchadnetzar, King of Babylon, rose against them and exiled them. Of this period, 440 years elapsed till King Shlomo built the Sanctuary, and another 410 years passed till the Chaldean host destroyed it.

When Israel entered the land, they were to dwell there eternally. For thus did God assure Avraham: 'For all the land that you see, to you I shall give it, and to your seed, unto eternity' (Bereishit 13). God imposed only one condition: 'And you shall observe all my statutes and all my judgments, and you shall do them — so that the land may not spit you out, wherein I bring you to dwell in it' (Vayikra 20). 'And that the land may not spit you out, if you should defile it, as it spat out the nation that was before you' (Vayikra 18).

'The matter may be likened to a prince who was fed some repulsive food, which he could not retain, and disgorged it. Similarly, the land of Israel does not sustain transgressors' (Rashi ibid.).

Of the twenty one generations who dwelt in the land the first time, there were numerous generations who failed to observe God's commandments, and defiled the land, with the execrations of idolatory. As a result, divine anger descended upon Yehudah and Yerushalayim. Prophets were sent to admonish them and to stir them towards repentance. But they would not listen.

'Also all the leaders of the cohanim and the people transgressed greatly by following the abominations of the nations; and they defiled the Lord's house which He had sanctified in Yerushalayim. And the Lord, the God of their fathers, sent to them by His messengers, sending betimes and often; because He had compassion upon His people, and upon His dwelling place; but they mocked the messengers of God, and despised His words, and scoffed at His prophets, until the wrath of the Lord rose against His people, till there was no remedy' (Second Divrey Hayamim 36).

The Sages said: 'To what were the ten tribes and the tribes of Yehudah and Binyamin likened ? To two persons who clothed themselves in a new garment during the rainy season. One pulled from one side, and the other from the other side, till they tore it. Likewise, did the ten tribes not stop from worshipping idols in Shomron, and the tribes of Yehudah and Binyamin worshipped idols in Yerushalayim, till they brought about the destruction of Yerushalayim' (Opening of Eichah Raba).

'And it was in the ninth year of his reign, in the tenth month, in the tenth (day) of the month, that Nebuchadnetzar King of Babylon came, he and all his hosts, upon Yerushalayim, and he encamped upon it and built forts around it. And the city came under siege till the eleventh year of King Tzidkiyahu. On the ninth of the month famine was intense in the city, the people had no bread, and the city was breached...' (Second Melachim 25).

'And in the fifth month, on the tenth of the month... Nebuchadnetzar came... and he burned the house of the Lord, and the King's house, and all the houses of Yerushalayim... and the entire wall surrounding Yerushalayim was destroyed ... and Nebuzaradan, the captain of the guard, exiled the remaining multitude' (Irmeyahu 52).

We see then, that the tenth of Tevet — on which the siege of Yerushalayim began, was the beginning of the whole chain of calamities which finally ended with the destruction of the *Beit Hamikdash.*

UNDER SIEGE AND TRAVAIL

'And the city came under siege ... and famine became intense in the city.' The daughters of Zion gathered in the market places, and upon seeing each other, one would say to the other: Why have you come out to the market place, for you have never done so? The other answered and said: Shall I hide it from you? The plague of famine is hard. I cannot bear it. They held on to each other, and went about the city seeking food, but did not find it. They embraced the pillars and died in every corner. Their suckling children crawled about on hand and foot, each one recognizing his mother, and seeking to nurse milk from her. When the child found no nourishment, his life was severed, and he died in his mother's lap' (Pesikta Raba 26).

'When that *rasha* (wicked one) came to Yerushalayim together with the kings, they thought that they would capture it in little time. But God strengthened the inhabitants of Yerushalayim till 'the third year' ... perhaps they would repent. There were numberless heroes in Yerushalayim who waged war with the Babylonians, and inflicted heavy losses upon them. There was one hero among them by the name of Avika Ben Gavrati, who used to catch in his hands, the rocks hurled by the enemy against the wall, and then throw them back upon the enemy soldiers — slaying many of them. He even began to stop the stones and to hurl them back with his foot. But because of our sins, a wind came and hurled him from the wall. He was shattered and died. At that hour Yerushalayim was breached, and the Babylonians entered' (Yalkut Shimony Eichah 1).

FASTING IN ORDER TO RECTIFY OUR SINS

'The essential significance of the fast of the Tenth of Tevet, as well as that of the other fast days, is not primarily the grief and mourning which they evoke: Their aim is rather to awaken the hearts towards repentance; to recall to us, both the evil deeds of our fathers, and our own evil deeds, which caused anguish to befall both them and us — and thereby to cause us to return towards the good. As it is said: 'And they shall confess their transgressions and the transgressions of their fathers' (Vayikra 26. Rambam Hilchot Ta'anit Chapter 5).

The Sages have said: 'Every generation in whose days the Sanctuary is not built, it is reckoned unto them, as if they had destroyed it' (Jerusalem Talmud, Tr. Yoma 1). For every generation has the capacity to 'awaken' Divine mercy, that Israel be redeemed; its exiles assembled to their land; and the Sanctuary rebuilt. How? By perfect repentance, and the correction of their previous transgressions. And as long as salvation fails to come, it is a sign that we have not yet repented from our sins, and that we are still suffering from the results of our own transgressions, as well as our repetition of our fathers' transgressions. It is therefore as if we were delaying the final redemption, and as if we ourselves had caused the destruction.

Even when the Sanctuary is destroyed and Israel dwell in exile; our inheritance is desolate, and in the hands of transgressors, God has not divorced His people, Heaven forbid; He has not decreed external exile for them, nor has He decreed eternal ruin for His Sanctuary. Exile, destruction and anguish, are all temporary, and may at any hour of Divine mercy be transformed into rejoicing. Habitation in the land and the building of the Sanctuary, are alone eternal.

EXPULSION BUT NOT SPITTING OUT

The verse which says: 'So that the land shall not spit you out when you defile it, as it spat out the nation which preceded you' (Vayikra 18), is not only a warning, but is also a promise. God here assures Israel that even if they should defile the land, it will not spit them out eternally. Only the nation which preceded us was eternally 'spat out' from the land. Not so Israel. We were expelled from it for our transgressions; we were exiled from it for our misdeeds. But we shall again return to it. We shall again possess it as an eternal inheritance. And the matter depends only upon repentance, and the action of Divine mercy in quickening the time of our final redemption.

The aim of fasting, therefore, is to subjugate our evil inclination by restriction of pleasure; to open our hearts and stir us to repentance and good deeds...through which the gates of Divine mercy might be opened for us.

Therefore, each person is obligated to take it to heart to examine his deeds and to repent during these days. As it is written of the people of Ninveh: 'And the Lord saw their actions' (Yonah 3) ... upon which the Rabis say: 'It is not said, He saw their sack cloth and fasting, but rather, their actions...' (Ta'anit 22). We see hence that the purpose of fasting is repentance.

'Therefore, the people who fast but engage in aimless walking about, and in pointless activities, grasp what is of secondary importance and forsake what is essential. Nevertheless, repentance alone, without fasting is insufficient. For during these days it is a positive commandment of Prophetic origin to engage in fasting' (Chayey Adam 133).

The Sages have stated: 'Of every fast whose intention is improper Scripture says: 'She raised her voice upon me, therefore I hated her' (Jerusalem Talmud, Ta'anit Chapter 2).

THE OBSERVANCE OF THE FAST

If a public fast falls on Shabat it is delayed till after Shabat... since fasting is not permitted on Shabat. The one exception is Yom Kipur, which is prescribed by the Torah, and hence is observed on the day of its occurrence even if it falls on Shabat. The 'Geonim' also write that the same was once true of the tenth of Tevet, since it is written of the tenth of Tevet: 'On this very day' (Yechezkel 2). In our calendar calculation, however, the tenth of Tevet can never fall on Shabat.

If a public fast occurs on Erev Shabat we fast the entire day till the conclusion of the fast, despite our entry into Shabat while fasting. Nowadays our calendar calculation is such that the only public fast which can fall on Erev Shabat is the tenth of Tevet.

During every public fast with the exception of Yom Kipur and the Ninth of Av, eating is permitted the previous night till daybreak. This is so, however, only if one has not slept regularly. If he has, it is as if he had already begun the fast upon going to bed, and he may not eat, even if he rose before the dawn. If however, it was his intention before going to bed, to rise from sleep and to eat before daybreak, he may do so. Further, if he habitually drinks something upon rising from bed, he may drink before daybreak even if he had not intended to do so.

During the Fast of Gedaliah, the tenth of Tevet, the Seventeenth of Tamuz and the Fast of Esther, washing, anointing and wearing shoes are permitted; these activities being forbidden only on Yom Kipur and the Ninth of Av. To wash one's mouth in the morning is however forbidden on every public fast. (In the view of the Magen Avraham washing the mouth is forbidden only if one uses as much as a 'revi'it' of water). And it certainly is prohibited to take any food into one's mouth, even if only for purposes of tasting.

The ill — even if their illness entails no danger ... pregnant women, nursing mothers, for whom fasting is difficult, as well as minors, are not obligated to fast these four fast days.

Those who are not obligated to fast, should nevertheless refrain from eating publicly, or from indulgence in eating, and they should eat only what is necessary for health. It is likewise proper to train minors by feeding them only what is necessary for them, and to diminish their pleasure, so that they might experience a sense of mourning with the community.

We are more lenient concerning the Fast of Esther, which originates in custom, than concerning the other fast days, which are of Prophetic origin.

(The rules of observance for Yom Kipur and the Ninth of Av are explained in their appropriate places.)

All the fast days which are days of mourning for the destruction of the 'Beit Hamikdash,' will be suspended in the days of the Messiah. They are even to become Yamim Tovim and days of rejoicing. As it is said: 'Thus did the Lord of Hosts say, the Fast of the Fourth and the Fast of the Fifth, and the Fast of the Seventh and the Fast of the Tenth, shall be to the House of Yehudah for rejoicing and happiness and for festivals' (Zechariah 8).

On the Shabat preceding the tenth of Tevet, and on that preceding the seventeenth of Tamuz, it is customary in the Sephardi communities for the cantor to announce: 'Our brethren, the house of Israel, hear! The Fast of the Fourth (or the Fast of the Tenth) shall be on (Sunday or Monday etc.). May

God transform it into rejoicing and happiness as it is written: 'Thus did the Lord of Hosts say, the Fast of the Fourth...'

THE PUBLIC FAST AND THE INDIVIDUAL FAST

If Beit Din proclaims a public fast over some trouble which has befallen the community, such as a drought, a plague, locusts or the like, the same *dinim* (laws) apply to them as to all the above mentioned public fasts, despite the fact that they are not fixed fast days. A fast over drought is an exception however, and its *dinim* are, at times, as severe as those of the Ninth of Av. Nowadays a public fast over drought does not differ from any other fast.

'It is a positive commandment in the Torah to cry out and to sound trumpets over any trouble that befalls the community. As it is said: '...against the enemy that oppresses you, then you shall sound and alarm with the trumpets' (Bamidbar 10). That is, when you face trouble... cry out and sound trumpets.

'And this matter is an aspect of *teshuvah* (repentance)... that in a time when trouble befalls, they should cry out and blow trumpets over it, that all might know that the evil befell them as a result of their evil actions. But if they will not cry out, and will not sound trumpets, and they will say: This matter is a natural occurrence, and this trouble is accidental — then their behavior is brutal, and it causes them to cleave to their evil actions; and their present trouble will lead to further troubles. Of this it is written in the Torah: 'And if you will walk contrary unto me; then I will walk contrary unto you in fury' (Vayikra 26. Rambam Hilchot Ta'anit 1).

Just as it is obligatory for the community to fast and pray over any troubles that befall it, likewise is it obligatory upon each individual to engage in fasting and in seeking Divine mercy if trouble befalls him.

Neither a public nor a private fast may be set for Shabat, Yom Tov, Rosh Chodesh, Chanukah or Purim; the one exception being a fast over a dream which is permitted even Shabat. It is however permissible to accept a personal fast upon oneself during 'minchah' on Shabat ... fast to be observed on a permitted day.

If an individual wishes to accept upon himself a personal fast, he should do so, through intention during minchah the previous day with silent reflection while saying the brachah 'shma kolenu'. After the conclusion of 'shmoneh esreh' (the silent prayer), he should state verbally: 'Tomorrow I will fast.' If he failed to state his acceptance of the fast verbally, but only intended to do so during minchah, he is nevertheless obligated to fast, so long as he made a verbal acceptance while it was yet day. But if he accepted the fast after dark, his fast does not have the formal status of a fast (which is regarded as a sacrificial offering for him), but he is yet obligated to fast in fulfillment of a vow. In either case, he adds the prayer of 'anenu' to his regular prayer.

Why is formal acceptance of the fast necessary? For a fast takes the place of a sacrificial offering through the lessening of one's own fat and blood, and a sacrifice always requires previous consecration.

In the case of a personal fast it is permissible to wash one's mouth in the morning and it is also permissible to taste food, though it may not be swallowed.

If one accepted a fast because of some trouble, and the trouble passed, he is yet obligated to complete his fast. Even if he has not yet begun, he is obligated to fulfill his pledge. If however, it later became known to him that at the very time of his acceptance of the fast, the ill person had already recovered or had died, then his very 'acceptance' was in error and he is not under obligation to complete his fast.

One who fasts — whether a public fast or a private one, says 'anenu,' during minchah of the fast day. If one forgets, and pronounces the Divine Name at the close of 'shma kolenu' without having said 'anenu,' he concludes the 'shmoneh esreh,' and says 'anenu' immediately preceding the verse, 'May the words of my mouth be accepted,' before stepping backwards upon the conclusion of 'shmoneh esreh.'

'Anenu' is not said during 'shacharit,' for some accident may occur to prevent his completion of the fast, in which case he would have prayed falsely. The Sephardi custom however, is to say 'anenu' even during 'shacharit.'

During the public fast, if there are at least seven persons present in the synagogue who completed their fast, then the cantor says 'anenu' both 'shacharit' and 'minchah' upon concluding the 'brachah,' 'See our afflictions,' and proceeds immediately with the next brachah, 'Heal us.' Unlike the individual, the cantor says 'anenu' as a separate brachah and concludes with: 'Blessed are You, O Lord, who answers in a time of trouble.'

The 'cohanim' pronounce their prescribed blessing during minchah on a public fast. (This blessing is not pronounced during minchah on any other day. Outside the Land of Israel, the blessing of the 'cohanim' is recited during minchah on a public fast day by the cantor.)

'Selichot' (penitential prayers) are said on a public fast day, and the passage 'Vayechal' is read in the Torah during 'shacharit' and 'minchah.' Only those who fast the whole day, are called to the Torah. If a 'cohen' is present who does not intend to complete

the fast, he should leave the synagogue, so that he might not be called to the Torah. If however, a non-fasting person is called, he should 'go up to the Torah' out of regard for its honor, so that it might not appear as if he were refusing to 'go up to the Torah.'

If one who fasts, forgetfully recites a brachah over food, but remembers his fast before eating, he says, 'Blessed is the Name of His glorious majesty unto eternity,' after the brachah which he had uttered for naught. If he remembers his fast after having eaten the equivalent of an olive-measure, or having drunk the equivalent of a mouthful, his fast is no longer valid if it be an individual fast; and he may subsequently eat as much as he desires. In case of a public fast however, he is still required to complete the day in fasting, and he is not required to fast another day but to make restitution for it, since he had been unintentionally remiss.

The ancient Sages considered it praiseworthy to give the food uneaten on a fast day, to the poor. In the absence of a poor man, the equivalent value of the food should be given for some sacred purpose. Likewise does the Jerusalem Talmud comment on King David's utterance; 'And I, in my affliction, have prepared unto the house of the Lord gold and silver' (I Chronicles 22) when King David afflicted himself by fasting, he contributed his meal for sacred purpose.

DAYS ON WHICH MANY FAST

The following are days on which calamities occurred to our fathers and it is proper for individuals to fast on them. Some authorities permit fasting on these days, even if they fall on Rosh Chodesh. It is however proper — in the case of those which fall on Rosh Chodesh — not to complete the fast.

The first of Nisan: The sons of Aharon died.

The tenth: Miriam died, and the miraculous spring which accompanied Israel in the wilderness through her merit, departed.

The 26th: Yehoshua, the son of Nun, died.

The tenth of Iyar: Eli, the Cohen, and his two sons died, and the Ark of God was captured by the Philistines.

The 28th: The Prophet Shmuel died.

The 23rd of Sivan: The bringing of *bikurim* (offering of first fruits) to Yerushalayim ceased, in the days of Yeroveam, the son of Nevat.

The 25th: Rabi Shimon, the son of Gamliel, Rabi Ishmael and Rabi Chanina were slain by the Romans. (The three were among the ten martyrs whom the Romans put to death in an effort to extirpate the study of Torah.)

The 27th: Rabi Chanina, the son of Teradyon, was burned alive together with a scroll of the Torah.

The first of Av: Aharon, the Cohen, died.

The 18th: The Eternal Lamp (in the *Beit Hamikdash*) was extinguished in the days of Ahaz.

The 17th of Elul: Those who brought forth slander against the land of Israel (the spies sent by Moshe), died.

The fifth of Tishrey: Twenty Jews were slain by the Romans (in a period of forced conversion) and Rabi Akiva was imprisoned.

The seventh: The decree was issued that our forefathers should die by sword, famine, and plague, because of the making of the golden calf.

The seventh of Mar-Cheshvan: The Babylonians blinded the eyes of King Tzidkiyahu, after having slaughtered his sons before his eyes.

The 28th of Kislev: King Yehoyakim burned the scroll dictated to Baruch Ben Neriah, by his teacher, the Prophet Irmeyahu.

The eighth of Tevet: The Torah was translated into

Greek in the days of King Ptolemy, and darkness came upon the world for three days.

The ninth: Ezra the Scribe, and Nechemiah, who both led the Jews on their return from Babylonian captivity, died.

The tenth: The Babylonians laid siege to Yerushalayim at the time of the destruction of the first *Beit Hamikdash.*

The fifth of Shevat: The last of the Elders who lived in the days of Yehoshua, died.

The 23rd: All Israel gathered to wage war against the Tribe of Binyamin over the matter of the 'concubine in Give'ah.'

The seventh of Adar: Moshe Rabenu died.

The ninth: The House-of-Shamai and the House-of-Hillel engaged in dispute.

Some authorities consider it praise-worthy for individuals to fast voluntarily every Monday and Thursday over the destruction of the Sanctuary, the burning of the Torah, and the desecration of God's Name. In the future God will transform these days to rejoicing and happiness.

SHOVAVIM TAT

Shovavim tat is an acrostic whose Hebrew letters comprise the first letters of each of the following *sidrot* (weekly portions read in the Torah) : *Shmot, Va'era, Bo, Beshalach, Yitro, Mishpatim, Trumah, Tetzaveh.*

During an intercalated year, whose winter is longer by one month than the winters of other years, it is the custom of the pious to voluntarily fast eight days: the eight Thursdays of the weeks when the above *sidrot* are read. These fast days are regarded in the *Halachah* as individual fast days, rather then public ones, but they do not require formal acceptance during minchah of the previous day, since they are fixed for every intercalated year.

If enough fast to comprise a *minyan* of ten, *Va'yechal*

is read during *minchah.* During *shacharit* however, the regular weekly portion is read.

The reason for these eight fast days is as follows:

The number of winter days in an intercalated year is more numerous than during other years. Therefore, there is an interruption of more than half a year between the fast days of BaHaB of Cheshvan and those of Iyar (see page 257). And since the pious fast *BaHaB*, in order to attain forgiveness for the entire community, for a period of half a year, these fast days are intended, to atone for Israel's transgressions during the intercalated month, which is added to the half year.

The essential aim of the fast is to pray for Israel's fruitfulness, and that no expectant mother might miscarry. Therefore, the fast was fixed for the fifth day of the week, on which the fish of the sea were created — who were given the blessing: 'be fruitful and multiply.'

In the first of these eight *sidrot* it is written: 'and for all that they afflicted them, so did they increase and so did they expand.' The final *sidra, Tetzaveh*, contains the conclusion of the commandment concerning the erection of the Tabernacle — through which God dwells in the midst of the children of Israel.

Shevat

SHEVAT ◆ SHABAT SHIRAH — THE SABBATH OF SONG ◆ THE SONG OF ALL EXISTENCE FROM THE THROAT OF ISRAEL ◆ GRATITUDE ◆ THE FIFTEENTH OF SHEVAT ◆ A WEEKDAY ROSH HASHANAH ◆ A PRAYER FOR A BEAUTIFUL ETROG ◆ LAWS CONCERNING BLESSINGS OVER FRUIT ◆ THE PRAISE-OF-THE-LAND-OF-ISRAEL ◆ FLOWING WITH MILK AND HONEY ◆ AT THE TIME OF THE REDEMPTION ◆ THE FOUR PARSHIYOT ◆ THE INTERRUPTIONS BETWEEN THE FOUR SPECIAL SABBATHS ◆ SHEKALIM ◆ SHABAT SHEKALIM IN THE SYNAGOGUE ◆ THE HEALING PRECEDES THE WOUND ◆ THE COLLECTION OF THE SHEKALIM IS MANDATORY ◆ ONLY HALF A SHEKEL ◆ A SMALL RANSOM AND GREAT FORGIVENESS ◆ A FIERY COIN ◆ THE UNITY OF ISRAEL ◆ THE DESIRE TO PERFORM A MITZVAH.

CHAPTER NINE

SHEVAT

The month of Shevat is the eleventh month counting from Nisan. In the general calendar year of Jewish tradition, which begins with Tishrey, it is the fifth month. In Scripture it is referred to as the eleventh month: 'and it was in the fortieth year, in the eleventh month...' (Dvarim 1); 'on the twenty-fourth day of the eleventh month, the month of Shevat...' (Irmeyahu 1).

Shevat is always a full month of thirty days, with its thirtieth day counting simultaneously as the first day of Rosh Chodesh Adar. The preceding month of Tevet is always an incomplete one; thus, Rosh Chodesh Shevat always consists of one day.

On the first of the month, Moshe spoke the Book of Dvarim to Israel. 'Beyond the Jordan, in the land of Moab, Moshe took upon him to expound this law, saying...' (Dvarim 1). He admonished them over their repeated rebelliousness against God during the forty years of their wanderings in the wilderness. He again expounded for them many of the mitzvot which had already been addressed to them on Mount Sinai or from the Tent-of-Meeting. And he also addressed to them a number of new mitzvot which had not previously been given them. He recounted the blessings or curses to which they would be subject; he prepared them for their entry into, and possession of the land of Canaan, and he concluded by blessing them before his death. For thirty-seven days, Moshe spoke these words to all Israel. He began the first of Shevat and ended the seventh of Adar. His first words were: 'you have dwelt long enough in this mountain. Turn and take your journey, and go to the hill-country of the Amonites, and to all the neighboring places... as far as the great rivers, the river Perat.' His concluding words were: 'Happy are you, Israel, who is like unto you? A people saved by the Lord, the shield of your help, and the sword of your excellency — and your enemies shall dwindle away before you; and you shall tread upon their high places' (Dvarim 33).

The later Sages have therefore said that the first of Shevat is comparable to the day of the giving of the Torah. Just as the sixth of Sivan, on which the Torah was given to Israel, remains forever especially suitable for the renewed acceptance of the Torah, similarly is the heart of the Jew newly receptive to the influence of Torah on the first of Shevat, since the 'repetition' of the Torah was given to Israel on the first of Shevat. All the intervening days between the first of Shevat and seventh of Adar are therefore particularly suited for renewed inspiration in the study of Torah and the practice of mitzvot.

SHABAT SHIRAH — THE SABBATH OF SONG

The Sabbath on which the *sidra* of *Beshalach* is read is called *Shabat Shirah*, because it contains the song sung by Israel after the splitting of the Red Sea.

In addition to the 'song of the sea' this portion contains many other themes: the Exodus from Egypt, the splitting of the sea, the statutes and judgments given in Marah, the *manna*, the well, the war with Amalek. Nevertheless, Israel selected only the theme of *shirah* as the name to be given to this Shabat. For whenever Israel utters this song throughout the generations it is as new for them. When they first sang it, God and His Hosts hearkened, as it were, to the utterance of their mouths. At that hour the souls of Israel attained the highest state of exaltation; their hearts became wellsprings overflowing with Torah, and the sound of their words was like the voice of the Almighty. Further, this Torah which welled up from within them preceded the Torah which they heard from the Almighty on Mount Sinai.

With the strength of this song they 'implanted' song and rejoicing in the heart of Israel till the end of the generations. And whenever Israel would hence be delivered from their enemies and saved from distress, their hearts would then sing in praise to the God who had delivered them, and their thanksgiving would be not only in behalf of themselves, but for all God's loving-kindness. The *shirah* begins with the introduction: 'and they spoke, saying.' That is to say, the song which they spoke then, caused them to continue uttering song in all the generations.

This song was uttered by them in perfect faith, and not because of the impact and impression of the miracles they had seen. For the emotion which results from a momentary impression is transitory, whereas true faith is enduring. And Israel did not utter song till they knew at heart that all the bondage and affliction which they had known and would know; that all the testing and purification to which they had been subject, were acts of God's eternal lovingkindness. They then knew that Israel has no joy and no life other than through faith in God. It is thus written: 'and to the upright of heart there is rejoicing' (Tehilim 97). 'And the just shall live by his faith' (Chavakuk 2). And in the words of the *shirah* it is said: 'and they had faith in the Lord and in Moshe his servant — then Israel sang.'

Then the song of the sea was uttered in its proper time and place; at a time when all the Heavenly Hosts and every earthly creature were filled with song to their King, and acknowledged that the Lord was greater than all the gods. When the glory of His sovereignty filled the world, Israel uttered song. As it is said, 'Then Moshe and the children of Israel sang:' then — and not before; then — and not later.

Had they delayed their song, all existence would not have responded after them in song, for the effect of the event would have worn off. Had they uttered song immediately upon their departure from Egypt, it might have been said to them: 'Thank Pharaoh, for he set you free. See that his horses and chariots, and all his might are still untouched, whereas you are lost in the wilderness. Now that Pharaoh's horses and riders, and his army were drowned in the sea, and Pharaoh has remained without strength and pride — at this hour song is fitting; 'I shall sing to the Lord for He is highly exalted; the horse and his rider He has thrown into the sea.'

THE SONG OF ALL EXISTENCE FROM THE THROAT OF ISRAEL

'I shall sing to the Lord' — To Him alone, for there is none beside Him!

'For He is highly exalted' — He alone is exalted. But the pride of man casts him down to the abyss, though he seeks to rise to the heavens.

'The horse' — The symbol of strength and might among earthly creatures.

'And His rider' — a person takes pride in his dominion over the forces of creation. He fancies himself their 'rider,' but who is man and what is his pride in the presence of the power of a single one of God's creatures in the presence of the might of the sea when its waves rise ?

'He has thrown into the sea' — He has thrown your might into the sea, like one throws from his hand some minute object.

But even the raging sea and all the might of its waves — what are they before the children of God's loved ones ? A wind comes forth from His nostrils and immediately —

'The waters were piled up' — as if they were sand rather than water.

'The floods stood upright as a heap' — as if they were building bricks rather than flowing water.

'The deeps were congealed in the heart of the sea' — as if they were blocks of ice rather than boiling streams of water.

'In the heart of the sea' — the deeps did not dry up.

Below, they continued to flow as they were created to do. But when they reached the place of the feet of God's loved ones, there they were congealed — 'in the heart of the sea.'

And who are we, with all our praise, before the majesty of the King of the Universe, Who created all, and Who acts with lovingkindness towards all? We entered the sea redeemed, freed from bondage, exalted; we came out of the sea, servants again. All the greatness and the pride we restore to You, our God — for we are Your servants, and You are our king —

'The Lord shall reign forever!'

No creature ever uttered a more beautiful song to God than this one. This song is therefore, beloved to Israel. They recite it daily, and they read it publicly one Shabat each year, with a special melody and with great rejoicing. Some follow the custom of standing when it is read. Special honor is accorded this Shabat and it is crowned by a special name: '*Shabat Shirah*' ('The-Sabbath-of-song').

GRATITUDE

On Shabat Shirah some practice the custom of scattering remnants from their Sabbath foods outside their homes, to feed the passing birds.

The portion of Torah which is read on this Sabbath contains the account of the *manna* which came down for Israel in the wilderness. Daily, the Israelites gathered *manna* in prescribed measure for each individual. On Friday they were instructed to gather double measures of manna, since no manna fell on the Sabbath. We are told however, 'and it was on the seventh day, some of the people went forth to gather, but they found none.' On which the Rabis comment, that those who went forth to gather the manna on Shabat day were iniquitous. Since they knew that the manna would not fall on the Shabat, as Moshe had said, they went forth during the night and scattered some of their leftover manna on the fields. Their intentions were to gather it in the morning and to bring it into the camp before the eyes of the people, so that the people might say that Moshe was deceitful and that he fabricated mitzvot himself. When morning came and they went for the manna they found none. The birds had preceded them and had gathered it up during the night, thereby vindicating Moshe's words and causing the Sabbath to be sanctified among the people. The birds therefore, receive their justified reward, when their righteousness is recalled in the reading of this *sidra.*

Others say that the reward they receive is accorded them for the song which they utter to God as they chirp daily. And when we read the Torah portion which contains our song, we also recall the song of the birds.

THE FIFTEENTH OF SHEVAT

The 15th of Shevat is one of the four 'Firsts-of-the-Year' *(Rosh Hashanahs)* which each year contains: the first of Nisan, the first of Elul, the first of Tishrey and the 15th of Shevat.

The first of Nisan is regarded as Rosh Hashanah with reference to counting the years in the reigns of the Kings of Israel, as well as with reference to the order of the pilgrim-festivals.

The first of Elul is Rosh Hashanah with reference to tithing of animals. All the animals which are born till the first of Elul are counted for the departing year; those born afterwards are counted for the new year and are tithed separately. Tithes may not be taken from animals born one year for those born another year. (since the animal tithe bears the sanctity of a sacrificial offering — unlike other tithes — it does not apply nowadays.)

The first of Tishrey is Rosh Hashanah for the judgment of mankind; for the count of *shmitah* and jubilee years; for counting the first three years *(orlah)* produce of newly planted trees; and for grain and vegetable tithes.

The 15th of Shevat is the Rosh Hashanah of trees, with reference to the different tithes which are brought each year, counting towards the seventh, *shmitah* year. The same applies to the conclusion of the *orlah* years. And some hold that it also applies to the fruit of the seventh year, so that fruits which begin to ripen before the 15th of Shvat of the eighth year have the status of fruit of the seventh year. (Fruits are regarded as having begun to ripen from the time of their appearance, but prior to having reached a third of their full size.)

Our Sages have designated the 15th of Shevat as the boundary between one year and another, since most of the rains of the previous year have already fallen. Any new growth of fruit after this day, is a result of the blessings of the new year. On the 15th of Shevat also, the soil is already saturated with the rains of the previous winter, so that trees newly planted after the 15th of Shevat are assured of taking firm root and bringing forth fruit.

A WEEKDAY ROSH HASHANAH

Although the 15th of Shevat is called Rosh Hashanah, the designation applies only to the above indicated matter of tithes that are due from fruit-of-the-trees. The day is not however, marked by prohibition of work, nor is it observed with festive meals, or by any direct reference in prayer.

Nevertheless, it is invested with a festive sense, *Tachanun* is not said during *shacharit* or during the preceding *minchah* service. Eulogies are not delivered for the dead, and if it falls on Shabat, *av harachamim* is not said (since *av harachamim* recalls the souls of the dead.)

It is customary to eat fruit which comes from the Land of Israel and to eat a new fruit, of which one had not yet partaken the present year, in order to recite *shehecheyanu*.

The reason for the festive mood of the Rosh Hashanah of trees (in contrast to the Rosh Hashanah of the first of Elul, which is observed without distinction from any other day), is that the 15th of Shevat bespeaks the praise of the Land of Israel, for on this day the strength of the soil of the land is renewed. And it is with reference to the fruits of the trees and the produce of the soil, that the Torah praises the Land of Israel: 'a land of wheat and barley and vines and fig trees and pomegranates, a land of olive trees and honey' (Dvarim 8). The Land of Israel is here praised with reference to two species of grain and five species of fruit, for the honey that is mentioned here, is the honey of dates.

When the soil of the Land of Israel renews its strength to give forth its riches, the people of Israel who love the land and yearn for it, also rejoice. And when Israel eats of the fruit of the land and derives pleasure from the goodness of its fruit, they utter blessing before their pleasure and after it, to the One who bequeathed the precious land unto them. They pray to Him that He might renew its youth, and their youth, as in the days of old, and in accord with all He promised their forefathers. As it is written in the passage which speaks the praise of the Land of Israel: 'and you shall eat and be satisfied, and bless the Lord your God for the good land which He has given you.'

Another reason for the special observance of the 15th of Shevat is that the time of Rosh Hashanah for the trees is also a time of prayer and judgment concerning the trees. For it is the way of Providence that whenever any of His creatures begins to grow, He surveys its entire future; it is proper hence at such a time, to pray that the new creature or being, might prosper. The Torah has compared Man to a tree of the field; hence this day also recalls the Divine judgment upon man who is compared to a tree. And such is the character of the people of Israel, that they rejoice on a day of judgment. Let the decision be what it may, but let all see that 'there is a law and that there is a Judge.'

A PRAYER FOR A BEAUTIFUL ETROG

It is written in the book of Benei Isaschar:

'We have it on tradition from our forefathers to pray on

the 15th of Shevat that God might provide us with a beautiful *etrog kasher*, when we shall need one for the fulfillment of the *mitzvah* for the *etrog* which we obtain, is in accord with the merit of each individual. Therefore, how good and how pleasant it is for a person to pray on that day — the beginning of the sprouting of new fruit — that God might provide — at the required time — a beautiful *etrog*. And in this instance, one's prayer yields fruit.'

LAWS CONCERNING BLESSING OVER FRUIT

Since it is customary to eat a variety of fruit on the 15th of Shevat, it is proper to review the following 'dinim,' (laws) so that a person might know the correct procedure in case of doubt, or to prevent one's uttering a 'brachah levatalah' (a brachah uttered in Vain).

One who eats fruit of the tree, whether not as part of a meal or in the midst of one, recites the blessing, 'bore peri ha'etz' before partaking of the fruit. And the 'hamotzi' which is recited at the beginning of every regular meal does not suffice for the fruit also, unless one uses the fruit as a relish together with bread. If one eats the fruit separately, he is required to recite a blessing over them even in the midst of a meal.

If one has a variety of fruit before him he recites the brachah over the fruit he prefers most, and his brachah then suffices for the other species of fruit.

If one has before him any of the species of fruit which are mentioned in the Torah with reference to the 'praise-of-the-Land-of-Israel' — olives, dates, grapes, figs and pomegranates — he recites the brachah over those fruit, though he may personally prefer one of the other species that are before him.

Among the fruit mentioned in the Torah with reference to the praise-of-the land, the preference fol-

lowed, corresponds to the order in which the various species are mentioned in the Torah:

'A land of wheat and barley, and vines, and fig-trees and pomegranates — a land of olive trees and honey' (Dvarim 8).

In the first part of the verse the order is: wheat, barley, vines, fig-trees and pomegranates. In the second part of the verse the order is olive trees and honey. Whichever species is closer to the word 'land' takes precedence. In the case of species which are of equal distance to the term 'land' in both parts of the verse, the species mentioned in the first part of the verse takes precedence. Hence, our final order of precedence in the case of fruit of the tree is as follows: olives, dates, grapes, figs and pomegranates. And even the last of these takes precedence over other fruit which are not mentioned with reference to the 'praise-of-the-land.'

One does not recite a brachah over food or drink till they are brought before him. If he did utter a brachah and food was brought before him afterwards, he should recite a brachah again, since there was nothing to which his first brachah could apply at the time when it was made. However, if food and drink were prepared in another place, and he knew at the time of the brachah that he would find them in their place, he is not required to recite another brachah.

If one recited a brachah over fruits that are before him, and afterwards other fruits of the same species — or of another species whose brachah is the same as that of the first — are brought before him, he is not required to make a second brachah. Some differ however with regard to this 'din' and they hold that a second brachah is not required only if the later fruit is of the same species as the first. It is proper to take care initially, to have it in mind that one's brachah should apply to whatever will be brought before him (provided the brachah is the appropriate one). In the case of a guest, even if various species were later brought before him, his first brachah suffices both for the species which had already been brought before him, as well as for any species which it was the intention of the host to serve later.

If one has before him a new fruit which he has not yet eaten the same season, he also recites the brachah 'shehecheyanu' immediately after the brachah 'peri ha'etz' — since the blessing over fruit is constant and 'shehecheyanu' is not canstant; in which case what is constant takes precedence. Others hold that 'shehecheyanu' takes precedence in this case, since shehecheyanu applies from the time when the new fruit are seen; hence since the obligation to utter shehecheyanu comes first, it is therefore recited first.

If one forgot to recite shehecheyanu and ate, he is not required to recite the brachah again.

In the case of a fruit which is the product of a grafting of two species forbidden by the 'halachah,' shehecheyanu is not recited.

If one has before him a variety of new species which require shehecheyanu — just as the recitation of the brachah, 'peri ha'etz,' over one of the fruit suffices for them all, similarly is it only necessary to recite shehecheyanu once.

If a variety of fruit is brought before a person, among which there are some which he has already eaten the same season, and therefore, is not required to utter shehecheyanu over them again — and there are also some fruit over which he is required to recite shehecheyanu, then if the fruit which required shehecheyanu also takes precedence with reference to the regular brachah, he recites both the regular brachah and shehecheyanu over it. If however the fruit which requires shehecheyanu does not take precedence over the other fruit before him, he then recites the regular brachah over the fruit which takes precedence, and when he later partakes of the fruit which requires shehecheyanu he then recites shehecheyanu alone. Some differ and they recite even the regular brachah over fruit, over the species which require shehecheyanu, despite the fact that that species comes later in the order of precedence. Some follow the practice of reciting shehecheyanu first over the mere sight of the new fruit, and subsequently they recite the regular brachah over the species which takes precedence.

If one eats fruit in the midst of a regular meal, then the 'birkat hamazon' (grace after meal) recited after the meal suffices for the fruit also. If one eats fruit apart from the meal, he afterwards recites the prescribed three-fold-brachah for fruit which are mentioned with reference to the 'praise-of-the-land.' For other fruit he recites 'bore nefashot.' If one eats both types of fruit, he recites the prescribed 'three-fold-brachah.'

THE PRAISE-OF-THE-LAND -OF-ISRAEL

Since the 15th of Shevat recalls for us the praise of the Land of Israel it is therefore proper to recall, on this day, some of the words of our Sages who extolled its unique excellence.

First in Precedence and First in Praise — 'You thus find concerning the ways of God that whoever was more beloved takes precedence. The Torah which is most beloved, was created before all else... the Land of Israel, which was most beloved... was created before all else... In the case of all other lands, each has something which the other lacks. The Land of Israel however, lacks nothing. As it is said: (Dvarim 8): 'A land in which you shall eat bread without scarcity, thou shall not lack anything' (Sifri Ekev).

The Chosen Land for the People That Is Chosen — 'And this is the land that shall fall to you for an inheritance' (Bamidbar 34) — God said: The Land is Mine... and Israel is Mine... it is best that I should bequeath My land to My servants' (Bamidbar Raba, Masey).

It is written: 'For the Lord has chosen Zion; He has desired it for a dwelling place for Him' (Tehilim 132). 'A land flowing with milk and honey, a land of brooks of water, of fountains and depths, springing forth in valleys and hills; a land of wheat and barley and vines and figtrees and pomegranates... You shall not lack anything in it; a land whose stones are iron, and out of whose hills you may dig copper, a land of hills and valleys, from the rains of whose heavens you shall drink water, a land which the Lord your God seeks. The eyes of the Lord your God are always upon it from the beginning of the year till the end of the year.' This may be compared to a King who has one son more beloved to him than all his other sons, and one vineyard excelling over all his other vineyards. He says: I shall give the choiceest vineyard to the best of the sons.

Likewise, Israel is chosen from among all the nations, and the Land of Israel is chosen among all the lands — let the chosen ones come and inherit the chosen inheritance.

For this land is not like all other lands. All other lands satisfy their inhabitants at times, and at times they are cursed; in either case its condition is not in accord with the ways of nature. When it is blessed, its yield is great, even if only little had been sown; little may be eaten, but the nourishment it provides is great. When it is not blessed, nothing avails to open its treasures — in defiance of the ways of nature. For the matter depends not on labor and toil alone, but rather: 'The blessing, that you hearken to the precepts of the Lord your God... and the curse if you will not hearken...' (Dvarim 11).

Desolation Which Contains Blessing — 'And I shall make the land desolate' (Vayikra 26) — this is a good measure; that Israel might not say: since we have been exiled from our land, enemies may now come and find satisfaction upon it. It is therefore said: 'And your enemies who dwell therein shall be desolate upon it' (ibid.). Even the enemies who come afterwards will not find satisfaction in it' (Sifri Bechukotai). Come and see: Although the land is still under its curse; although the Lord has not yet visited His land with a full remembrance, and for two thousand years its enemies have diligently sought to destroy it — even now — how sweet its fruit are! How much more will the land radiate light and blessing upon its returning sons, at the time of God's total remembrance — may it come soon, in our days! How great is the majesty and the glory for which this land is destined at the time of its final redemption.

The Fruit of the Land of Israel Bear the Tiding of Redemption — 'And Rabi Aba said: There is no greater manifestation of the final redemption than this. As it is said: 'And you, mountains of Israel, you shall give forth your branches, and you shall bear your fruit for My people Israel, because they have come near' (Yechezkel 36). When the Land of Israel will give forth its fruit bountifully, then the redemption will draw near, and there is no greater manifestation of the redemption than this' (Rashi, ibid.).

In Her First Days — 'And the land which you crossed over thither to possess it, is a land of hills and valleys' (Dvarim 8). Does not this verse speak in fault of the land, since it mentions hills? (The implication is that the land is rocky and infertile). What then does the reference to valleys teach us ? Just as valleys add to the excellence of the land (for the level surface of valleys is good for sowing), likewise do hills add to the 'praise-of-the-land.' Further, both the hills and the valleys yield fruit with specific qualities; while fruit grown on the hills are light, the fruit of the valley are heavy.

'Rabi Shimon Ben Yochai says: Twelve (types of) lands were given, corresponding to the twelve tribes, and the fruit of one tribe's land tasted differently from the fruit of another's.

'And he dips his foot in oil' (Dvarim 33). We learn from this that the land of Asher was greatly rich in oil. It once happened that the people of Ludkia were in need of oil. They appointed an official and said to him: 'Go and acquire oil for us for a hundred times ten thousand...' He went to Yerushalayim and said: 'I am in need of oil for a hundred times ten thousand...' They answered: 'Go to Tzor.'

'He went to Tzor and said: 'I am in need of oil for a hundred times ten thousand...'

'Go to Gush Chalav.'

'He went to Gush: 'I am in need of oil for a hundred times ten thousand...'

'Go to so and so.'

'He went to the person's house and did not find him. They said to him:

'He is in the field.' He went and found him tending the olive trees. He said to him:

'I am in need of oil of a hundred times ten thousand...'

'Wait for me till I finish tending the olive tree.' When he finished his work he took his utensils on his back and came. The official thought: Is it possible that this one has a hundred times ten thousand worth of oil? It seems that the Jews have been scoffing at me. When he (the man of Gush Chalav) reached his house, his maidservant brought forth pitchers of warm water, and he washed his hands and feet. She then brought forth a gold container filled with oil, in which he dipped his hands and feet, to fulfill what was said: 'And he dips his foot in oil.' Bread was put before him, and he ate and drank. After eating and drinking, he arose and measured (for the official) oil worth one hundred times ten thousand... He said to him:

'Do you want more?'

'I have no money.'

'Take, and I will come with you to take my money.'

'He then rose and measured oil for another eighteen times ten thousand.

'They said: That man did not leave a mule or camel in the Land of Israel which he did not bring with him (for loading)... the people of Ludkia... greatly praised him. He said to them: 'Address your praise only towards this person, for all the credit is due him. Furthermore, I am indebted to him in the sum of eighteen times ten thousand! As it is said: 'Some appear wealthy and they have nothing; some appear poor and are exceedingly wealthy' (Yalkut Shimony).

FLOWING WITH MILK AND HONEY

'Rami, the son of Yechezkel, visited Beney Berak, and he saw goats grazing under a fig-tree. Honey dripped from the fig-tree, and milk dripped from the goats and both intermixed. Whereupon he said: Behold! A land flowing with milk and honey...' (Tr. Ketubot 111).

'Rabi said to Rabi Preda: Are you not going to show me the clusters in your vineyard. He answered: Yes. Rabi Preda went out to show them to him: He (Rabi) looked far ahead and saw what seemed like an ox among the vines. Said he to Rabi Preda: Does not this ox ruin the vine? Rabi Preda answered: This ox which you see — is a cluster of grapes...

'It happened that a person had a row of fig-trees. He came and found a fence of honey surrounding them...' (Jerusalem Talmud, Pe'ah 7).

'Rabi Shimon Ben Chalafta said: It happened that Rabi Yehudah said to his son in Sichnin: Go and bring us a dried fig from the barrel. He went up, and upon stretching forth his hand, found that it was filled with honey. Said he: Father! It has honey in it. Rabi Yehudah answered: Immerse your hand and you will bring up dried figs' (ibid.).

'Rav Chisda said: It is written: 'And I have given you a precious land, a deer-like inheritance' (Irmeyahu 3). Why is the Land of Israel compared to a deer? To teach you: Just as a deer does not have sufficient skin to contain his flesh, likewise is the Land of Israel unable to contain all its fruit' (Tr. Ketubot 112).

AT THE TIME OF THE REDEMPTION

'Yerushalayim is destined to be like the Land of Israel, and the Land of Israel will be like the entire world...' (Psikta Rabati Chapter 1). 'When the Lord your God will expand your boundary' (Dvarim 12)...is it possible that God can expand the Land of Israel? Rabi Itzchak said: No one knows the length and breadth of a scroll, and its real dimensions become known only when it is opened. Likewise, the Land of Israel mainly consists of hills and valleys...as it is said: 'And the land which you are crossing over thither to possess it, is a land of hills and valleys' (Dvarim 11)... Of the future however, it is said: 'Every valley shall be lifted up, and every mountain and hill shall be made low; and the rugged shall be made level, and the rough places a plain' (Yeshayahu 40). At that time its true dimensions will become known' (Dvarim Raba 4).

'A stalk of wheat will one day rise high like a palm, and will reach up to the mountain tops' (Tr. Ketubot 111).

'And you shall gather your corn, your wine and your oil' (Dvarim 11) — the Land of Israel will be filled with corn, wine, and oil, and all the lands...will fill her with silver and gold' (Sifri Ekev 51).

THE FOUR PARASHIOT

Moshe Rabenu ordained the public reading of the Torah

every Sabbath and Festival. On each Sabbath of the year we read the respective *sidra* of the week, to which seven persons are called. After the conclusion of the *sidra,* an eighth person is called for *maftir* which consists of a repetition of the last few verses of the *sidra* (a minimum of three verses). After *maftir* a Prophetic portion is read whose theme bears a relation to the theme of the *sidra.*

During Festivals a passage relating to the respective Festival is read, and five persons are called to the Torah (on Yom Kipur, six). The *maftir* is taken from the *sidra* of *Pinchas,* and it recounts the special additional offerings brought on the respective Festival. The Prophetic reading likewise relates to the theme of the day.

On Rosh Chodesh the Torah reading is an account of the special sacrificial offerings of the day and is taken from *Pinchas.* Four persons are called. In the case of a Festival which falls on the Shabat (the same is true of Rosh Hashanah and Yom Kipur when they fall on Shabat) the regular portion of the week is not read. The prescribed reading for the respective Festival alone is read, but it is sub-divided into seven portions, and seven persons are called to the Torah. The *maftir* is also that of the respective festival.

When Rosh Chodesh, Purim and Chanukah fall on Shabat, the regular portion of the week is read; seven persons are called to the Torah, the *maftir* is taken from another portion and relates to the theme of the day, as does the Prophetic portion also.

Whenever the Torah reading is taken from two different portions (on Festivals; when Rosh Chodesh and Chanukah fall on Shabat; when Rosh Chodesh Tevet falls on one of the weekdays of Chanukah) two Torah scrolls are drawn from the Ark; with each of them rolled to their respective portion. Two Torah Scrolls are taken out to keep from 'burdening the congregation,' through the delay occasioned by rolling the same scroll from one portion to another.

Similarly, on a day when the Reading is taken from three separate portions, three Torah scrolls are taken out. This occurs only on Simchat Torah; when Rosh Chodesh Tevet, Adar, Nisan fall on Shabat — as will be explained later.

There are four Sabbaths in the year which do not coincide with either a Festival, or Rosh Chodesh, or Chanukah, or Purim, but on which nevertheless, two portions are read, and hence two Torah scrolls are taken out. And if one of these also coincides with Rosh Chodesh, three Torah scrolls are taken out for the reading of three portions.

These four Sabbaths fall as follows: The last Shabat of Shevat (if the year is a regular one, and is not intercalated), and three Sabbaths in Adar (during most years); or, the four Sabbaths of the month of Adar; and one in Nisan (in a minority of years) as will be explained later.

In a leap year which has two months of Adar, only the second Adar, which immediately precedes Nisan, is counted with reference to this matter; in which case the first four of these special Sabbaths coincide with the last Shabat of Adar I.

During these four Sabbaths the regular portion of the week is read and seven persons are called to the Torah. The maftir is taken from another portion and relates to the theme of the respective special Sabbath, as does the Prophetic portion

The portions read for maftir during these Sabbaths are as follows: On the first Sabbath; a passage from *Ki tisa,* which contains the account of the obligatory half-*shekel*-offering, is read. It is hence called: *Parshat shekalim.* On the second Shabat the maftir is taken from the end of *Ki tetze* — 'Remember what Amalek did to you,' and it is called, *parshat* zachor (remember). On the third Shabat the account of the 'red heifer' is read from *Chukat,* and it is called *parshat parah* (heifer). On the fourth Shabat the *maftir* is taken from *Bo* — 'This month shall be to you the first of months.' And it is called: *parshat hachodesh* (the month).

THE INTERRUPTIONS BETWEEN THE FOUR SPECIAL SABBATHS

The above mentioned four *parshiot: shekalim, zachor, parah, hachodesh,* never follow each other consecutively, but there is always an interruption between them; at times by one intervening Shabat, and at times by two. The time that is designated for these four *parshiot,* is dependent on the following four rules:

1. *Shabat shekalim* always falls at the advent of Adar, but never after Adar has already begun. If Rosh Chodesh falls on Shabat, *shekalim* is read the same day; if Rosh Chodesh Adar falls on a weekday, the portion of *Shekalim* is read on the Shabat which precedes Rosh Chodesh.
2. *Shabat zachor* always falls directly before Purim.
3. *Shabat parah* always immediately precedes *hachodesh.*
4. *Shabat hachodesh* always occurs at the advent of Nisan, but not after Nisan has already begun. If Rosh Chodesh Nisan falls on Shabat, the portion of *hachodesh* is read the same day; if it falls on a weekday, the portion of hachodesh is read on the Shabat which immediately precedes Rosh Chodesh.

Therefore, if one wishes to know which are the intervening Sabbaths in a given year, he needs only to know on which day Rosh Chodesh Adar falls (the Adar which immediately precedes Nisan), and he will know the order of the four parshiot, and the interruptions between them.

The theme of the four parshiot will be discussed separately in the forthcoming chapters.

SHEKALIM

When the Sanctuary stood, a positive *mitzvah* was incumbent upon every Jew to contribute half a *shekel* yearly for the purchase of the communal-offerings brought in the Sanctuary. During a given year the offerings had to be purchased from the half *shekel* contributions of the same year.

This mitzvah was incumbent upon everyone; even upon a poor person dependent upon charity. If one lacked a half *shekel*, he borrowed from others, pawned or sold one of his garments, in order to be able to give the required silver *half-shekel*. As it is said: 'The rich shall not increase, and the poor shall not diminish from a *half-shekel*' (Shmot 30).

The half-shekel is not to be given in installments, a little at a time, but is to be given all at once.

All the shekalim were due in the Sanctuary by Rosh Chodesh Nisan each Year, since on Rosh Chodesh Nisan allocations were made from the chamber in which the shekalim were kept, towards the purchase of the communal offerings that were to be brought later.

On Rosh Chodesh Nisan public announcements were therefore made for the bringing in of the shekalim, so that each person might have sufficient time to prepare his half-shekel, and to give it at the proper time. On the 15th of Adar collectors sat in each city and requested the voluntary bringing in of the shekalim, but no coercion was applied as yet to anyone who had not yet brought in his half-shekel. On the 25th of the month the collectors sat in the Sanctuary, and henceforth the collections were mandatory.

The Sages enacted, that on the Shabat immediately preceding Adar or on the Shabat on which Rosh Chodesh Adar fell, the passage on shekalim was to be read from the Torah, since, on Shabat the people all gather in the synagogue to hear the reading of the Torah. This reading of the portion of shekalim was therefore the first call for the fulfillment of the mitzvah in its proper time.

Now that the Sanctuary no longer exists, and we no longer bring offerings, and the mitzvah of the half-shekel does not apply, we nevertheless read this portion from the Torah in the proper time, so that the Torah Reading might be regarded as equal to the practical fulfillment of the mitzvah. As it is written: 'And we shall pay for oxen — with our lips' (Hoshea 14).

Another reason for the enactment of the Sages, that we read the portion of shekalim even nowadays, is our anticipation of the speedy rebuilding of the Sanctuary, which makes it necessary for us to be familiar with the proper manner of performing the mitzvah.

This mitzvah is beloved to Israel, for we learn from it to love every individual Jew greatly — since all Jews are regarded as equal before God; and the most important of the sacred services — the bringing of the communal-offerings of atonement — was performed by all Israel in equality. Before God none was poor and none wealthy; none were near and none were distant, but all were near in the attainment of forgiveness for Israel.

SHABAT SHEKALIM IN THE SYNAGOGUE

If *Shabat Shekalim* falls in the last days of Shevat, two Torah scrolls are taken out; in one the regular portion of the week is read and seven persons are called, and in the second the *maftir* is read from *Ki tisa,* (it contains the mitzvah of the half-shekel.) If Shabat shekalim falls on Rosh Chodesh Adar three Torah scrolls are taken out; in the first the regular weekly portion is read and six persons are called; in the second the portion relating to Rosh Chodesh is read from *Pinchas,* and the seventh person is called; and in the third, the passage relating to the half-shekel is read from *Ki tisa.*

Although two or three *parshiot* are read this Shabat from the Torah, the Prophetic portion relates only to the theme of *shekalim,* and it recounts the action of Yehoyada, the Cohen, and King Yehoash, through whose efforts the people contributed towards the repair of the Sanctuary. The reason for limiting the Prophetic Reading to only one theme is that the Prophetic Reading always relates to the theme of the concluding portion read from the Torah.

Since the portion of the week is regular, it is read first. Since the Reading for Rosh Chodesh is read more frequently than the portion of shekalim, it is read next. The portion of shekalim, which is read only once, is read last.

We have said above that the reason for the taking out of two Torah scrolls, is the intent not 'to burden the congregation.' It would seem that on Shabat shekalim only one scroll be read from, since the regular portion of the week is always close to *Ki tisa* (which contains the portion of shekalim), nevertheless, the prevalent custom has become to take out two or three scrolls even on Shabat shekalim. It is the custom in many Ashkenazi communities to add *yotzrot* to the regular *shacharit* prayers on Shabat shekalim. In some communities *yotzrot* are said only during *musaf*. In many Jerusalem synagogues the custom is to recite *yotzrot* during these Sabbaths after the cantor's repetition of the *amidah*, and before the Torah reading. In the *Sephardi* communities, however, *yotzrot* are not said at all.

THE HEALING PRECEDES THE WOUND

Why does *shekalim* precede *zachor* ? It has already been said above that the reason for reading of the mitzvah of the half-shekel on the Shabat preceding Adar, is that the collection of shekalim was announced on the first of Adar. But this itself requires explanation. Is there not another mitzvah in Adar — that of remembering the injunction to wipe out Amalek — and was not the command to wipe out Amalek addressed to Israel before that of the half-shekel ?

The answer is that through the mitzvah of shekalim we achieve the merit of being able to wipe out Amalek. And God has bidden Israel to give a half-shekel as a 'soul-ransom,' so that 'the healing might precede the wound.'

'Resh Lakish said: It was revealed and known before the One whose word created the world, that Haman (descendant of Amalek) would weigh out the *shekalim* in order to attain the assent of Achashverosh to destroy Israel: He therefore, preceded their shekalim to his, and for this reason we learn: On the first of Adar announcement is made concerning shekalim...' (Tr. Megilah 13).

THE COLLECTION OF THE SHEKALIM IS MANDATORY

'Why is the half-shekel collection imposed even by force, and even if the givers have to mortgage themselves to make their contributions ? They made a parable; to what is the thing similar ? to one on whose foot a wound arose. The doctor bound him, and made an incision in his foot in order to heal him. Likewise, did God say: Let Israel mortgage themselves for their shekalim, so that communal offerings might be available from them; since communal offerings attain reconciliation and atonement beween Israel and our Father in Heaven' (Yalkut Shimony, Ki-tisa).

ONLY HALF A SHEKEL

Why did the Torah prescribe the giving of half a shekel and not a whole one ? Since the shekalim came to atone for the sin of the golden calf, and Israel committed this transgression only half the day, from the seventh hour of the 40th day after Moshe's ascent to heaven, till evening, God therefore said: The sustenance you drew during the six hours which you served idols, you are to return to Me... The Sages therefore prescribed: 'Since they sinned half the day, let them give a half-shekel' (Jerusalem Talmud, Shekalim, Chapter 2).

The later Sages have found in this matter various allusions and insights, which lead a person towards the love and fear of God.

Why a half-shekel ? A person is taught thereby to know, that for all his efforts in the service of God, would that he attain to half of his capacity. And let him not be arrogant at heart and say, 'I have served God with all my strength.'

Another reason: These shekalim come to atone for the making of the golden calf. But since the Women did not commit the sin of the calf, and a man without a woman is only half a person, a half-shekel is therefore sufficient for each person.

Another reason: Atonement is never required for more than 'half' a person, whereas his second 'half' (his soul) is always pure and is never blemished. Hence it needs no atonement.

A person has a 'root' and 'branches.' His root is in the Heavens: It consists of the pure soul given to man, which is hewn from the most exalted heights and retains its purity forever. His branches are on earth, and they are the manifest powers of the soul and the means of physical action. Any blemish caused through a man's sins, adhere only to these branches, which he has separated from their roots above. When a person repents, he needs only to attach the branches again to their uppermost root — to elevate his powers and actions and to draw them near to the yearnings of the soul.

In the portion of shekalim it is written: 'When you will lift up the heads of the children of Israel' — which has been explained to mean: Lift up their stature — elevate their actions to the roots of their souls, and they will become whole again. They do not require to be totally recreated anew after sin, since 'half' of them lives and endures in purity at all times. They need only to give a half-shekel for the redemption of their souls. And with this half, the *shekel* by which they are 'weighed' becomes indeed a 'whole shekel.'

In the additional *yotzrot* prayers for Shabat shekalim we therefore say: 'And a shekel will I bear in the established and exalted house.' That is to say, If we now bring this half-shekel, we will indeed have in hand a whole shekel by which 'to be seen in the presence of our God.' For this reason we do not say, 'I will bear a half-shekel,' but rather, 'a shekel will I bear.'

And this is a source of encouragement for those who

pursue *teshuvah.* For the Torah says to them: Know that your soul is always bound to merit, and sin can only blemish part of you, but not all of you. Rectify the part which has been blemished, and all of you will be rectified.

A SMALL RANSOM AND GREAT FORGIVENESS

'Rabi Yehudah, the son of Rabi Shimon, said in the name of Rabi Yochanan: Moshe heard three things from God which caused him to turn back in dread: When God said to him, 'and they shall give each man, ransom for his soul,' Moshe said: Who is capable of giving ransom for his soul? 'Skin for skin, and all that a man has, he shall give for his life' (Job 2), and it will still not suffice... God said to him: I do not ask in accord with My strength but in accord with theirs. 'This they shall give' ... Likewise, God said to him: 'Command the children of Israel, and say to them: My bread which is offered to Me by fire, which is of a sweet savour unto me, this shall you observe to offer unto Me in due season.' To which Moshe answered: Who can provide Him with His bread? ... Similarly, God said to him: 'And they shall make for Me a Sanctuary, and I shall dwell in their midst,' and Moshe answered: Who can make a Sanctuary for Him to dwell in? (Bamidbar Raba 12).

'And they shall give, each man, ransom for his soul.' When Moshe heard this he was filled with fear... Said Rabi Yehudah, the son of Ilai: Moshe deduced: We find that ransom for the life of a person consists of a *kikar* of silver, as it is said: And your life shall be instead of his life, or you shall weigh out a kikar of silver' (First Melachim 20).

'Rabi Yosi said: Moshe deduced it from the law of a slanderer of whom it is said: 'And they shall penalize him a hundred silver pieces' (Dvarim 22). We too have brought forth slander and said (of the golden calf): This is your god Israel.' Each one of us is required therefore to give one hundred silver pieces.

'Resh Lakish said: Moshe deduced it from one who coerced

a maiden. It is written there: 'And the man... shall give ransom to the father of the maiden 50 silver pieces' (ibid.) We have coerced the Divine Word, 'You shall have no other gods before Me,' and we have made idols — each of us is required to give 50 silver pieces.

'Rabi Yehudah, the son of Simon, said: Moshe deduced it from a goring ox, as it is said: 'If the ox shall gore a slave or a maidservant, he (the owner) shall give to his master 30 silver shekalim...' (Shmot 21). We too have exchanged God's glory for that of an ox, as it said: 'And they exchanged their glory for the mold of an ox' (Tehilim 106). Ea. 1 one of us is therefore required to give thirty shekalim.

'God knew what was in the heart of Moshe, but He said to him: By your life ! Not a silver *kikar*, nor a hundred silver pieces, nor fifty shekalim, nor thirty shekalim, but — This they shall give, all who pass over among the counted, a half-shekel' (Yalkut Shimony, Ki tisa).

A FIERY COIN

If a person commits a grave transgression and forfeits his life to the government, can he ransom himself with money ? And even if there were a monetary ransom for one found guilty before a king of flesh and blood, is there a monetary ransom for one found guilty before the King of Kings, the Holy One Blessed-be-He? And even if he were able to ransom his life with money, could he do so with some small coin ? And Israel was found liable to a death penalty before the King of Kings, but God bade them only to give half-a-shekel!

Moshe was perplexed and could not understand this matter. How could this small coin suffice to be a life ransom for those who bowed down to the calf, and said to it: 'This is your god, O Israel, which has brought you forth from the Land of Egypt ?' 'Rabi Meir said: God brought forth the likeness of a fiery coin from underneath the Throne of His Glory: He showed it to Moshe and said to him: 'This they shall give.' The likeness of this they shall give' (Jerusalem Talmud, Shekalim Chapter 1).

We are taught thereby: A person may give much silver and gold without attaining any forgiveness for his sin, if he fails to repent, and remains immersed in sin.

On the other hand, a person may give a small coin as ransom for his soul and attain complete forgiveness, provided that he has completely 'uprooted' himself from his sin, and has repented with all his heart. In such an instance, even the inanimate silver coin which he gives in quest of forgiveness, rises upwards (though it normally is pulled downwards), till it becomes likened in his hand to fire (which ascends upwards). And even this coin, though it is small, attains forgiveness for him.

Further, — if a person gives it wholeheartedly and with fiery devotion — God treasures this coin beneath His Throne of Glory. For thus did the Sages say: 'Repentance is great for it reaches the Throne of Glory!'

For this reason did they say: 'This they shall give — the likeness of this they shall give:' A small coin from a heart filled with love of God, and burning with Divine Fire.

THE UNITY OF ISRAEL

The Torah prescribes: 'This they shall give, everyone that passes among those who are numbered, half-a-shekel...' (Shmot 30). Why does the Torah find it necessary to add, 'the rich shall not give more, and the poor shall not give less?' Since the Torah itself indicates no difference between the poor and the rich, would we then, on our own, make such a distinction?

It may be answered that the Torah refers only to the kinderhearted among Israel, whose hearts are wealthy in the quality of benevolence and who wish to give their all to attain atonement. Of these the Torah said that they ought not to give more than the prescribed half-shekel. For if they should do so, the hard-hearted among the people would withhold their contributions completely, since they would say that the only acceptable contribution is the contribution of a person's total wealth. The people would hence be divided in two, the hard hearted and the open hearted.

The Torah has therefore said: Let the charitable person show his benevolence by restraining its extent, and thereby he will open a door of kind heartedness for others, who might then say: If this is all that the charitable give, I will give the same. Thus, the entire people will become unified in the quality of benevolence.

We may learn from this that a small mitzvah which Israel performs in unity, is more beloved before God than a great mitzvah performed only by Israel's great men. For thus did the Torah say: 'The rich shall not give more,' in order that 'the poor shall not give less.'

THE DESIRE TO PERFORM A MITZVAH

There is benevolence in action, and benevolence in will and desire. Our sins have caused us the loss of the Sanctuary; there are no sacrificial offerings; the mitzvah of the half-shekel does not apply. Nevertheless, the mitzvah of reading the portion of shekalim from the Torah has not ceased. For the essence of the mitzvah of the half-shekel is to awaken the benevolent desire of a person's heart towards the fulfillment of his Creator's will; and this awakening of the heart's desire always applies, and it is achieved when a Jew reads from the Torah the passages on this theme.

Furthermore, at times the desire to give is greater than the contribution itself. And though we are not capable of contributing towards the services of the Sanctuary, nevertheless, since we yearn to do so and rejoice in the mitzvah as we read it in the Torah, the Torah regards it as if we had fulfilled the mitzvah. Thereby, we may also merit its practical fulfillment, speedily, in our days.

GLOSSARY AND INDEX